From Master Student to Master Employee, 3e

Based on Dave Ellis' Becoming a Master Student

Doug Toft, Contributing Editor

CUSTOM TABLE OF CONTENTS

From master student to master employee

ONCE UPON A TIME, people thought of education as an enterprise set apart from the business of daily life. The halls of colleges, universities, and other schools were described as ivory towers—places where scholars retreated from the world of work to pursue knowledge.

Today, a different point of view prevails. The boundaries between classroom, office, and factory floor are fluid and flexible. Learning includes practicum experience, internships, work-study assignments, and other career-related experiences. Many students work full-time while attending classes.

Instead of competing, workplaces and classrooms can now complement each other. This development mirrors some key discoveries in the psychology of learning: that we learn by immersing ourselves in concrete experiences, reflecting on them, constructing theories, and then testing those theories in action.

Pioneers of both liberal education and modern work methods would agree. In his classic book *The Idea of a University,* John Henry Newman wrote that "all Knowledge is a whole and the separate Sciences parts of one"—leaving no room to divorce theory from practice or knowledge from application.[1] And Henry Ford said, "The only real security that a person can have in this world is a reserve of knowledge, experience, and ability. Without these qualities, money is practically useless."[2]

The purpose of this book is to build two kinds of bridges between your classroom experiences and your career. One is the bridge of skills—your ability to perform tasks that are valued by employers. The other is the bridge of learning—the ability to update your skills and acquire new ones any time you choose.

As a student, you are now involved in a multibillion-dollar enterprise called higher education. By focusing on the skills you acquire and the results you create, you can move between the role of student and the role of employee as easily as you change clothes. As a student, you are also at work, performing in ways that produce measurable results. This is natural because both roles draw on a common set of skills. The phrases *master student* and *master employee* are terms for qualities that live inside you, waiting only to be discovered. ✳

critical thinking exercise

1 Textbook reconnaissance

Start becoming a master student this moment by doing a 15-minute "textbook reconnaissance." Here's how.

First, read this book's Table of Contents. Do it in three minutes or less. Next, look at every page in the book. Move quickly. Scan headlines. Look at pictures. Notice forms, charts, and diagrams. Don't forget the last few pages in back, which include extra copies of planning forms that you might find useful.

A textbook reconnaissance shows you where a course is going. It gives you the big picture. That's useful because brains work best when going from the general to the specific. Getting the big picture before you start makes it easier to recall and understand details later on.

Your textbook reconnaissance will work even better if, as you scan, you look for ideas you can use. When you find one, write the page number and a short description of the idea. If you run out of room, just continue your list on a separate sheet of paper. You also can use Post-It Notes to flag the pages that look useful. You could even use notes of different colors to signal priority, such as green for ideas to use right away and yellow for suggestions to apply later. The idea behind this technique is simple: It's easier to learn when you're excited, and it's easier to get excited about a course if you know it's going to be useful, interesting, or fun.

Remember, look at every page, and do it quickly. Another useful tip for the master student is this: Do it now.

Page Number   **Description**

_____

_____

_____

_____

_____

 Complete this exercise online.

This book is worthless—
if you just read it

FROM MASTER STUDENT TO MASTER EMPLOYEE is worthless, *if* reading it is all you do. Until you take action and use the ideas to change your behavior, this book will make little difference in your life.

The purpose of this book is to help you make successful transitions to higher education and the workplace, and to set up a pattern of success that will last the rest of your life. You probably won't take action and use the ideas in this book until you are convinced that you have something to gain. That's one reason for providing this Introduction—to persuade you to use this book actively.

Before you stiffen up and resist this sales pitch, remember that you have already bought the book. Now you can get something for your money by committing yourself to take action—in other words, by committing yourself to becoming a master student. Here's what's in it for you.

Andersen Ross/Getty

Pitch #1: You can save money now and make more money later. Start with money. Your college education is one of the most expensive things you will ever buy. You might find yourself paying $30 to $100 an hour to sit in class. (See Critical Thinking Exercise 37: "Education by the Hour" on page 291 to come up with a specific figure that applies to your own education.)

As a master student, you control the value you get out of your education, and that value can be considerable. The joy of learning aside, college graduates make more money during their lifetimes than do their non-degreed peers.[3] The income advantage you might gain through higher education could total hundreds of thousands of dollars. It pays to be a master student.

Pitch #2: You can rediscover the natural learner in you. Joy is important, too. As you become a master student, you will learn to gain knowledge in the most effective way possible—by discovering the joyful, natural learner within you.

Children are great natural students. They quickly master complex skills, such as language, and they have fun doing it. For young children, learning is a high-energy process involving experimentation, discovery, and sometimes broken dishes. Then comes school. For some students, drill and drudgery replace discovery and dish breaking. Learning can become a drag. You can use this book to reverse that process and rediscover what you knew as a child—that laughter and learning go hand in hand.

Sometimes—and especially in college—learning does take effort. As you become a master student, you will learn many ways to work hard and have fun.

Pitch #3: You can choose from hundreds of techniques. *From Master Student to Master Employee* is packed with hundreds of practical, nuts-and-bolts techniques. The best part is, you can begin using them immediately. For example, during Critical Thinking Exercise 1: "Textbook Reconnaissance" on page 1, you might find three powerful learning techniques in one 15-minute exercise. Even if you doze in lectures, drift off during tests, or dawdle on term papers, you'll find ideas in this book that you can use to become a more effective student.

Not all of these ideas will work for you. That's why there are so many of them in this book. You can experiment with the techniques. As you discover what works, you will develop a unique style of learning that you can use for the rest of your life.

Pitch #4: You get the best suggestions from thousands of students. The concepts and techniques in this book are here not just because learning theorists, educators, and psychologists say they work. They are here because tens of thousands of students from all kinds of backgrounds have tried them and agree that they work. These people are students who dreaded giving speeches, couldn't read their own notes, and fell behind in their course work. Then they figured out how to solve those problems. Now you can use their ideas.

Pitch #5: You can learn about yourself. The process of self-discovery is an important theme in *From Master Student to Master Employee*. Throughout the book, you can use Discovery Statements and Intention Statements for everything from organizing your desk to choosing long-term goals. Studying for an organic chemistry quiz is a lot easier with a clean desk and a clear idea of the course's importance to you.

Pitch #6: You can use a proven product. The previous editions of this book have proved successful for thousands of students. Student feedback has been positive. In particular, students with successful histories have praised the techniques in this book.

Pitch #7: You can learn the secret of student success. If this sales pitch still hasn't persuaded you to use this book actively, maybe it's time to reveal the secret of student success. (Provide your own drum roll here.) The secret is . . . there are no secrets. Perhaps the ultimate formula is to give up formulas, keep experimenting, and find strategies that actually help you meet your goals.

The strategies that successful students use are well known. You have hundreds of them at your fingertips right now, in this book. Use them. Modify them. Invent new ones. You're the authority on what works for you.

However, what makes any technique work is commitment—and action. Without them, the pages of *From Master Student to Master Employee* are just two pounds of expensive mulch. Add your participation to the mulch, and these pages become priceless. ✳

This book is worth $1,000

Cengage Learning is proud to present three students each year with a $1,000 scholarship for tuition reimbursement. Any post-secondary school in the United States and Canada can nominate one student for the scholarship. To be considered, the student must write an essay that answers the question, "How do you define success?"

 For more details, visit the *From Master Student to Master Employee* Web site.

Get the most out of this book

1. Get used to a new look and tone. This book looks different from traditional textbooks. *From Master Student to Master Employee* presents major ideas in magazine-style articles. You will discover lots of lists, blurbs, one-liners, pictures, charts, graphs, illustrations, and even a joke or two.

Note: As a strategy for avoiding sexist language, this book alternates the use of feminine and masculine pronouns.

2. Rip 'em out. The pages of *From Master Student to Master Employee* are perforated because some of the information here is too important to leave in the book, and there are some pages your instructor might want to see. For example, Journal Entry 2 asks you to list some important things you want to get out of your education. To keep yourself focused on these goals, you could rip that page out and post it on your bathroom mirror or some other place where you'll see it several times a day.

You can reinsert the pages later by sticking them into the spine of the book. A piece of tape will hold them in place.

3. Skip around. You can use this book in several different ways. Read it straight through. Or pick it up, turn to any page, and find an idea you can use. Look for ideas you can use right now. For example, if you are about to choose a major or want to learn how to set goals, skip directly to the articles on these topics on pages 78 and 94, respectively.

You might find that this book presents similar ideas in several places. This repetition is intentional. Repetition reinforces key points. Also, a technique that works in one area of your life might work in others as well. Look especially to the Power Processes in this text for ideas that you can apply in many ways.

4. If it works, use it. If it doesn't, lose it. If there are sections of this book that don't apply to you at all, skip them—unless, of course, they are assigned. In that case, see if you can gain value from those sections anyway. When you are committed to getting value from this book, even an idea that seems irrelevant or ineffective at first can turn out to be a powerful tool.

5. Put yourself into the book. As you read about techniques in this book, create your own scenarios and cast yourself in the title role. For example, when reading through Critical Thinking Exercise 1: "Textbook Reconnaissance," picture yourself using this technique on your math textbook.

6. Listen to your peers. At the beginning of each chapter you will find a feature titled "Master Employee in Action." These include quotations from people who demonstrate the attitudes and strategies presented in this text. As you dig into each chapter, think about what you would say if you could add your voice to theirs.

7. Own this book. Right now, put your name, address, and related information on the inside cover of this book. Don't stop there, though. Determine what you want to get out of school, and create a record of how you intend to get it by reading the Power Processes and completing the Journal Entries in this Introduction. Every time your pen touches a page, you move closer to mastery.

8. Do the Critical Thinking Exercises. Critical Thinking Exercises appear throughout this book. Their purpose is to help you stretch your mind and get some practice in solving problems. Use these exercises to explore new ways of thinking about chapter topics. Note that other elements of this text, including Chapter 8: "Thinking" and Journal Entries, also promote critical thinking.

The Critical Thinking Exercises are based on a single idea: Ideas are meant to be *used*. Exercises invite you to write, touch, feel, move, see, search, ponder, speak, listen, recall, choose, commit, and create. You might even sing and dance. Learning often works best when it involves action.

To get the most out of this book, do most of the exercises. Also remember that it's never too late to go back and do the ones you skipped.

9. Learn about learning styles. Check out the Learning Styles Inventory and related articles in Chapter 1: "First Steps." This material can help you discover your preferred learning styles and allow you to explore new styles. Then, throughout the rest of this book, you'll find suggestions for applying your knowledge of learning styles. The modes of learning can be accessed by asking four basic questions: *Why? What? How?* and *What if?*

10. Navigate through learning experiences with the Master Student Map. You can orient yourself for maximum learning every time you open this book by asking those same four questions: *Why? What? How?* and *What if?* That's the idea behind the Master Student Map included on the first page of each chapter, which includes sample answers to those questions. Remember that you can use the four-part structure of this map to cycle through several learning styles and effectively learn anything.

11. Link to the Web. Throughout this book, you'll notice reminders to visit the Web site for *From Master Student to Master Employee*. When you see these notices, go to the Web site for articles, online exercises, and links to other useful Web sites.

12. Read the sidebars. Look for sidebars—short bursts of words and pictures placed between longer articles—throughout this book. These short pieces might offer insights that transform your experience of higher education. ✳

2 critical thinking exercise
Commitment

This book is worthless unless you actively participate in its activities and exercises. One powerful way to begin taking action is to make a commitment. Conversely, if you don't make a commitment, then sustained action is unlikely. The result is a worthless book. Therefore, in the interest of saving your valuable time and energy, this exercise gives you a chance to declare your level of involvement upfront. From the following options, choose the sentence that best reflects your commitment to using this book. Write the number in the space provided at the end of the list.

1. "Well, I'm reading this book right now, aren't I?"

2. "I will skim the book and read the interesting parts."

3. "I will read the book, think about it, and do the exercises that look interesting."

4. "I will read the book, do some exercises, and complete some of the Journal Entries."

5. "I will read the book, do some exercises and Journal Entries, and use some of the techniques."

6. "I will read the book, do most of the exercises and Journal Entries, and use some of the techniques."

7. "I will study this book, do most of the exercises and Journal Entries, and use some of the techniques."

8. "I will study this book, do most of the exercises and Journal Entries, and experiment with many of the techniques in order to discover what works best for me."

9. "I promise myself that I will create value from this course by studying this book, doing all the exercises and Journal Entries, and experimenting with most of the techniques."

10. "I will use this book as if the quality of my education depends on it—doing all the exercises and Journal Entries, experimenting with most of the techniques, inventing techniques of my own, and planning to reread this book in the future."

Enter your commitment level and today's date here:

Commitment level _____ Date _____

If you selected commitment level 1 or 2, you might consider passing this book on to a friend. If your commitment level is 9 or 10, you are on your way to terrific success in school. If your level is somewhere in between, experiment with the techniques and learning strategies you will find in this book. If you find that they work, consider returning to this exercise and raising your level of commitment.

Complete this exercise online.

Link to the work world

ONE THEORY of education separates life into two distinct domains: work and school. One is the "real" world. The other is the place where you attend classes to prepare for the real world.

Consider another point of view: Success in higher education promotes success on the job. You can link school experiences to the work world, starting today.

When you graduate from school, you don't leave your capacity for mastery locked inside a classroom. Excellence in one setting paves the way for excellence in other settings. A student who knows how to show up for class on time is ready to show up for work on time. And a student who's worked cooperatively in a study group brings people skills to the table when joining a project team at work.

To stimulate your thinking, experiment with this strategy: Whenever you go to class, imagine that you're actually at work. Then act accordingly. When you read, think like an employee who is gathering information to include in a bid for a multimillion-dollar project. When you take notes, imagine that you're documenting the results of a corporate board meeting. Whenever you complete a class assignment, imagine that you're about to be paid for the quality of your work.

This is not a far-fetched idea. In some career and technical schools, students are required to dress as they would in the workplace. They know that *dressing* the part of an employee makes it easier for them to *act* the part.

Psychologist William James promoted this strategy nearly a century ago. He wrote that when you act repeatedly in a new and constructive way, you're likely to stimulate new feelings and gain new habits in the process.[4] Another name for this is the "act as if" technique. In other words, act as if you are a master employee right now.

Starting with this page, read this book with a mental filter in place. Ask yourself:

- How can I use these ideas to meet my career goals?
- How can I use these techniques at my current job?
- How can these strategies help me to get a better job—one with more pay, more recognition, and more opportunities to do what I love to do?

For example, suggestions from "*Making the Transition to Higher Education*" (page 13) can also help you make the transition to a new career.

The techniques presented in "*Setting and Achieving Goals*" (page 94) can help you plan and complete work-related projects on time.

The article "*20 Memory Techniques*" (page 122) will come in handy as you learn the policies and procedures for a new job.

Use the techniques presented in Chapter 5: "Reading," starting with "*How Muscle Reading Works*" (page 140), to keep up with journals and books in your career field. This set of techniques can also help you extract valuable information from Web sites, keep up with ever-increasing volumes of e-mail, and reduce mountains of interoffice memos to manageable proportions.

Adapt the ideas mentioned in "*Cooperative Learning: Working in Teams*" (page 193) in order to collaborate more effectively with coworkers.

The suggestions in "*Thriving with Diversity*" (page 252) can assist you in adapting to the culture of a new company.

Ideas from "*Managing Conflict*" (page 255) can help you defuse tensions among coworkers.

These are just a few examples. Take any idea that you gain from this book and put it to the test. Use it, modify it, expand it, or replace it with one of your own. When you start looking for ways to break down the barriers between higher education and higher achievement on the job, there's no limit to the possibilities. ✳

The Discovery and Intention Journal Entry system

One way to become a better student is to grit your teeth and try harder. There is a better way: The Discovery and Intention Journal Entry system. This system can increase your effectiveness by showing you how to focus your energy.

USING THE DISCOVERY and Intention Journal Entry system is a little like flying an airplane. Airplanes are seldom exactly on course. Human and automatic pilots are always checking an airplane's positions and making corrections. The resulting flight path looks like a zigzag. The plane is almost always flying in the wrong direction, but because of constant observation and course correction, it arrives at the right destination.

As a student, you can use a similar approach. Journal Entries throughout this book are labeled as Discovery Statements, Intention Statements, or Discovery/Intention Statements. Each Journal Entry will contain a short set of instructions to direct your writing.

Through Discovery Statements, you gain awareness of "where you are." These statements are a record of what you are learning about yourself as a student—both your strengths and your weaknesses. Discovery Statements can also be declarations of your goals, descriptions of your attitudes, statements of your feelings, transcripts of your thoughts, and chronicles of your behavior.

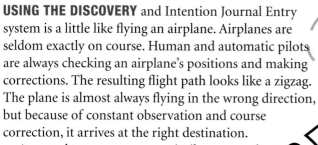

Sometimes Discovery Statements chronicle an "aha!" moment—a flash of insight that results when you connect a new idea with your prior experiences, preferred styles of learning, or both. Perhaps a solution to a long-standing problem suddenly occurs to you, or a life-changing insight wells up from the deepest recesses of your mind. Don't let such moments disappear. Capture them in Discovery Statements.

Intention Statements can be used to alter your course. These statements are about your commitment to take action based on increased awareness. An intention arises out of your choice to direct your energy toward a specific task and to aim at a particular goal. The processes of discovery and intention reinforce each other.

Even simple changes in behavior can produce results. If you feel like procrastinating, then tackle just one small, specific task related to your intention. Find something you can complete in five minutes or less, and do it *now*. For example, access just one Web site related to the topic of your next assigned paper. Spend just three minutes previewing a reading assignment. Taking "baby steps" like these can move you into action with grace and ease.

That's the system in a nutshell. Discovery leads to awareness. Intention leads to commitment. And *intention leads naturally to focused action*.

The process of discovery, intention, and action creates a dynamic and efficient cycle. The purpose of this system is not to get you pumped up and excited to go out there and try harder. In fact, Discovery and Intention Statements are intended to help you work smarter rather than harder.

First, you write Discovery Statements about where you are now. Next, you write Intention Statements about where you want to be, and the specific steps you will take to get there. Finally, you follow up with action—the sooner, the better.

Then you start the cycle again. Write Discovery Statements about whether or how you act on your Intention Statements—and what you learn in the process. Follow up with more Intention Statements about what you will do differently in the future. Then move into action and describe what happens next.

This process never ends. Each time you repeat the cycle, you get new results. It's all about getting what you want and becoming more effective in everything you do. This is the path of mastery—a path that you can travel for the rest of your life.

Sometimes a Discovery or Intention Statement will be long and detailed. Usually, it will be short—maybe just a line or two. With practice, the cycle will become automatic.

Don't panic when you fail to complete an intended task. Straying off course is normal. Simply make the necessary corrections. Mastery is not an end state or final goal. Rather, mastery is a process that never ends.

Miraculous progress might not come immediately. Do not be concerned. Stay with the cycle. Give it time. Use Discovery Statements to get a clear view of your world. Then use Intention Statements to direct your actions. Whenever you notice progress, record it.

Even if the following statement strikes you as improbable, just consider the possibilities: It can take the same amount of energy to get what you *don't* want in school as it takes to get what you *do* want. Sometimes getting what you don't want takes even more effort. An airplane burns the same amount of fuel flying away from its destination as it does flying toward it. It pays to stay on course.

You can use the Discovery and Intention Journal Entry system to stay on your own course and get what you want out of school. Start with the Journal Entries included in the text. Then go beyond them. Write Discovery and Intention Statements of your own at any time, for any purpose. Create new strategies whenever you need them, based on your current situation.

Once you get the hang of it, you might discover you can fly. ✳

Hello Author I Agree ☺

Rewrite this book

Some books should be preserved in pristine condition. This book isn't one of them.

Something happens when you interact with your book by writing in it. *From Master Student to Master Employee* is about learning, and learning results when you are active. When you make notes in the margin, you can hear yourself talking with the author. When you doodle and underline, you see the author's ideas taking shape. You can even argue with the author and come up with your own theories and explanations. In all of these ways, you can become a coauthor of this book. Rewrite it to make it yours.

While you're at it, you can create symbols or codes that will help you when reviewing the text later on. You might insert a "Q" where you have questions or put exclamation points next to important ideas. You could also circle words to look up in a dictionary.

Remember, if any idea in this book doesn't work for you, you can rewrite it. Change the exercises to fit your needs. Create a new technique by combining several others. Create a technique out of thin air!

Find something you agree or disagree with on this page, and write a short note in the margin about it. Or draw a diagram. Better yet, do both. Let creativity be your guide. Have fun.

Begin rewriting now.

Discovery and Intention Statement guidelines

Discovery Statements

1 Record the specifics about your thoughts, feelings, and behavior. Thoughts include inner voices. We talk to ourselves constantly in our heads. When internal chatter gets in your way, write down what you are telling yourself. If this seems difficult at first, just start writing. The act of writing can trigger a flood of thoughts.

Thoughts also include mental pictures. These images are especially powerful. Picturing yourself flunking a test is like a rehearsal to do just that. One way to take away the power of negative images in your mind is to describe them in detail.

Also notice how you feel when you function well. Use Discovery Statements to pinpoint exactly where and when you learn most effectively.

In addition, observe your actions and record them accurately. Use facts. If you spent 90 minutes chatting online with a favorite cousin instead of reading your anatomy text, write about it and include the details, such as when you did it, where you did it, and how it felt. Record your observations quickly, as soon as you make them.

2 Use discomfort as a signal. When you approach a daunting task, such as a difficult math problem, notice your physical sensations—a churning stomach, perhaps, or shallow breathing or yawning. Feeling uncomfortable, bored, or tired might be a signal that you're about to do valuable work. Stick with it. Tell yourself you can handle the discomfort just a little bit longer. You will be rewarded.

You can experience those rewards at any time. Just think of the problem that poses the biggest potential barrier to your success in school. Choose a problem that you face right now, today. (Hint: It might be the thing that's distracting you from reading this article.) If you have a lot of emotion tied up in this problem, that's even better. Write a Discovery Statement about it.

3 Suspend judgment. When you are discovering yourself, be gentle. Suspend self-judgment. If you continually judge your behaviors as "bad" or "stupid" or "galactically imbecilic," sooner or later your mind will revolt. Rather than put up with the abuse, it will quit making discoveries. For your own benefit, be kind to yourself.

4 Tell the truth. Suspending judgment helps you tell the truth about yourself. The saying "The truth will set you free" endures for a reason. The closer you get to the truth, the more powerful your Discovery Statements will be. And if you notice that you are avoiding the truth, don't blame yourself. Just tell the truth about it.

Intention Statements

1 Make intentions positive. The purpose of writing Intention Statements is to focus on what you want rather than what you don't want. Instead of writing "I will not fall asleep while studying chemistry," write, "I intend to stay awake when studying chemistry." Also avoid the word *try*. Trying is not doing. When we hedge our bets with *try*, we can always tell ourselves, "Well, I *tried* to stay awake." We end up fooling ourselves into thinking we succeeded.

2 Make intentions observable. Experiment with an idea from educational trainer Robert Mager, who suggests that goals be defined through behaviors that can be observed and measured.[5] Rather than writing "I intend to work harder on my history assignments," write, "I intend to review my class notes, and I intend to make summary sheets of my reading." Then, when you review your progress, you can determine more precisely whether you have accomplished what you intended.

3 Make intentions small and achievable. Give yourself opportunities to succeed by setting goals you can meet. Break large goals into small, specific tasks that can be accomplished quickly. Small and simple changes in behavior—when practiced consistently over time—can have large and lasting effects. If you want to get an A in biology, ask yourself, "What can I do today?" You might choose to study biology for an extra hour. Make that your intention.

When setting your goals, anticipate self-sabotage. Be aware of what you might do, consciously or unconsciously, to undermine your best intentions. If you intend to study differential equations at 9 p.m., notice what you're doing when you sit down to watch a two-hour movie that starts at 8 p.m.

Also, be careful with intentions that depend on other people. If you write that you intend for your study group to complete an assignment by Monday, then your success depends on the other students in the group.

4 **Set timelines that include rewards.** Timelines can focus your attention. For example, if you are assigned to write a paper, break the assignment into small tasks and set a precise due date for each one. You might write, "I intend to select a topic for my paper by 9 a.m. Wednesday."

Timelines are especially useful when your intention is to experiment with a technique suggested in this book. The sooner you act on a new idea, the better. Consider practicing a new behavior within four hours after you first learn about it.

Remember that you create timelines to help yourself, not to feel guilty. In addition, you can always change a timeline.

When you meet your goal on time, reward yourself. Rewards that are an integral part of a goal are powerful. For example, your reward for earning a degree might be the career you've always dreamed of. External rewards, such as a movie or an afternoon in the park, are also valuable. These rewards work best when you're willing to withhold them. If you plan to take a nap on Sunday afternoon whether or not you've finished your English chemistry assignment, the nap is not an effective reward.

Another way to reward yourself is to sit quietly after you have finished your task and savor the feeling. One reason why success breeds success is that it feels good. ✳

journal entry ①

Discovery Statement

Recalling excellence

Welcome to the first Journal Entry in this book. You'll find Journal Entries in every chapter, all with a similar design that allows space for you to write.

Reflect on your personal experience of mastery. In the following space, write a description of a time in your life when you did something well. This experience does not need to be related to school. Describe the details of the situation, including the place, time, and people involved. Also describe the physical sensations and emotions you associate with the event.

I discovered that . . .

_____

_____

_____

_____

_____

_____

The value of higher education

THE POTENTIAL BENEFITS of higher education are enormous. To begin with, there are economic benefits. Over their lifetimes, college graduates on average earn much more than high school graduates. That's just one potential payoff. Consider the others explained in the following text.

Gain a broad vision

It's been said that a large corporation is a collection of departments connected only by a plumbing system. As workers in different fields become more specialized, they run the risk of forgetting how to talk to one another.

Higher education can change that. One benefit of studying the liberal arts is the chance to gain a broad vision. People with a liberal arts background are aware of the various kinds of problems tackled in psychology and theology, philosophy and physics, literature and mathematics. They understand how people in all of these fields arrive at conclusions and how these fields relate.

Master the liberal arts

According to one traditional model, education means mastering two essential tasks: the use of language and the use of numbers. To acquire these skills, students once immersed themselves in seven subjects: grammar, rhetoric, logic, arithmetic, geometry, music, and astronomy. These subjects, called the liberal arts, complemented the fine arts (such as poetry) and the practical arts (such as farming).

This model of liberal arts education still has something to offer. Today we master the use of language through the basic processes of communication: reading, writing, speaking, and listening. In addition, courses in mathematics and science help us understand the world in quantitative terms. The abilities to communicate and calculate are essential to almost every profession.

The word *liberal* comes from the Latin verb *libero*, which means "to free." Liberal arts are those that

(money) © Don Farrall/Getty, (statue) © Ron Dahlquist/Getty, (nurse, woman in pink) © Masterfile Royalty Free, (nest) © Judith Collins/Alamy

promote critical thinking. Studying them can free us from irrational ideas, half-truths, racism, and prejudice. The liberal arts grant us freedom to explore alternatives and create a system of personal values. These benefits are the very basis of personal fulfillment and political freedom.

Discover your values

Our values define how we spend our time and money. Higher education offers the opportunity to question and refine our values.

In addition, we do not spend all of our waking hours at our jobs. That fact leaves us with a decision that affects the quality of our lives: how to spend leisure time. By cultivating our interest in the arts and community affairs, the liberal arts provide us with many options for activities outside work. Our studies add a dimension to life that goes beyond having a job and paying the bills.

Discover new interests

Taking a broad range of courses has the potential to change your direction in life. A student previously committed to a career in science might try out a drawing class and eventually switch to a degree in studio arts. Or a person who swears that she has no aptitude for technical subjects might change her major to computer science after taking an introductory computer course.

To make effective choices about your long-term goals, base those choices on a variety of academic and personal experiences. Even if you don't change majors or switch career directions, you might discover an important avocation or gain a complementary skill. For example, science majors who will eventually write for professional journals can benefit from taking English courses.

Hang out with the greats

The poet Ezra Pound defined literature as "news that stays news."[6] Most of the writing in newspapers and magazines becomes dated quickly. In contrast, many of the books you read in higher education have passed the hardest test of all—time. Such works have created value for people for decades, sometimes for centuries. These creations are inexhaustible. We can return to them time after time and gain new insights. These are the works we can justifiably deem great. Hanging out with them transforms us. Getting to know them exercises our minds, just as running exercises our bodies.

Learn skills that apply across careers

Jobs that involve responsibility, prestige, and higher incomes depend on self-management skills. These skills include knowing ways to manage time, resolve conflicts, set goals, learn new skills, and relate to people of diverse cultures. Higher education is a place to learn and practice such skills.

Join the conversation

Long ago, before the advent of printing presses, televisions, and computers, people educated themselves by conversing with each other. Students in ancient Athens were often called *peripatetic* (a word that means "walking around") because they were frequently seen strolling around the city, engaged in heated philosophical debate.

Since then, the debate has deepened and broadened. The world's finest scientists and artists have joined voices in a conversation that spans centuries and crosses cultures. This conversation is about the nature of truth and beauty, knowledge and compassion, good and evil—ideas that form the very basis of human society.

Robert Hutchins, former president of the University of Chicago, called this exchange the "great conversation."[7] By studying this conversation, we take on the most basic human challenges: coping with death and suffering, helping create a just global society, living with meaning and purpose.

Our greatest thinkers have left behind tangible records. You'll find them in libraries, concert halls, museums, and scientific laboratories across the world. Through higher education, you gain a front-row seat for the great conversation—and an opportunity to add your own voice. ✳

You don't *need* this course— but you might *want* it

Some students don't believe they need a student success course. They might be right. These students may tell you that many schools don't even offer such a class. That's true.

Consider the benefits of taking this course anyway.

Start with a single question: What's one new thing that you could do on a regular basis to make a significant, positive difference in your life? This question might be the most important thing you ask yourself this term. The answer does not have to involve a huge behavior change. Over weeks and months, even a small shift in the way you take notes, read a textbook, or interact with instructors can make a major difference in how well you do in school.

Students who open up to this idea experience benefits. These comments from a recent student success course evaluation are typical:

I didn't expect to get anything out of this course except an easy 'A.' Boy, was I ever wrong. This course has changed my life.

I entered college with no confidence. Now that I have taken this class, I feel like I can succeed in any class.

This course has truly showed that I have the power to change any situation for the better.

I am now ready for the rest of my college years.

A student success course gives you dozens of strategies for creating the life of your dreams. It's possible that you might arrive at these strategies on your own, given enough time. Why wait, however? Approach this book and your course as if the quality of your education depends on them. Then watch the benefits start to unfold.

You share one thing in common with other students at your career school, college, or university: Entering higher education represents a major change in your life. You've joined a new culture with its own set of rules, both spoken and unspoken.

© Andresr/Shutterstock

Making the transition to higher education

WHETHER YOU'VE JUST GRADUATED from high school or have been out of the classroom for decades, you'll discover many differences between secondary and post-secondary education. The sooner you understand such differences, the sooner you can deal with them. Some examples of what you might face include the following:

■ *New academic standards.* Once you enter higher education, you'll probably find yourself working harder in school than ever before. Instructors will often present more material at a faster pace. There probably will be fewer tests in higher education than in high school, and the grading might be tougher. Compared to high school, you'll have more to read, more to write, more problems to solve, and more to remember.

■ *A new level of independence.* College instructors typically give less guidance about how or when to study. You may not get reminders about when assignments are due or when quizzes and tests will take place. You probably won't get study sheets the night before a test. And anything that's said in class or included in assigned readings might appear on an exam. Overall, you might receive less consistent feedback about how well you are doing in each of your courses. Don't let this tempt you into putting off work until the last minute. You will still be held accountable for all course work.

■ *Differences in teaching styles.* Instructors at colleges, universities, and vocational schools are often steeped in their subject matter. Many did not take courses on how to teach and might not be as interesting as some of your high school teachers. In addition, some professors might seem more focused on research than on teaching.

■ *A larger playing field.* The institution you've just joined might seem immense, impersonal, and even frightening. The sheer size of the campus, the variety of courses offered, the large number of departments—all of these opportunities can add up to a confusing array of options.

■ *More students and more diversity.* The school you're attending right now might enroll hundreds or thousands more students than your high school. And the range of diversity among these students might surprise you.

In summary, you are now responsible for structuring your time and creating new relationships. Perhaps more than ever before, you'll find that your life is your own creation. You are free to set different goals, explore alternative ways of thinking, change habits, and expand your circle of friends. All this can add up to a new identity—a new way of being in the world.

At first, this world of choices might seem overwhelming or even frightening. You might feel that you're just going through the motions of being a student or playing a role that you've never rehearsed.

That feeling is understandable. Use it to your advantage. Consider that you *are* assuming a new role in life—that of being a student in higher education. And just as actors enter the minds of the characters that they portray, you can take on the character of a master student.

When you're willing to take responsibility for the quality of your education, you can create the future of your dreams. Keep the following strategies in mind.

Decrease the unknowns. Before classes begin, get a map of the school property and walk through your first day's schedule, perhaps with a classmate or friend. Visit your instructors in their offices and introduce yourself. Anything you can do to get familiar with the new routine will help.

Admit your feelings—whatever they are. School can be an intimidating experience for new students. Anyone can feel anxious, isolated, homesick, or worried. People of diverse cultures, adult learners, commuters, and people with disabilities may feel excluded.

Those emotions are common among new students, and there's nothing wrong with them. Simply admitting the truth about how you feel—to yourself and to someone else—can help you cope. And you can almost always do something constructive in the present moment, no matter how you feel.

If your feelings about this transition make it hard for you to carry out the activities of daily life—going to class, working, studying, and relating to people—then get professional help. Start with a counselor at the student health service on your campus. The mere act of seeking help can make a difference.

Allow time for transition. You don't have to master the transition to higher education right away. Give it some time. Also, plan your academic schedule with your needs in mind. Balance time-intensive courses with others that don't make as many demands.

Find resources. A supercharger increases the air supply to an internal combustion engine. The resulting difference in power can be dramatic. You can make just as powerful a difference in your education if you supercharge it by using all of the resources available to students. In this case, your "air supply" includes people, campus clubs and organizations, and school and community services.

Of all resources, people are the most important. You can isolate yourself, study hard, and get a good education. However, doing this is not the most powerful use of your tuition money. When you establish relationships with teachers, staff members, fellow students, and employers, you can get a *great* education. Build a network of people who will personally support your success in school.

Accessing resources is especially important if you are the first person in your family to enter higher education. As a first-generation student, you are having experiences that people in your family may not understand. Talk to your relatives about your activities at school. If they ask how they can help you, give specific answers. Also, ask your instructors about programs for first-generation students on your campus.

Meet with your academic advisor. One person in particular—your academic advisor—can help you access resources and make the transition to higher education. Meet with this person regularly. Advisors generally know about course requirements, options for declaring majors, and the resources available at your school. Peer advisors might also be available.

When you work with an advisor, remember that you're a paying customer and have a right to be satisfied with the service you get. Don't be afraid to change advisors when that seems appropriate.

Learn the language of higher education. Terms such as *grade point average (GPA)*, *prerequisite*, *accreditation*, *matriculation*, *tenure*, and *syllabus* might be new to you. Ease your transition to higher education by checking your school catalog or school Web site for definitions of these words and others that you don't understand. Also ask your academic advisor for clarification.

Show up for class. In higher education, teachers generally don't take attendance. Yet you'll find that attending class is essential to your success. The amount that you pay in tuition and fees makes a powerful argument for going to classes regularly and getting your money's worth. In large part, the material that you're tested on comes from events that take place in class.

Showing up for class occurs on two levels. The most visible level is being physically present in the classroom. Even more important, though, is showing up mentally. This kind of attendance includes taking detailed notes, asking questions, and contributing to class discussions.

Research on college freshmen indicates a link between regular class attendance and academic success.[8] Succeeding in school can help you get almost anything you want, including the career, income, and relationships you desire. Attending class is an investment in yourself.

Manage out-of-class time. For students in higher education, time management takes on a new meaning. What you do *outside* class matters as much as—or even more than—what you do in class. Instructors give you the raw materials for understanding a subject while a class meets. You then take those materials, combine them, and *teach yourself* outside of class.

To allow for this process, schedule two hours of study time for each hour that you spend in class. Also, get a calendar that covers the entire academic year. With the syllabus for each of your courses in hand, note key events for the entire term—dates for tests, papers, and other projects. Getting a big picture of your course load makes it easier to get assignments done on time and avoid all-night study sessions.

Experiment with new ways to study. You can cope with increased workloads and higher academic expectations by putting all of your study habits on the table and evaluating them. Don't assume that the learning strategies you used in the past—in high school or the workplace—will automatically transfer to your new role in higher education. Keep the habits that serve you, drop those that hold you back, and adopt new ones to promote your success. On every page of this book, you'll find helpful suggestions.

Classroom civility—what's in it for you

A student arrives 15 minutes late to a lecture and lets the door slam behind her. She pulls a fast-food burger out of a paper bag (hear the sound of that crackling paper). Then her cell phone rings at full volume—and she answers it. Behaviors like these send a message to everyone in the room: "I'm ignoring you."

Civility means treating people with politeness and respect. Even a small problem with classroom civility can create a barrier for everyone. Learning gets interrupted. Trust breaks down. Your tuition dollars go down the drain.

When you treat instructors with respect, you're more likely to be treated that way in return. A respectful relationship with an instructor could turn into a favorable reference letter, a mentorship, a job referral, or a friendship that lasts for years after you graduate from school. Politeness pays.

Classroom civility does not mean that you have to be passive or insincere. You can present your opinions with passion and even disagree with an instructor. And you can do so in a way that leaves everyone enriched rather than threatened.

Many schools have formal policies about classroom civility. Find out what policies apply to you.

The basics of classroom civility are summarized in the following suggestions. They reflect common sense, and they make an uncommon difference.

Attend classes regularly. Show up for classes on time. If you know that you're going to miss a class or be late, then let your instructor know. Take the initiative to ask your instructor or another student about what you missed.

If you arrive late, do not disrupt class. Close the door quietly and take a seat. When you know that you will have to leave class early, tell your instructor before class begins, and sit near an exit. If you leave class to use the restroom or handle an emergency, do so quietly.

During class, participate fully. Take notes and join in discussions. Turn off your cell phone or any other electronic device that you don't need for class. Remember that sleeping, texting, or doing work for another class is a waste of your time and money.

Instructors often give assignments or make a key point at the end of a class period. Be there when it happens. Wait until class has been dismissed before you pack up your notebook and other materials.

Communicate respect. When you speak in class, begin by addressing your instructor as *Ms., Mrs., Mr., Professor,* or whatever the teacher prefers.

Discussions gain value when everyone gets a chance to speak. Show respect for others by not monopolizing class discussions. Refrain from side conversations and profanity. When presenting viewpoints that conflict with those of classmates or your instructor, combine passion for your opinion with respect for the opinions of others.

Respect gets communicated in the smallest details. Maintain good hygiene. Avoid making distracting noises, and cover your mouth if you yawn or cough. Also avoid wearing inappropriate revealing clothing. Even if you meet your future spouse in class, refrain from public displays of affection.

If you disagree with a class requirement or grade you received, then talk to your instructor about it after class. Your ideas will get more attention if they are expressed in a private setting and in a respectful manner.

See civility as a contribution. Every class you enter has the potential to become a community of people who talk openly, listen fully, share laughter, and arrive at life-changing insights. Anything you do to make that vision a reality is a contribution to your community.

Take the initiative in meeting new people.
Take time before or after class to introduce yourself to classmates and instructors. Most of the people in this new world of higher education are waiting to be welcomed. Plugging into the social networks at any school takes time, but it's worth the effort. Connecting to school socially as well as academically promotes your success and your enjoyment.

Become a self-regulated learner. Reflect on your transition to higher education. Think about what's working well, what you'd like to change, and ways to make those changes. Psychologists use the term *self-regulation* to describe this kind of thinking.[9] Self-regulated learners set goals, monitor their progress toward those goals, and change their behavior based on the results they get.

From Master Student to Master Employee promotes self-regulation through the ongoing cycle of discovery, intention, and action. Write Discovery Statements to monitor your behavior and evaluate the results you're currently creating in any area of your life. Write about your level of commitment to school, your satisfaction with your classes and grades, your social life, and your family's support for your education.

Based on your discoveries, write Intention Statements about your goals for this term, this year, next year, and the rest of your college career. Describe exactly what you will do to create new results in each of these time frames. Then follow through with action. In this way, you take charge of your transition to higher education, starting now. ✳

 Find more strategies for mastering the art of transition online.

Extracurricular activities: Reap the benefits

As you enter higher education, you may find that you are busier than you've ever been before. Often that's due to the variety of extracurricular activities available to you: athletics, fraternities, sororities, student newspapers, debate teams, study groups, service learning projects, internships, student government, and political action groups, to name just a few. Your school might also offer conferences, films, concerts, museums, art galleries, and speakers—all for free or reduced prices. Student organizations help to make these activities possible, and you can join any of them.

Extracurricular involvement comes with potential benefits. People who participate in extracurricular activities are often excellent students. Such activities help them bridge the worlds inside and outside the classroom. They develop new skills, explore possible careers, build contacts for jobs, and build a lifelong habit of giving back to their communities. They make new friends among both students and faculty, work with people from other cultures, and sharpen their conflict resolution skills.

Getting involved in these organizations also comes with some risks. When students don't balance extracurricular activities with class work, their success in school can suffer. They can also compromise their health by losing sleep, neglecting exercise, skipping meals, or relying on fast food. These costs are easier to avoid if you keep a few suggestions in mind:

- *Make conscious choices* about how to divide your time between schoolwork and extracurricular activities. Decide up-front how many hours each week or month you can devote to a student organization. Leave room in your schedule for relaxing and for unplanned events. For more ideas, see Chapter 3: "Time."

- *Look to the future* when making commitments. Write down three or four of the most important goals you'd like to achieve in your lifetime. Then choose extracurricular activities that directly support those goals.

- *Create a career plan* that includes a list of skills needed for your next job. Then choose extracurricular activities to develop those skills. If you're unsure of your career choice, then get involved in campus organizations to explore your options.

- *Whenever possible, develop leadership experience* by holding an office in an organization. If that's too much of a commitment, then volunteer to lead a committee or plan a special event.

- *Get involved in a variety of extracurricular activities.* Varying your activities demonstrates to future employers that you can work with a variety of people in a range of settings.

- *Recognize reluctance* to follow through on a commitment. You might agree to attend meetings and find yourself forgetting them or consistently showing up late. If that happens, write a Discovery Statement about the way you're using time. Follow that with an Intention Statement about ways to keep your agreements—or consider renegotiating those agreements.

- *Check out the rules* before joining any student organization. Ask about dues and attendance requirements.

Connect to resources

AS A STUDENT IN higher education, you can access a world of student services and community resources. Any of them can help you succeed in school. Many of them are free.

Name a problem that you're facing right now or that you anticipate facing in the future: finding money to pay for classes, resolving conflicts with a teacher, lining up a job after graduation. Chances are that a school or community resource can help you. The ability to access resources is a skill that will serve you long after you've graduated.

Resources often go unused. Following are some examples of resources that might be available to you. Check your school and city Web sites for more options.

Academic advisors can help you select courses, choose a major, plan your career, and adjust in general to the culture of higher education.

Arts organizations connect you to local museums, concert venues, clubs, and stadiums.

Athletic centers often open weight rooms, swimming pools, indoor tracks, basketball courts, and racquetball and tennis courts to all students.

Child care is sometimes made available to students at a reasonable cost through the early childhood education department on campus or community agencies.

Churches, synagogues, mosques, and temples have members who are happy to welcome fellow worshippers who are away from home.

Computer labs on campus are places where students can go to work on projects and access the Internet. Computer access is often available off-campus as well. Check public libraries for this service. Some students get permission to use computers at their workplace after hours.

Consumer credit counseling can help even if you've really blown your budget. Best of all, it's usually free. Do your research, and choose a reputable and not-for-profit consumer credit counselor.

Counseling centers in the community can assist you with a problem when you can't get help at school. Look for career-planning services, rehabilitation offices, outreach programs for veterans, and mental health clinics.

The *financial aid office* assists students with loans, scholarships, work-study, and grants.

Governments (city, county, state, and federal) often have programs for students. Check the government listings in your local telephone directory.

Hotlines offer a way to get emergency care, personal counseling, and other kinds of help via a phone call. Do an Internet search on *phone hotlines* in your area that assist with the specific kind of help you're looking for, and check your school catalog for more resources.

Job placement offices can help you find part-time employment while you are in school and a full-time job after you graduate.

Legal aid services provide free or inexpensive assistance to low-income people.

Libraries are a treasure on campus and in any community. They employ people who are happy to help you locate information.

Newspapers published on campus and in the local community list events and services that are free or inexpensive.

The *school catalog* lists course descriptions and tuition fees, requirements for graduation, and information on everything from the school's history to its grading practices.

School security agencies can tell you what's safe and what's not. They can also provide information about parking, bicycle regulations, and traffic rules.

Special needs and disability services assist college students who have learning disabilities or other disabilities.

Student health clinics often provide free or inexpensive counseling and other medical treatment.

Student organizations present opportunities for extracurricular activities. Explore student government, fraternities, sororities, service clubs, religious groups, sports clubs, and political groups. Find women's centers; multicultural student centers; and organizations for international students, students with disabilities, and gay and lesbian students.

Support groups exist for people with almost any problem, from drug addiction to cancer. You can find people with problems who meet every week to share suggestions, information, and concerns about problems they share.

Tutoring is usually free and is available through academic departments or counseling centers. ✳

Leading the way—succeeding as a first-generation student

AMERICAN HISTORY CONFIRMS that people who are the first in their family to enter higher education can succeed. Examples range from the former slaves who enrolled in the country's first African-American colleges to the ex-soldiers who used the GI Bill to win advanced degrees. From their collective experience, you can take some life-changing lessons.

Remember your strengths

The fact that you're reading this book right now is a sign of your accomplishments. You applied to school. You got admitted. You've already taken a huge step to success: You showed up.

Celebrate every one of your successes in higher education, no matter how small they seem. Every assignment you complete, every paper you turn in, and every quiz question you answer is a measurable and meaningful step to getting a degree.

Discover more of your strengths by taking any fact that others might see as a barrier and looking for the hidden advantage. Did you grow up in a family that struggled to make ends meet financially? Then you know about living on a limited budget. Did you work to help support your family while you were in high school? Then you know about managing your time to balance major commitments. Did you grow up in a neighborhood with people of many races, religions, and levels of income? Then you already have an advantage when it comes to thriving with diversity.

Put your strengths in writing. Write Discovery Statements about specific personal, academic, and financial challenges you faced in the past. Describe how you coped with them. Then follow up with Intention Statements about ways to meet the challenges of higher education.

Also keep showing up. Going to every class, lab session, and study group meeting is a way to squeeze the most value from your tuition bills.

Expect change—and discomfort

Entering higher education means walking into a new culture. At times you might feel that all the ground rules have changed, and you have no idea how to fit in. This is normal.

When you walked into your first class this semester, you carried your personal hopes for the future along with the expectations of your parents, siblings, and other relatives. Those people might assume that you'll return home and be the same person you were last year.

The reality is that you will change while you're in school. Your beliefs, your friends, and your career goals may all shift. You might feel critical of people back home and think that some of their ideas are limited. And in turn, they might criticize you.

First-generation students sometimes talk about standing between two worlds. They know that they're changing. At the same time, they are uncertain about what the future holds.

This, too, is normal. Education is all about change. It can be exciting, frustrating, and frightening—all at once. Making mistakes and moving through disappointments is part of the process.

Ask for support

You don't have to go it alone. Your tuition buys access to many services. These are sources of academic and personal support. You'll find examples listed in "Connect to Resources" on page 17. Ask your school about any programs geared specifically to first-generation students.

The key point is to *ask for help right away*. Do this as soon as you feel stuck in class or experience conflict in a relationship.

Also keep a list of every person who stands behind you—relatives, friends, instructors, advisors, mentors, tutors, and counselors. Remind yourself that you are surrounded by people who want you to succeed. Furthermore, thank each of them for their help.

Pay it forward

You are an inspiration to your family, friends, and fellow students. Several people you know might apply to school on the strength of your example. Talk to these people about what you've learned. Your presence in their lives is a contribution. ✳

Succeeding in higher education— at any age

David Buffington/BlendImages/Getty

> If you're returning to school after a long break from the classroom, there's no reason to feel out of place. Returning adults and other nontraditional students are a majority of the student body in some schools.

BEING AN ADULT LEARNER puts you on strong footing. With a rich store of life experiences, you can ask meaningful questions and make connections between course work and daily life.

Following are some suggestions for adult learners who want to ease their transition to higher education. If you're a younger student, commuting student, or community college student, look for useful ideas here as well.

Be clear about why you're back in school. Deborah Davis, author of *The Adult Learner's Companion*, suggests that you state your reason for entering higher education in a single sentence or phrase.[10] For example:

- To be a role model for my family.
- To finish a degree that I started work on years ago.
- To advance in my current job.
- To increase my income and career prospects over the long term.

Make your statement brief, memorable, and personally inspiring. Recall it whenever you're buried in the details of writing papers, reading textbooks, and studying for tests.

Ease into it. If you're new to higher education, consider easing into it. You can choose to attend school part-time before making a full-time commitment. If you've taken college-level classes in the past, find out if any of those credits will transfer into your current program.

Plan your week. Many adult learners report that their number one problem is time. One solution is to plan your week. By planning ahead a week at a time, you get a bigger picture of your multiple roles as a student, an employee, and a family member. With that awareness, you can make conscious adjustments in the number of hours you devote to each domain of activity. For many more suggestions on this topic, see Chapter 3: "Time."

Delegate tasks. Consider hiring others to do some of your household work or errands. Yes, this costs money. It's also an investment in your education and future earning power.

If you have children, delegate some of the chores to them. Or start a meal co-op in your neighborhood. Cook dinner for yourself and someone else one night each week. In return, ask that person to furnish you with a meal on another night. A similar strategy can apply to child care and other household tasks.

Get to know other returning students. Introduce yourself to other adult learners. Being in the same classroom gives you an immediate bond. You can exchange work, home, or cell phone numbers and build a network of mutual support. Some students adopt a buddy system, pairing up with another student in each class to complete assignments and prepare for tests.

Find common ground with traditional students. You share a central goal with younger students: to succeed in school. It's easier to get past the generation gap when you keep this in mind. Traditional and nontraditional students have many things in common. They seek to gain knowledge and skills for their chosen careers. They desire financial stability and personal fulfillment. And, like their older peers, many younger students are concerned about whether they have the skills to succeed in higher education.

Consider pooling resources with younger students. Share notes, edit papers, and form study groups. Look for ways to build on each other's strengths. If you want help with using a computer for assignments, you might find a younger student to help. In group projects and case studies, expand the discussion by sharing insights from your experiences.

David Buffington/BlendImages/Getty

Enlist your employer's support. Employers often promote continuing education. Further education can increase your skills in a specific field while enhancing your ability to work with people. That makes you a more valuable employee or consultant.

Let your employer in on your educational plans. Point out how the skills you gain in class will help you meet work objectives. Offer informal seminars at work to share what you're learning in school.

Get extra mileage out of your current tasks. You can look for specific ways to merge your work and school lives. Some schools offer academic credit for work and life experience. Your company might reimburse its employees for some tuition costs or even grant time off to attend classes.

Experiment with combining tasks. For example, when you're assigned a research paper, choose a topic that relates to your current job tasks.

Look for child care. For some students, returning to class means looking for child care outside the home. Many schools offer childcare facilities at reduced rates for students.

Review your subjects before you start classes. Say that you're registered for trigonometry and you haven't taken a math class since high school. Consider brushing up on the subject before classes begin. Also talk with future instructors about ways to prepare for their classes.

Be willing to adopt new study habits. Rather than returning to study habits from previous school experiences, many adult learners find it more effective to treat their school assignments exactly as they would treat a project at work. They use the same tactics in the library as they do on the job, which often helps them learn more actively.

Integrate class work with daily experiences. You can start by remembering two words: *why* and *how*.

Why prompts you to look for a purpose and benefit in what you're learning. Say that your psychology teacher lectures about Abraham Maslow's ideas on the hierarchy of human needs. Maslow stated that the need for self-actualization is just as important as the need for safety, security, or love.[11]

As you learn what Maslow meant by *self-actualization*, ask yourself why this concept would make a difference in your life. Perhaps your reason for entering higher education is connected to your own quest for self-actualization, that is, for maximizing your fulfillment in life and living up to your highest potential. The theory of self-actualization could clarify your goals and help you get the most out of school.

How means looking for immediate application. Invent ways to use and test concepts in your daily life—the sooner, the better. For example, how could you restructure your life for greater self-actualization? What would you do differently on a daily basis? What things would you acquire that you don't have now? And how would you be different in your moment-to-moment relationships with people?

"Publish" your schedule. After you plan your study and class sessions for the week, hang your schedule in a place where others who live with you will see it.

Enroll family and friends in your success. The fact that you're in school will affect the key relationships in your life. Attending classes and doing homework could mean less time to spend with others. You can prepare family members by discussing these issues ahead of time. For ways to prevent and resolve conflict, see Chapter 9: "Communicating."

You can also involve your spouse, partner, children, or close friends in your schooling. Offer to give them a tour of the campus and encourage them to attend social events at school with you.

Take this process a step further and ask the key people in your life for help. Share your reason for getting a degree, and talk about what your whole family has to gain from this change in your life. Ask them to think of ways that they can support your success in school. Make your own education a joint mission that benefits everyone. ✳

Discovery Statement

Choosing your purpose

Success is a choice—your choice. To *get* what you want, it helps to *know* what you want. That is the purpose of this two-part Journal Entry.

You can begin choosing success by completing this Journal Entry right now. If you choose to do it later, plan a date, time, and place and then block out the time on your calendar.

Date: _____

Time: _____

Place: _____

Part 1

Select a time and place when you know you will not be disturbed for at least 20 minutes. (The library is a good place to do this exercise.) Relax for two or three minutes, clearing your mind. Next, complete the following sentences—and then keep writing.

When you run out of things to write, stick with it just a bit longer. Be willing to experience a little discomfort. Keep writing. What you discover might be well worth the extra effort.

What I want from my education is . . .

_____

_____

_____

_____

When I complete my education, I want to be able to . . .

_____

_____

_____

_____

I also want . . .

_____

_____

_____

_____

_____

Part 2

After completing Part 1, take a short break. Reward yourself by doing something that you enjoy. Then come back to this Journal Entry.

Now, review the list you just created of things that you want from your education. See if you can summarize them in one sentence. Start this sentence with; "My purpose for being in school is. . . ."

Allow yourself to write many drafts of this mission statement, and review it periodically as you continue your education. With each draft, see if you can capture the essence of what you want from higher education and from your life. State it in a vivid way—in a short sentence that you can easily memorize, one that sparks your enthusiasm and makes you want to get up in the morning.

You might find it difficult to express your purpose statement in one sentence. If so, write a paragraph or more. Then look for the sentence that seems most charged with energy for you.

Following are some sample purpose statements:

- My purpose for being in school is to gain skills that I can use to contribute to others.

- My purpose for being in school is to live an abundant life that is filled with happiness, health, love, and wealth.

- My purpose for being in school is to enjoy myself by making lasting friendships and following the lead of my interests.

Write at least one draft of your purpose statement in the following space:

_____

_____

_____

_____

_____

_____

_____

_____

THE Power Processes

A User's Guide

A *Power Process* is a suggestion to shift your perspective and try on a new habit or way of seeing the world. This book includes a baker's dozen of them. Reviewers of *From Master Student to Master Employee* consistently refer to the power of the Power Processes. Many students point to these short, offbeat, and occasionally outrageous articles as their favorite part of the book.

Why use the Power Processes?

People operate like holograms. Holograms are three-dimensional pictures made by using lasers and a special kind of film. You can cut holographic film into tiny pieces and reproduce the entire image from any piece. Each piece contains the whole.

Scientists have observed the same principle at work in biology, physics, sociology, politics, and management. Biologists know that the chromosomes in each cell are the blueprints for that whole organism. Careful study of any one cell can show a plan for the entire body.

The hologram-like nature of human behavior can be summed up in the word *process*. We have a natural tendency to live in patterns—to act out of habit. You can harness this idea for practical benefit. Altering a single attitude or basic behavior is like changing the blueprint for your life. One small change can open the door to many other changes, with a cascading series of positive effects. That's the reason why the word *power* goes with the term *process*.

Becoming a master student means setting up patterns of success that will last the rest of your life. The Power Processes in this book offer many more examples of this approach.

How do I use the Power Processes?

Approach each Power Process with an open mind. Then experiment with it right away. See if it works for you.

Psychologists have written thousands of pages on the subject of personal change. You can find countless personality theories, techniques for reinforcing behaviors, and other complex schemes.

As an alternative, consider that personal change is simple. Just do something differently. Do it now. Then see what happens.

People often make personal change more complicated. They spend years trying to enhance their self-discipline, unearth their childhood memories, search for their hidden sources of motivation, discover their higher self, and on and on.

Another option is to just change, starting today. That's the idea behind the Power Processes. You'll find 13 of them in this book:

- Discover what you want, page 23
- Ideas are tools, page 49
- Risk being a fool, page 81
- Be here now, page 113
- Love your problems (and experience your barriers), page 133
- Notice your pictures and let them go, page 159
- I create it all, page 183
- Detach, page 211
- Find a bigger problem, page 239
- Employ your word, page 271
- Choose your conversations (and your community), page 293
- Surrender, page 313
- Be it, page 353

To start unleashing the power, turn the page now. ✳

Excerpts from Creating Your Future. Copyright © 1998 by David B. Ellis. Reprinted with permission of the author.

Discover What You Want

Excerpts from Creating Your Future.
Copyright © 1998 by David B. Ellis.
Reprinted with permission of the author.

Imagine a person who walks up to a counter at the airport to buy a plane ticket for his next vacation. "Just give me a ticket," he says to the reservation agent. "Anywhere will do."

The agent stares back at him in disbelief. "I'm sorry, sir," she replies. "I'll need some more details. Just minor things—such as the name of your destination city and your arrival and departure dates."

"Oh, I'm not fussy," says the would-be vacationer. "I just want to get away. You choose for me."

Compare this scene with that of another traveler who walks up to the counter and says, "I'd like a ticket to Ixtapa, Mexico, departing on Saturday, March 23, and returning Sunday, April 7. Please give me a window seat, first class, with vegetarian meals."

Now, ask yourself which traveler is more likely to end up with an enjoyable vacation. The same principle applies in any area of life. Knowing where we want to go increases the probability that we will arrive at our destination. Discovering what we want makes it more likely that we'll attain it. Once our goals are defined precisely, our brains reorient our thinking and behavior to align with those goals—and we're well on the way there.

The example about the traveler with no destination seems far-fetched. Before you dismiss it, though, do an informal experiment: Ask three other students what they want to get out of their education. Be prepared for hemming and hawing, vague generalities, and maybe even a helping of pie-in-the-sky à la mode.

These responses are amazing, considering the stakes involved. Our hypothetical vacationer is about to invest a couple weeks of his time and hundreds of dollars, all with no destination in mind. Students routinely invest years of their lives and thousands of dollars with an equally hazy idea of their destination in life.

Now suppose that you ask someone what she wants from her education and you get this answer: "I plan to get a degree in journalism with double minors in earth science and Portuguese so that I can work as a reporter covering the environment in Brazil." Chances are you've found a master student. The details of a person's vision offer a clue to mastery.

Discovering what you want greatly enhances your odds of succeeding in higher education. Many students quit school simply because they are unsure about what they want from it. With well-defined goals in mind, you can look for connections between what you want and what you study. The more connections you discover, the more likely you'll stay in school—and the more likely you'll get what you want in every area of life.[12]

Learn more about using this Power Process online.

1 | First Steps

Master Student Map

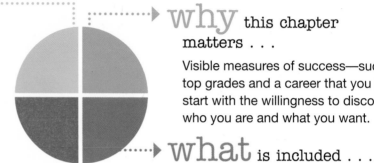

as you read, ask yourself

what if . . .

I could discover my interests, skills, and passions—and build a successful education and career with them?

why this chapter matters . . .

Visible measures of success—such as top grades and a career that you love—start with the willingness to discover who you are and what you want.

how

you can use this chapter . . .

- Experience the power of telling the truth about your current skills.
- Discover your preferred learning styles and develop new ones.
- Define what you want from your education and your career.

what is included . . .

MASTER EMPLOYEE in *action*

The skills I learned in college are initiative and being pro-active. Similar to making the effort to attend office hours to speak with a professor about a project, I have been pro-active in reaching out to people within my division to learn more about their job responsibilities. Through doing so, I have been able to gain insights as to areas I may want to learn more about as well as further my knowledge about how our jobs are connected.

—KRISTEN OATS, FINANCIAL ANALYST

Photo courtesy of Kristen Oats

First Step:
Truth is a key to mastery

THE FIRST STEP technique is simple: Tell the truth about who you are and what you want. End of discussion. Now proceed to Chapter 2: "Careers."

Well, it's not *quite* that simple.

The First Step is one of the most valuable tools in this book. It magnifies the power of all the other techniques. It is a key to becoming a master student.

Urging you to tell the truth sounds like moralizing, but there is nothing moralizing about a First Step. It is a practical, down-to-earth way to change behavior. No technique in this book has been field-tested more often or more successfully—or under tougher circumstances.

The principle of telling the truth is applied universally by people who want to turn their lives around. For members of Alcoholics Anonymous, the First Step is acknowledging that they are powerless over alcohol. For people who join Weight Watchers, the First Step is admitting how much they weigh.

It's not easy to tell the truth about our weaknesses. For some of us, it's even harder to recognize our strengths. Maybe we don't want to brag. Maybe we're attached to a poor self-image. Yet using the First Step technique in *From Master Student to Master Employee* means we must tell the truth about our positive qualities, too.

It might help to remember that weaknesses are often strengths taken to an extreme. The student who carefully revises her writing can make significant improvements in a term paper. If she revises too much and hands in the paper late, though, her grade might suffer. Any success strategy carried too far can backfire.

Whether written or verbal, the ways that we express our First Steps are more powerful when they are specific rather than judgmental. For example, if you want to improve your note-taking skills, you might write, "I am an awful note taker." It would be more effective to write, "I can't read 80 percent of the notes I took in Introduction to Psychology last week, and I have no idea what was important in that class." Be just as specific about what you plan to achieve. You might declare, "I want to take legible notes that help me predict what questions will be on the final exam."

Completing the exercises in this chapter can help you tap resources you never knew you had. They're all First Steps. It's just that simple. The truth has power. ✳

journal entry ③

Discovery/Intention Statement

Create value from this chapter

Take five minutes to skim the Discovery Wheel exercise starting on page 27. Find one statement that describes a skill you already possess—a personal strength that will promote your success in school. Write that statement here:

_____

_____

_____

_____

_____

The Discovery Wheel might also prompt some thoughts about skills you want to acquire. Describe one of those skills by completing the following sentence.

I discovered that . . .

_____

_____

_____

_____

Now, skim the appropriate chapter in this book for at least three articles that could help you develop this skill. For example, if you want to take more effective notes, turn to Chapter 6: "Notes." List the names of your chosen articles here.

I intend to read . . .

_____

_____

_____

_____

_____

3 critical thinking exercise
Taking the First Step

The purpose of this exercise is to give you a chance to discover and acknowledge your own strengths, as well as areas for improvement. For many students, this exercise is the most difficult one in the book. To make the exercise worthwhile, do it with courage.

Some people suggest that looking at areas for improvement means focusing on personal weaknesses. They view it as a negative approach that runs counter to positive thinking. Well, perhaps. Positive thinking is a great technique. So is telling the truth, especially when we see the whole picture—the negative aspects as well as the positive ones.

If you admit that you can't add or subtract and that's the truth, then you have taken a strong, positive First Step toward learning basic math. On the other hand, if you say that you are a terrible math student and that's not the truth, then you are programming yourself to accept unnecessary failure.

The point is to tell the truth. This exercise is similar to the Discovery Statements that appear in every chapter. The difference is that, in this case, for reasons of confidentiality, you won't write down your discoveries in the book.

Be brave. If you approach this exercise with courage, you are likely to disclose some things about yourself that you wouldn't want others to read. You might even write down some truths that could get you into trouble. Do this exercise on separate sheets of paper; then hide or destroy them. Protect your privacy.

To make this exercise work, follow these suggestions.

Be specific. It is not effective to write, "I can improve my communication skills." Of course you can. Instead, write down precisely what you can *do* to improve your communication skills—for example, "I can spend more time really listening while the other person is talking, instead of thinking about what I'm going to say next."

Look beyond the classroom. What goes on outside school often has the greatest impact on your ability to be an effective student. Consider your strengths and weaknesses that you may think have nothing to do with school.

Be courageous. This exercise is a waste of time if it is done half-heartedly. Be willing to take risks. You might open a door that reveals a part of yourself that you didn't want to admit was there. The power of this technique is that once you know what is there, you can do something about it.

Part 1

Time yourself, and for 10 minutes write as fast as you can, completing each of the following sentences at least 10 times with anything that comes to mind. If you get stuck, don't stop. Just write something—even if it seems crazy.

- I never succeed when I . . .
- I'm not very good at . . .
- Something I'd like to change about myself is . . .

Part 2

When you have completed the first part of the exercise, review what you have written, crossing off things that don't make any sense. The sentences that remain suggest possible goals for becoming a master student.

Part 3

Here's the tough part. Time yourself, and for 10 minutes write as fast as you can, completing the following sentences with anything that comes to mind. As in Part 1, complete each sentence at least 10 times. Just keep writing, even if it sounds silly.

- I always succeed when I . . .
- I am very good at . . .
- Something I like about myself is . . .

Part 4

Review what you have written, and circle the things that you can fully celebrate. This list is a good thing to keep for those times when you question your own value and worth.

 Complete this exercise online.

4 critical thinking exercise
The Discovery Wheel

The Discovery Wheel is another opportunity to tell the truth about the kind of student you are and the kind of student you want to become.

This is not a test. There are no trick questions, and the answers will have meaning only for yourself.

Here are two suggestions to make this exercise more effective. First, think of it as the beginning of an opportunity to change. There is another Discovery Wheel at the end of this book. You will have a chance to measure your progress there, so be honest about where you are now. Second, lighten up. A little laughter can make self-evaluations a lot more effective.

Here's how the Discovery Wheel works. By the end of this exercise, you will have filled in a circle similar to the one on this page. The Discovery Wheel circle is a picture of how you see yourself as a student. The closer the shading comes to the outer edge of the circle, the higher the evaluation of a specific skill. In the example to the right, the student has rated her reading skills low and her note-taking skills high.

The terms *high* and *low* are not meant to reflect judgment. The Discovery Wheel is not a permanent picture of who you are. It is a picture of how you view your strengths and weaknesses as a student today. To begin this exercise, read the following statements and award yourself points for each one, using the point system described below. Then add up your point total for each section, and shade the Discovery Wheel on page 30 to the appropriate level.

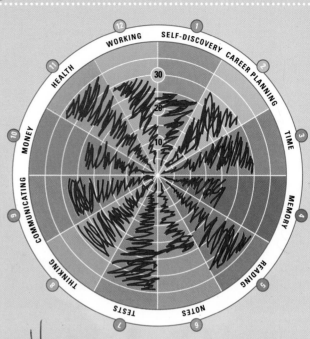

5 points:	This statement is always or almost always true of me.
4 points:	This statement is often true of me.
3 points:	This statement is true of me about half the time.
2 points:	This statement is seldom true of me.
1 point:	This statement is never or almost never true of me.

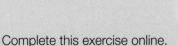

Complete this exercise online.

1. __4__ I enjoy learning.

2. __3__ I understand and apply the concept of multiple intelligences.

3. __2__ I connect my courses to my purpose for being in school.

4. __3__ I make a habit of assessing my personal strengths and areas for improvement.

5. __2__ I am satisfied with how I am progressing toward achieving my goals.

6. __4__ I use my knowledge of learning styles to support my success in school.

7. __5__ I am willing to consider any idea that can help me succeed in school—even if I initially disagree with that idea.

8. __4__ I regularly remind myself of the benefits I intend to get from my education.

__21__ **Total score (1) Self-discovery**

1. __3__ I relate school to what I plan to do for the rest of my life.

2. __1__ I plan my career with a detailed knowledge of my skills.

3. __4__ I relate my career plan to my interests, attitudes, and core values.

4. _3_ I can effectively use a variety of resources to research possible careers.

5. _1_ I use the career planning services offered by my school.

6. _1_ I am planning a career that contributes something worthwhile to the world.

7. _1_ I have a written career plan and I update it regularly.

8. _2_ I use internships, extracurricular activities, information interviews, and on-the-job experiences to test and refine my career plan.

_16_ **Total score (2) Career Planning**

1. _3_ I set long-term goals and periodically review them.

2. _3_ I set short-term goals to support my long-term goals.

3. _3_ I write a plan for each day and each week.

4. _5_ I assign priorities to what I choose to do each day.

5. _2_ I plan review time so I don't have to cram before tests.

6. _5_ I plan regular recreation time.

7. _3_ I adjust my study time to meet the demands of individual courses.

8. _1_ I have adequate time each day to accomplish what I plan.

_25_ **Total score (3) Time**

1. _2_ I am confident of my ability to remember.

2. _2_ I can remember people's names.

3. _4_ At the end of a lecture, I can summarize what was presented.

4. _2_ I apply techniques that enhance my memory skills.

5. _3_ I can recall information when I'm under pressure.

6. _3_ I remember important information clearly and easily.

7. _2_ I can jog my memory when I have difficulty recalling.

8. _4_ I can relate new information to what I've already learned.

_22_ **Total score (4) Memory**

1. _3_ I preview and review reading assignments.

2. _3_ When reading, I ask myself questions about the material.

3. _4_ I underline or highlight important passages when reading.

4. _2_ When I read textbooks, I am alert and awake.

5. _4_ I relate what I read to my life.

6. _1_ I select a reading strategy to fit the type of material I'm reading.

7. _4_ I take effective notes when I read.

8. _2_ When I don't understand what I'm reading, I note my questions and find answers.

_23_ **Total score (5) Reading**

1. _4_ When I am in class, I focus my attention.

2. _4_ I take notes in class.

3. _2_ I am aware of various methods for taking notes and choose those that work best for me.

4. _3_ I distinguish important material and note key phrases in a lecture.

5. _3_ I copy down material that the instructor writes out and displays to the class.

6. _3_ I can put important concepts into my own words.

7. _5_ My notes are valuable for review.

8. _1_ I review class notes within 24 hours.

_25_ **Total score (6) Notes**

1. _3_ I use techniques to manage stress related to exams.

2. _5_ I manage my time during exams and am able to complete them.

3. _1_ I am able to predict test questions.

4. _3_ I adapt my test-taking strategy to the kind of test I'm taking.

5. _4_ I understand what essay questions ask and can answer them completely and accurately.

6. _1_ I start reviewing for tests at the beginning of the term.

7. _1_ I continue reviewing for tests throughout the term.

8. _5_ My sense of personal worth is independent of my test scores.

23 Total score (7) Tests

1. _4_ I have flashes of insight and think of solutions to problems at unusual times.

2. _3_ I use brainstorming to generate solutions to a variety of problems.

3. _3_ When I get stuck on a creative project, I use specific methods to get unstuck.

4. _5_ I see problems and tough choices as opportunities for learning and personal growth.

5. _5_ I am willing to consider different points of view and alternative solutions.

6. _3_ I can detect common errors in logic.

7. _4_ I construct viewpoints by drawing on information and ideas from many sources.

8. _3_ As I share my viewpoints with others, I am open to their feedback.

30 Total score (8) Thinking

1. _2_ I am candid with others about who I am, what I feel, and what I want.

2. _5_ Other people tell me that I am a good listener.

3. _3_ I can communicate my upset and anger without blaming others.

4. _2_ I can make friends and create valuable relationships in a new setting.

5. _2_ I am open to being with people I don't especially like in order to learn from them.

6. _4_ I can effectively plan and research a large writing assignment.

7. _4_ I create first drafts without criticizing my writing, then edit later for clarity, accuracy, and coherence.

8. _2_ I know ways to prepare and deliver effective speeches.

23 Total score (9) Communicating

1. _2_ I am in control of my personal finances.

2. _3_ I can access a variety of resources to finance my education.

3. _4_ I am confident that I will have enough money to complete my education.

4. _3_ I take on debts carefully and repay them on time.

5. _1_ I have long-range financial goals and a plan to meet them.

6. _1_ I make regular deposits to a savings account.

7. _1_ I pay off the balance on credit card accounts each month.

8. _1_ I can have fun without spending money.

16 Total score (10) Money

1. _3_ I have enough energy to study and work—and still enjoy other areas of my life.

2. _2_ If the situation calls for it, I have enough reserve energy to put in a long day.

3. _1_ The way I eat supports my long-term health.

4. _5_ The way I eat is independent of my feelings of self-worth.

5. _2_ I exercise regularly to maintain a healthy weight.

6. _3_ My emotional health supports my ability to learn.

7. _1_ I notice changes in my physical condition and respond effectively.

8. _4_ I am in control of any alcohol or other drugs I put into my body.

21 Total score (11) Health

1. _4_ In work settings, I look for models of success and cultivate mentors.

2. _5_ My work creates value for my employer.

3. _4_ I see working as a way to pursue my interests, expand my skills, and develop mastery.

4. _5_ I support other people in their career planning and job hunting—and am willing to accept their support.

5. _3_ I can function effectively in corporate cultures and cope positively with office politics.

6. _2_ I am skilled at discovering job openings and moving through the hiring process.

7. ___1___ I regularly update and take action on my career plan.

8. ___5___ I see learning as a lifelong process that includes experiences inside and outside the classroom.

___29___ **Total score (12) Working**

Filling in your Discovery Wheel

Using the total score from each category, shade in each section of the Discovery Wheel. Use different colors, if you want. For example, you could use green to denote areas you want to work on. When you have finished, complete Journal Entry 4.

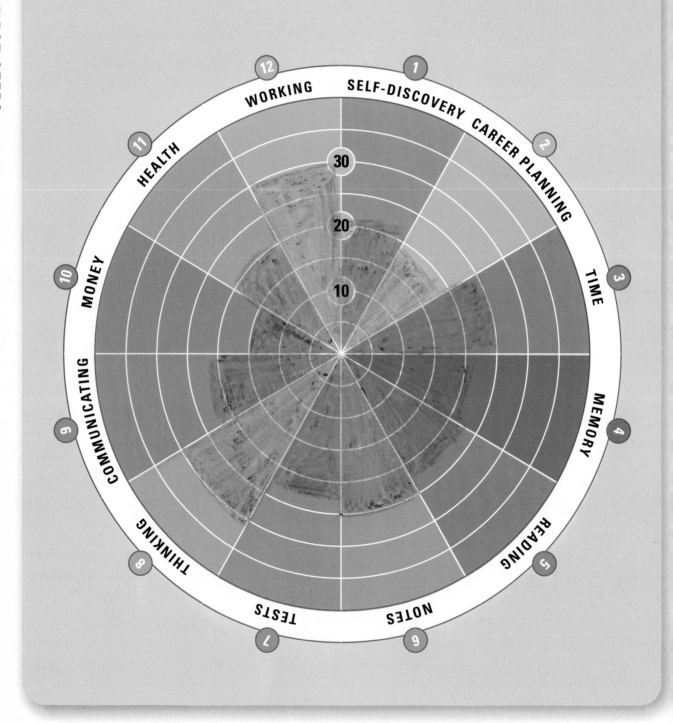

Discovery/Intention Statement

Roll your Discovery Wheel

Now that you have completed your Discovery Wheel, it's time to get a sense of its weight, shape, and balance. Can you imagine running your hands around it? If you could lift it, would it feel light or heavy? How would it sound if it rolled down a hill? Would it roll very far? Would it wobble? Make your observations without judging the wheel as good or bad. Simply be with the picture you have created.

After you have spent a few minutes studying your Discovery Wheel, complete the following sentences in the spaces below them. Don't worry about what to write. Just put down whatever comes to mind. Remember, this is not a test.

This wheel is an accurate picture of my ability as a student because . . .

This wheel is accurate because I am a hard worker, and I am always thinking. I need to work on communicating my ideas to others. Regarding school I need improvement in test taking, reading, and memory. Especially memory

My self-evaluation surprises me because . . .

I am surprised at how little I've planned for a career. I love writing lists, planning and taking notes but was also surprised that I to find that is probably a better way to take notes I write too much.

The two areas in which I am strongest are . . .

My strongest areas in the discovery wheel are working and thinking.

The areas in which I want to improve are . . .

I feel there is always room for improvement is all areas. Judging by my Discovery wheel I need significat improvement in money managment and Career Planning. Personally I would like to improve my communication skills and memory.

I want to concentrate on improving these areas because . . .

Each part of the wheel is important. A good career plan will help me achive goals and better my future.

Now, select one of your discoveries, and describe how you intend to benefit from it. Complete the statement below.

To gain some practical value from this discovery, I will . . .

I

Learning styles: Discovering how you learn

what if ◄········· ········► why

how ◄········· ·······► what

RIGHT NOW, you are investing substantial amounts of time, money, and energy in your education. What you get in return for this investment depends on how well you understand the process of learning and use it to your advantage.

If you don't understand learning, you might feel bored or confused in class. After getting a low grade, you might have no idea how to respond. Over time, frustration can mount to the point where you question the value of being in school.

Some students answer that question by dropping out of school. These students lose a chance to create the life they want, and society loses the contributions of educated workers.

You can prevent that outcome. Gain strategies for going beyond boredom and confusion. Discover new options for achieving goals, solving problems, listening more fully, speaking more persuasively, and resolving conflicts between people. Start by understanding the different ways that people create meaning from their experience and change their behavior. In other words, learn about *how* we learn.

We learn by perceiving and processing

When we learn well, says psychologist David Kolb, two things happen.[1] First, we *perceive*—that is, we notice events and "take in" new experiences. Second, we *process,* or "deal with," experiences in a way that helps us make sense of them.

Some people especially enjoy perceiving through *concrete experience.* They like to absorb information through their five senses. They learn by getting directly involved in new experiences. When solving problems, they rely on intuition as much as intellect. These people typically function well in unstructured classes that allow them to take initiative.

Other people favor perceiving by *abstract conceptualization.* They take in information best when they can think about it as a subject separate from themselves. They analyze, intellectualize, and create

theories. Often these people take a scientific approach to problem solving and excel in traditional classrooms.

People also process experiences differently. Some people favor processing information by *reflective observation.* They prefer to stand back, watch what is going on, and think about it. They consider several points of view as they attempt to make sense of things and generate many ideas about how something happens. They value patience, good judgment, and a thorough approach to learning.

Other people like to process experience by *active experimentation.* They prefer to jump in and start doing things immediately. These people do not mind taking risks as they attempt to make sense of things; this helps them learn. They are results-oriented and look for practical ways to apply what they have learned.

Perceiving and processing—an example

Suppose that you get a new cell phone. It has more features than any phone you've used before. You have many options for learning how to use it. For example, you could do any of the following:

- Just get your hands on the phone right away, press some buttons, and see if you can dial a number or send a text message.

- Read the instruction manual and view help screens on the phone before you try to make a call.

- Recall experiences you've had with phones in the past and what you've learned by watching other people use their cell phones.

- Ask a friend who owns the same type of phone to coach you as you experiment with making calls and sending messages.

These actions illustrate the different ways of perceiving and processing:

- Getting your hands on the phone right away and seeing if you can make it work is an example of learning through concrete experience.

- Reading the manual and help screens before you use the phone is an example of learning through abstract conceptualization.

- Recalling what you've experienced in the past is an example of learning through reflective observation.

- Asking a friend to coach you through a "hands-on" activity with the phone is an example of learning through active experimentation.

Four modes of learning and four questions

Your learning style is the unique way in which you blend the possible ways of perceiving and processing experience. Learning styles can be described in many ways. To keep things simple, just think in terms of four *modes* of learning.

Mode 1 learners are concrete and reflective. They seek a purpose for new information and a personal connection with the content. They want to know that a course matters, and how it challenges or fits in with what they already know. These learners embrace new ideas that relate directly to their current interests and career plans. In summary, Mode 1 learners ask, *Why* learn this?

Mode 2 learners are abstract and reflective. They crave information. When learning something, they want to know the main facts, ideas, and procedures. They seek a theory to explain events and are interested in what experts have to say. Often these learners like ideas that are presented in a logical, organized way. They break a subject down into its key elements or steps and master each one in a systematic way. Mode 2 learners ask, *What* is the content?

Mode 3 learners are abstract and active. They hunger for an opportunity to try out what they're studying. They want to take theories and test them by putting them into practice. These learners thrive when they have well-defined tasks, guided practice, and frequent feedback. Mode 3 learners ask, *How* does this work?

Mode 4 learners are concrete and active. They get excited about going beyond classroom assignments. They apply what they're learning in various situations and use theories to solve real problems. Mode 4 learners ask, *What if* I tried this in a different setting?

The four modes—an example

From Master Student to Master Employee is specifically designed to move you through all four modes of learning.

At the beginning of each chapter, you complete a Journal Entry designed to connect the chapter content to your current life experience. The aim is to help you see the chapter's possible benefits and discover a purpose for reading further. You answer the Mode 1 question—*Why* learn this?

Next, you read articles that are filled with ideas and suggestions for succeeding in school and the workplace. All these readings are answers to the Mode 2 question—*What* is the content?

You also use exercises to practice new skills with and get feedback from your instructor and other students. These exercises are answers to the Mode 3 question—*How* does this work?

Finally, at the end of each chapter, a "Career Application" article and "Focus on Transferable Skills" exercise helps you apply the chapter content to different situations and choose your next step toward mastery. You discover answers to the Mode 4 question—*What if* I tried this in a different setting?

Also notice the Master Student Map at the beginning of each chapter. It presents the chapter content as answers to these four questions. For example, the Master Student Map for this chapter (page 24) suggests *why* this chapter matters: "Success starts with telling the truth about what *is* working—and what *isn't*—in our lives right now." There's a list of *what* topics are included and suggestions for *how* you can use this chapter. Finally, you're encouraged to ask, "*What if* I could create new outcomes in my life by accepting the way I am right now?"

Becoming a flexible learner

Kolb believes that effective learners are flexible. They can learn using all four modes. They consistently ask *Why? What? How?* and *What if?*—and use a full range of activities to find the answers.

Becoming a flexible learner promotes your success in school and in the workplace. By developing all four modes of learning, you can excel in many types of courses. You can learn from instructors with many different styles of teaching. You can expand your options for declaring a major and choosing a career. You can experiment with a variety of strategies and create new options for learning *anything*.

Above all, you can recover your natural gift for learning. Rediscover a world where the boundaries between learning and fun, between work and play, all disappear. While immersing yourself in new experiences, blend the sophistication of an adult with the wonder of a child. This path is one that you can travel for the rest of your life.

The following elements of this chapter are designed to help you take the next steps toward becoming a flexible learner:

- To discover how you currently prefer to learn, take the Learning Style Inventory on this page.

- Read the article "Using Your Learning Style Profile to Succeed" to learn ways to expand on your preferences.

- For additional perspectives on learning styles, see the articles "Claim Your Multiple Intelligences" and "Learning by Seeing, Hearing, and Moving—The VAK System."

Directions for completing the Learning Style Inventory

To help you become more aware of learning styles, Kolb developed the Learning Style Inventory (LSI). This inventory is included on the next several pages. Responding to the items in the LSI can help you discover a lot about ways you learn.

The LSI is not a test. There are no right or wrong answers. Your goal is simply to develop a profile of your current learning style. So, take the LSI quickly. You might find it useful to recall a recent time when you learned something new at school, at home, or at work. However, do not agonize over your responses.

Note that the LSI consists of twelve sentences, each with four different endings. You will read each sentence, and then write a "4" next to the ending that best describes the way you currently learn. Then you will continue ranking the other endings with a "3," "2," or "1," representing the ending that least describes you. You must rank each ending. *Do not leave any endings blank.* Use each number only once for each question.

Following are more specific directions:

1. Read the instructions at the top of page LSI-1. When you understand example A, you are ready to begin.

2. Before you write on page LSI-1, remove the sheet of paper following page LSI-2.

3. While writing on page LSI-1, *press firmly* so that your answers will show up on page LSI-3.

4. After you complete the twelve items on page LSI-1, go to page LSI-3. ✳

 Find more information and examples related to learning styles online.

Discovery Statement

Prepare for the Learning Style Inventory

As a "warm-up" for the LSI and articles that follow, spend a minute or two thinking about times in the past when you felt successful at learning. Underline or highlight any of the following statements that describe those situations:

- I was in a highly structured setting, with a lot of directions about what to do and feedback on how well I did at each step. I was free to learn at my own pace and in my own way.

  I learned as part of a small group.

  I learned mainly by working alone in a quiet place.

- I learned in a place where there was a lot of activity going on.

- I learned by forming pictures in my mind.

- I learned by *doing* something—moving around, touching something, or trying out a process for myself.

  I learned by talking to myself or explaining ideas to other people.

  I got the "big picture" before I tried to understand the details.

  I listened to a lecture and then thought about it after class.

- I read a book or article and then thought about it afterward.

- I used a variety of media—such as videos, films, audio recordings, or computers—to assist my learning.

  I went beyond taking notes and wrote in a personal journal.

  I was considering where to attend school and knew I had to actually set foot on each campus before choosing.

  I was shopping for a car and paid more attention to how I felt about test driving each one than to the sticker prices or mileage estimates.

  I was thinking about going to a movie and carefully read the reviews before choosing one.

Reviewing this list, do you see any patterns in the way you prefer to learn? If you do see any patterns, briefly describe them here.

_____

_____

_____

Learning Style Inventory

Complete items 1–12 below. Use the following example as a guide:

A. When I learn: _2_ I am happy.   _3_ I am fast.   _4_ I am logical.   _1_ I am careful.

Remember: **4** = Most like you   **3** = Second most like you   **2** = Third most like you   **1** = Least like you

Before completing the items, remove the sheet of paper following this page. While writing, press firmly.

1. When I learn:	1	I like to deal with my feelings.	3	I like to think about ideas.	2	I like to be doing things.	4	I like to watch and listen.
2. I learn best when:	4	I listen and watch carefully.	1	I rely on logical thinking.	3	I trust my hunches and feelings.	2	I work hard to get things done.
3. When I am learning:	1	I tend to reason things out.	2	I am responsible about things.	3	I am quiet and reserved.	4	I have strong feelings and reactions.
4. I learn by:	4	feeling.	3	doing.	1	watching.	2	thinking.
5. When I learn:	3	I am open to new experiences.	4	I look at all sides of issues.	2	I like to analyze things, breaking them down into their parts.	1	I like to try things out.
6. When I am learning:	4	I am an observing person.	1	I am an active person.	3	I am an intuitive person	2	I am a logical person.
7. I learn best from:	2	observation.	4	personal relationships.	1	rational theories.	3	a chance to try out and practice.
8. When I learn:	3	I like to see results from my work.	4	I like ideas and theories.	1	I take my time before acting.	2	I feel personally involved in things.
9. I learn best when:	3	I rely on my observations.	2	I rely on my feelings.	4	I can try things out for myself.	1	I rely on my ideas.
10. When I am learning:	2	I am a reserved person.	3	I am an accepting person.	4	I am a responsible person.	1	I am a rational person.
11. When I learn:	3	I get involved.	4	I like to observe.	2	I evaluate things.	1	I like to be active.
12. I learn best when:	3	I analyze ideas.	4	I am receptive and open-minded.	1	I am careful.	2	I am practical.

LSI-1

Take a snapshot of your learning styles

This page is intended to be completed as a culminating exercise. Before you work on this exercise, complete the Learning Styles Inventory and read the following articles:

Learning styles: Discovering how you learn, page 32

Using your learning style profile to succeed, page 35

Claim your multiple intelligences, page 37

Learning by seeing, hearing, and moving—the VAK system, page 39

An inventory of your learning styles is just a snapshot that gives a picture of who you are today. Your answers are not right or wrong. Your score does not dictate who you can become in the future. The key questions are simply "How do I currently learn?" and "How can I become a more successful learner?"

Take a few minutes right now to complete the following sentences describing your latest insights into the way you learn. When you finish, plan to follow up on those insights.

If someone asked me, "What do you mean by learning styles, and can you give me an example?" I'd say. Each person learns differently. Some are hands on learners, picking something up and playing with it to figure it out.

I would describe my current learning style(s) as . . .

If someone asked me to define intelligence, I'd say . . .

When learning well, I tend to use the following senses . . .

I apply my knowledge of learning styles and multiple intelligences by using certain strategies, such as .

When I study or work with people whose learning styles differ from mine, I will respond by . . .

To explore new learning styles, I will . . .

Learning Style Graph

3 Remove the sheet of paper that follows this page. Then transfer your totals from Step 1 on page LSI-3 to the lines on the Learning Style Graph below. On the brown (F) line, find the number that corresponds to your "**Brown F**" total from page LSI-3. Then write an X on this number. Do the same for your "**Teal W**," "**Purple T**," and "**Orange D**" totals. The graph on this page is yours to keep and to refer to and the graph on page LSI-7 is for you to turn into your professor if he or she requires it.

4 Now, pressing firmly, draw four straight lines to connect the four X's and shade in the area to form a kite. (For an example, see the illustration to the right.) This is your learning style profile. Each X that you placed on these lines indicates your preference for a different aspect of learning:

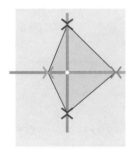

Concrete experience ("feeling"). The number where you put your X on this line indicates your preference for learning things that have personal meaning

and have connections to experiences in your life. The higher your score on this line, the more you like to learn things that you feel are important and relevant to yourself.

Reflective observation ("watching"). Your number on this line indicates how important it is for you to reflect on the things you are learning. If your score is high on this line, you probably find it important to watch others as they learn about an assignment and then report on it to the class. You probably like to plan things out and take the time to make sure that you fully understand a topic.

Abstract conceptualization ("thinking"). Your number on this line indicates your preference for learning ideas, facts, and figures. If your score is high on this line, you probably like to absorb many concepts and gather lots of information on a new topic.

Active experimentation ("doing"). Your number on this line indicates your preference for applying ideas, using trial and error, and practicing what you learn. If your score is high on this line, you probably enjoy hands-on activities that allow you to test out ideas to see what works.

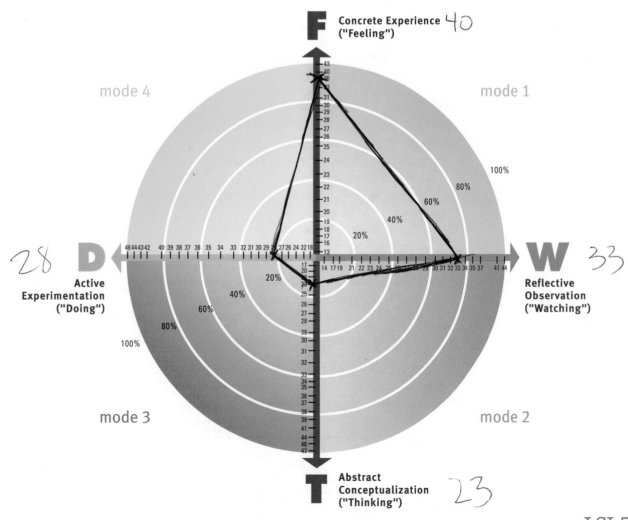

Learning styles across the curriculum

Y ou can get another perspective on learning styles by thinking about ways to succeed in the various subjects that you study. For example, a math course will draw on different ways of perceiving and processing information than a course in African-American literature or modern dance. When you feel stuck in a particular subject, see if you can get unstuck by applying a strategy based on your knowledge of learning styles. The following chart offers some examples. Start with them, and create more on your own.

Subject Area	Possible Strategies for Mastery
Humanities: English, literature, public speaking, history, religion, philosophy, fine arts	• Deepen your reading skills by previewing and reviewing each assignment (see Chapter 5: "Reading"). • Keep a dictionary handy and create an updated list of new words and their definitions. • Experiment with several different formats for taking notes (see Chapter 6: "Notes"). • Keep a personal journal to practice writing and make connections between the authors and ideas that you're studying. • Take part in class discussions and welcome chances to speak in front of groups.
Math and natural sciences: algebra, geometry, calculus, chemistry, biology, physics	• Before registering for a course, make sure that you are adequately prepared through prior course work. • In your notes, highlight basic principles—definitions, assumptions, axioms. • Learn concepts in the sequence presented by your instructor. • If you feel confused, ask a question immediately. • Attend all classes, practice solving problems every day, and check your work carefully. • Translate word problems into images or symbols; translate images and symbols into words. • Balance abstract ideas with concrete experiences, including laboratory sessions and study groups. • Take math courses back to back so you can apply what you learn in one level of a math course immediately to the next level.
Social sciences: sociology, psychology, economics, political science, anthropology, geography	• Pay special attention to theories—key terms and statements that are used to explain relationships between observations and predict events. • Expect complex and contradictory theories, and ask your instructor about ways to resolve disagreements among experts in the field. • Ask your instructor to explain the scientific method and how it is used to arrive at theories in each social science. • Ask about the current state of evidence for each theory. • Ask for examples of a theory and look for them in your daily life.
Foreign languages: learning to speak, read, and write any language that is new to you	• Pay special attention to the "rules"—principles of grammar, noun forms, and verb tense. For each principle, list correct and incorrect examples. • Spend some time reading, writing, or speaking the language every day. • Welcome the opportunity to practice speaking in class, where you can get immediate feedback. • Start or join a study group in each of your language classes. • Spend time with people who are already skilled in speaking the language. • Travel to a country where the language is widely spoken. • Similar to math courses, take your language courses back to back to ensure fluency.

Returning to the big picture about learning styles

This chapter introduces many ideas about how people learn—four modes, multiple intelligences, and the VAK system. That's a lot of information! And these are just a few of the available theories. You may have heard about inventories other than the Learning Style Inventory, such as the Myers-Briggs Type Indicator® (MBTI®) Instrument.* Do an Internet search on *learning styles,* and you'll find many more.

To prevent confusion, remember that there is one big idea behind these theories about learning styles. They all promote *metacognition* (pronounced "metta-cog-NI-shun"). *Meta* means "beyond" or "above." *Cognition* refers to everything that goes on inside your brain—perceiving, thinking, and feeling. So, metacognition refers to your ability to view your attitudes and behaviors from beyond—that is, understand more fully the way you learn. From that perspective, you can choose to think and act in new ways. *Metacognition is one of the main benefits of higher education.*

In addition, theories about learning styles share the following insights:

- People differ in important ways.
- We can see differences as strengths—not deficits.
- Relationships improve when we take differences into account.
- Learning is continuous—it is a *process,* as well as a series of outcomes.
- We *create* knowledge rather than simply absorbing it.
- We have our own preferences for learning.
- We can often succeed by matching our activities with our preferences.
- Our preferences can expand as we experiment with new learning strategies.
- The deepest learning takes place when we embrace a variety of styles and strategies.

Remember that teachers in your life will come and go. Some will be more skilled than others. None of them will be perfect. With a working knowledge of learning styles, you can view any course as one step along a path to learning what you want, using the ways that *you* choose to learn. Along this path toward mastery, you become your own best teacher.

*MBTI and Myer-Briggs Type Indicator are registered trademarks of Consulting Psychologists Press, Inc.

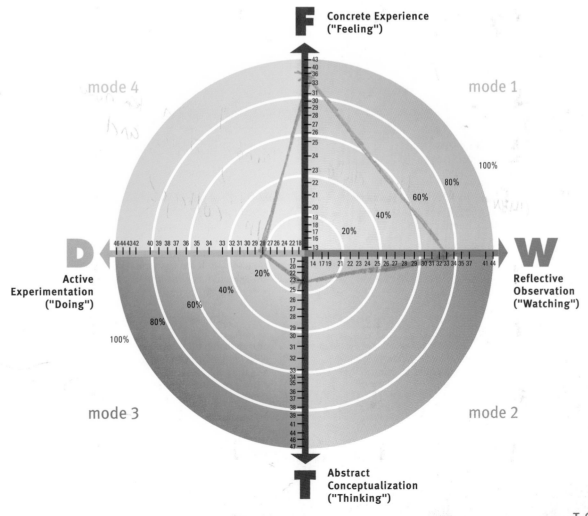

Balancing your preferences

The chart below identifies some of the natural talents as well as challenges for people who have a strong preference for any one mode of learning. For example, if most of your kite is in Mode 2 of the Learning Style Graph, then look at the lower right-hand corner of the following chart to see if this is an accurate description of yourself.

After reviewing the description of your preferred learning mode, read all of the sections for the other modes that start with the words "People with other preferred modes." These sections explain what actions you can take to become a more balanced learner.

Concrete Experience

mode 4

Strengths:
- Getting things done
- Leadership
- Risk taking

Too much of this mode can lead to:
- Trivial improvements
- Meaningless activity

Too little of this mode can lead to:
- Work not completed on time
- Impractical plans
- Lack of motivation to achieve goals

People with other preferred modes can develop Mode 4 by:
- Making a commitment to objectives
- Seeking new opportunities
- Influencing and leading others
- Being personally involved
- Dealing with people

mode 1

Strengths:
- Imaginative ability
- Understanding people
- Recognizing problems
- Brainstorming

Too much of this mode can lead to:
- Feeling paralyzed by alternatives
- Inability to make decisions

Too little of this mode can lead to:
- Lack of ideas
- Not recognizing problems and opportunities

People with other preferred modes can develop Mode 1 by:
- Being aware of other people's feelings
- Being sensitive to values
- Listening with an open mind
- Gathering information
- Imagining the implications of ambiguous situations

Active Experimentation

Reflective Observation

Strengths:
- Problem solving
- Decision making
- Deductive reasoning
- Defining problems

Too much of this mode can lead to:
- Solving the wrong problem
- Hasty decision making

Too little of this mode can lead to:
- Lack of focus
- Reluctance to consider alternatives
- Scattered thoughts

People with other preferred modes can develop Mode 3 by:
- Creating new ways of thinking and doing
- Experimenting with fresh ideas
- Choosing the best solution
- Setting goals
- Making decisions

Strengths:
- Planning
- Creating models
- Defining problems
- Developing theories

Too much of this mode can lead to:
- Vague ideals ("castles in the air")
- Lack of practical application

Too little of this mode can lead to:
- Inability to learn from mistakes
- No sound basis for work
- No systematic approach

People with other preferred modes can develop Mode 2 by:
- Organizing information
- Building conceptual models
- Testing theories and ideas
- Designing experiments
- Analyzing quantitative data

mode 3

mode 2

Abstract Conceptualization

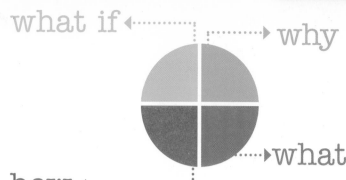

Using your learning style profile to succeed

Develop all four modes of learning

Each mode of learning highlighted in the Learning Style Inventory represents a unique blend of concrete experience, reflective observation, abstract conceptualization, and active experimentation. You can explore new learning styles simply by adopting new habits related to each of these activities. Consider the following suggestions as places to start. Also remember that any insight derived from exploring learning styles will make a difference in your life only when it leads to changes in your behavior.

To gain concrete experiences:

- Attend a live demonstration or performance related to your course content.

- Engage your emotions by reading a novel or seeing a video related to your course.

- Interview an expert in the subject you're learning or a master practitioner of a skill you want to gain.

- Conduct role-plays, exercises, or games based on your courses.

- Conduct an informational interview with someone in your chosen career or "shadow" that person for a day on the job.

- Look for a part-time job, internship, or volunteer experience that complements what you do in class.

- Deepen your understanding of another culture and extend your foreign language skills by studying abroad.

To become more reflective:

- Keep a personal journal, and write about connections among your courses.

- Form a study group to discuss and debate topics related to your courses.

- Set up a Web site, computer bulletin board, e-mail listserv, or online chat room related to your major.

- Create analogies to make sense of concepts; for instance, see if you can find similarities between career planning and putting together a puzzle.

- Visit your course instructor during office hours to ask questions.

- Take time during social events with friends and relatives to briefly explain what your courses are about.

To develop abstract thinking:

- Take notes on your reading in outline form; consider using word-processing software with an outlining feature.

- Supplement assigned texts with other books, magazine and newspaper articles, and related Web sites.

- Attend lectures given by your current instructors and others who teach the same subjects.

- Take ideas presented in text or lectures and translate them into visual form—tables, charts, diagrams, and maps (see Chapter 6: "Notes").

- Create visuals and use computer software to recreate them with more complex graphics and animation.

To become more active:

- Conduct laboratory experiments or field observations.

- Go to settings where theories are being applied or tested; for example, volunteer at a local business or observe a lab school classroom.

- Make predictions based on theories you learn, and then see if events in your daily life confirm your predictions.

- Try out a new behavior described in a lecture or reading, and observe its consequences in your life.

Use the modes to explore your major

If you enjoy learning in Mode 1, you probably value creativity and human relationships. When choosing a major, consider the arts, English, psychology, or political science.

If Mode 2 is your preference, then you enjoy gathering information and building theories. A major related to math or science might be ideal for you.

If Mode 3 is your favorite, then you like to diagnose problems, arrive at solutions, and use technology. Again, a major related to health care, engineering, or economics is a logical choice for you.

And if your preference is Mode 4, you probably enjoy taking the initiative, implementing decisions, teaching, managing projects, and moving quickly from planning into action. Consider a major in business or education.

As you prepare to declare a major, remain flexible. Use your knowledge of learning styles to open up possibilities rather than restrict them.

Use the modes of learning to explore your career

People who excel at Mode 1 are often skilled at "tuning in" to the feelings of clients and coworkers. These people can listen with an open mind, tolerate confusion, be sensitive to people's feelings, open up to problems that are difficult to define, and brainstorm a variety of solutions. If you like Mode 1, you may be drawn to a career in counseling, social services, the ministry, or another field that centers on human relationships. You might also enjoy a career in the performing arts.

People who prefer Mode 2 like to do research and work with ideas. They are skilled at gathering data, interpreting information, and summarizing—activities that help them arrive at the "big picture." They may excel at careers that center on science, math, technical communications, or planning. Mode 2 learners may also work as college teachers, lawyers, technical writers, or journalists.

People who like Mode 3 are drawn to solving problems, making decisions, and checking on progress toward goals. Careers in medicine, engineering, information technology, or another applied science are often ideal for them.

People who enjoy Mode 4 like to influence and lead others. These people are often described as "doers" and "risk takers." They like to take action and complete projects. Mode 4 learners often excel at managing, negotiating, selling, training, and teaching. They might also work for a government agency.

Keep in mind that there is no strict match between certain learning styles and certain careers. Learning is essential to success in all careers. Also, any career can attract people with a variety of learning styles.

Accommodate differing styles

Once you've discovered differences in styles, look for ways to accommodate them in your dealings with other people.

Remember that some people want to reflect on the "big picture" first. When introducing a project plan, you might say, "This process has four major steps." Before explaining the plan in detail, talk about the purpose of the project and the benefits of completing each step.

Allow time for active experimentation and concrete experience. Offer people a chance to try out a new product or process for themselves—to literally "get the feel of it."

Allow for abstract conceptualization. When leading a study group or conducting a training session, provide handouts that include plenty of visuals and step-by-step instructions. Visual learners and people who like to think abstractly will appreciate these materials. Also schedule periods for questions and answers.

When working on teams, look for ways that members can complement one another's strengths. If you're skilled at planning, find someone who excels at doing. Also seek people who can reflect on and interpret the team's experience. Pooling different styles allows you to draw on everyone's strengths. ✳

Use the modes to learn from any instructor

Students who experience difficulty in school might say, "The tests are too hard for me." Or "In class, we never have time for questions." Or "The instructor doesn't teach to my learning style."

Such statements prevent you from taking responsibility for your education. To stay in charge of your learning, consider adopting attitudes such as the following:

I will look for the value in this information.

I can learn something useful in any situation.

I will experiment with this suggestion to see if it works.

No matter who's teaching this course, I am responsible for what I learn.

I will master this subject by using several modes of learning.

You can take action on such statements even if you don't fully agree with them. One way to change your attitudes is to adopt new behaviors, see how they work, and watch for new results.

FIRST STEPS

1

(man) © Tanya Constantine/Getty, (fern) © Tim Laman/Getty, (ballet shoes) © Scott T. Baxter/Getty, (protractor) © Vladimir Godnik/Getty, (meditating woman) © Meg Takamura, (easel) © Stockbyte/Getty, (microphone) © George Doyle/Getty, (holding hands) © DougMenuez/Getty, (music) © Gregor Schuster/Getty

Claim your multiple intelligences

PEOPLE OFTEN THINK that being smart means the same thing as having a high IQ, and that having a high IQ automatically leads to success. However, psychologists are finding that IQ scores do not always foretell which students will do well in academic settings—or after they graduate.[2]

Howard Gardner of Harvard University believes that no single measure of intelligence can tell us how smart we are. Instead, Gardner defines intelligence in a flexible way as "the ability to solve problems, or to create products, that are valued within one or more cultural settings." He also identifies several types of intelligence:[3]

People using **verbal/linguistic intelligence** are adept at language skills and learn best by speaking, writing, reading, and listening.

People who use **mathematical/logical intelligence** are good with numbers, logic, problem solving, patterns, relationships, and categories.

When people learn visually and by organizing things spatially, they display **visual/spatial intelligence.**

People using **bodily/kinesthetic intelligence** prefer physical activity, and they would rather participate in games than just watch.

Individuals using **musical/rhythmic intelligence** enjoy musical expression through songs, rhythms, and musical instruments.

People using **intrapersonal intelligence** are generally reserved, self-motivated, and intuitive.

Outgoing people show evidence of **interpersonal intelligence** and do well with cooperative learning, often making good leaders.

People using **naturalist intelligence** love the outdoors and recognize details in plants, animals, rocks, clouds, and other natural formations.

Experiment with learning in ways that draw on a variety of intelligences. When we acknowledge all of our intelligences, we can constantly explore new ways of being smart. ✳

5 critical thinking exercise
Develop your multiple intelligences

In the following chart, place a check mark next to any of the "Possible Characteristics" that describe you. Also check off the "Possible Learning Strategies" that you intend to use. Finally, underline or highlight any of the "Possible Careers" that spark your interest.

Remember that the chart is *not* an exhaustive list or a formal inventory. Take what you find merely as points of departure. You can identify other characteristics and invent strategies of your own to cultivate different intelligences.

Type of intelligence	Possible characteristics	Possible learning strategies	Possible careers
Verbal/linguistic	☑ You enjoy writing letters, stories, and papers. ☑ You take excellent notes from textbooks and lectures.	☑ Highlight, underline, and write notes in your textbooks. ☑ Rewrite and edit your class notes.	English teacher, editor, jou ist, lawyer, librarian, radio television announcer
Mathematical/logical	☐ You prefer math or science class over English class. ☑ You want to know how and why things work.	☑ Group concepts into categories, and look for underlying patterns. ☐ Convert text into tables, charts, and graphs.	Accountant, actuary, audi computer programmer, ec mist, mathematician, matl science teacher, tax prepa
Visual/spatial	☐ You draw pictures to give an example or clarify an explanation. ☑ You assemble things from illustrated instructions.	☐ When taking notes, create concept maps, mind maps, and other visuals (see Chapter 6). ☑ When your attention wanders, focus it by sketching or drawing.	Architect, cartographer, c mercial artist, engineer, fir artist, graphic designer, in decorator, photographer
Bodily/kinesthetic	☐ You tend not to sit still for long periods of time. ☐ You enjoy working with your hands.	☐ Carry materials with you and practice studying in several different locations. ☐ Create hands-on activities related to key concepts.	Actor, athlete, athletic coa chiropractor, dancer, phys education teacher, physic therapist
Musical/rhythmic	☑ You often sing in the car or shower. ☑ You play a musical instrument.	☑ During a study break, play music or dance to restore energy. ☑ Relate key concepts to songs you know.	Musician, music teacher, therapist
Intrapersonal	☑ You enjoy writing in a journal and being alone with your thoughts. ☑ You prefer to work on individual projects over group projects.	☑ Connect course content to your personal values and goals. ☑ Connect readings and lectures to a strong feeling or significant past experience.	Freelance writer, owner o home-based business
Interpersonal	☐ You have plenty of friends and regularly spend time with them. ☑ You prefer talking and listening over reading or writing.	☐ Create flash cards and use them to quiz study partners. ☐ Volunteer to give a speech or lead group presentations.	Counselor, manager, nurs school administrator, teac
Naturalist	☑ You enjoy being outdoors. ☑ You find that important insights occur during times you spend in nature.	☑ Post pictures of outdoor scenes where you study and play recordings of outdoor sounds while you read. ☐ Invite classmates to discuss course work while taking a hike.	Biologist, construction wo environmental activist, pa ranger, recreation supervi woodworker

Learning by seeing, hearing, and moving: The VAK system

YOU CAN APPROACH the topic of learning styles with a simple and powerful system—one that focuses on just three ways of perceiving through your senses:

- Seeing, or *visual learning*.
- Hearing, or *auditory learning*.
- Movement, or *kinesthetic learning*.

To recall this system, remember the letters *VAK*, which stand for visual, auditory, and kinesthetic. The theory is that each of us prefers to learn through one of these sense channels. In addition, we can enrich our learning with activities that draw on the other channels.

To reflect on your VAK preferences, answer the following questions. Each question has three possible answers. Circle the answer that best describes how you would respond in the stated situation. This is not a formal inventory—just a way to prompt some self-discovery.

When you have problems spelling a word, you prefer to:

1. Look it up in the dictionary.
2. Say the word out loud several times before you write it down.
3. Write out the word with several different spellings and then choose one.

You enjoy courses the most when you get to:

1. View slides, overhead displays, videos, and readings with plenty of charts, tables, and illustrations.
2. Ask questions, engage in small-group discussions, and listen to guest speakers.
3. Take field trips, participate in lab sessions, or apply the course content while working as a volunteer or intern.

When giving someone directions on how to drive to a destination, you prefer to:

1. Pull out a piece of paper and sketch a map.
2. Give verbal instructions.
3. Say, "I'm driving to a place near there, so just follow me."

When planning an extended vacation to a new destination, you prefer to:

1. Read colorful, illustrated brochures or articles about that place.
2. Talk directly to someone who's been there.
3. Spend a day or two at that destination on a work-related trip before taking a vacation there.

You've made a commitment to learn to play the guitar. The first thing you do is:

1. Go to a library or music store and find an instruction book with plenty of diagrams and chord charts.
2. Pull out your favorite CDs, listen closely to the guitar solos, and see if you can sing along with them.
3. Buy or borrow a guitar, pluck the strings, and ask someone to show you how to play a few chords.

You've saved up enough money to lease a car. When choosing from among several new models, the most important factor in your decision is:

1. The car's appearance.
2. The information you get by talking to people who own the cars you're considering.
3. The overall impression you get by taking each car on a test drive.

Now take a few minutes to reflect on the meaning of your responses. All of the answers numbered "1" are examples of visual learning. The "2" refer to auditory learning, and the "3" illustrate kinesthetic learning. Finding a consistent pattern in your answers indicates that you prefer learning through one sense channel more than the others. Or you might find that your preferences are fairly balanced.

The following list includes suggestions for learning through each sense channel. Experiment with these examples, and create more techniques of your own. Use the suggestions to build on your current preferences and develop new options for learning.

To enhance visual learning:

- Preview reading assignments by looking for elements that are highlighted visually—bold headlines, charts, graphs, illustrations, and photographs.

- When taking notes in class, leave plenty of room to add your own charts, diagrams, tables, and other visuals later.

- Whenever an instructor writes information on a blackboard or other display, copy it exactly in your notes.

- Transfer your handwritten notes to your computer. Use word-processing software that allows you to format your notes in lists, add headings in different fonts, and create visuals in color.

- Before you begin an exam, quickly sketch a diagram on scratch paper. Use this diagram to summarize the key formulas or facts you want to remember.

- During tests, see if you can visualize pages from your handwritten notes or images from your computer-based notes.

To enhance auditory learning:

- Reinforce memory of your notes and readings by talking about them. When studying, stop often to recite key points and examples in your own words.

- After reciting several summaries of key points and examples, record your favorite version or write it out.

- Read difficult passages in your textbooks slowly and out loud.

- Join study groups, and create short presentations about course topics.

- Visit your instructors during office hours to ask questions.

To enhance kinesthetic learning:

- Look for ways to translate course content into three-dimensional models that you can build. While studying biology, for example, create a model of a human cell using different colors of clay.

- Supplement lectures with trips to museums, field observations, lab sessions, tutorials, and other hands-on activities.

- Recite key concepts from your courses while you walk or exercise.

- Intentionally set up situations in which you can learn by trial and error.

- Create a practice test, and write out the answers in the room where you will actually take the exam.

One variation of the VAK system has been called VARK.[4] The *R* describes a preference for learning by reading and writing. People with this preference might benefit from translating charts and diagrams into statements, taking notes in lists, and converting those lists into possible items on a multiple-choice test. ✳

Reminder: Go back to page LSI-2 to complete the "Take a Snapshot of Your Learning Styles" exercise.

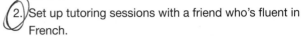

In 1482, Leonardo da Vinci wrote a letter to a wealthy baron, applying for work. Here is an excerpt from the letter: "I can contrive various and endless means of offense and defense. . . . I have all sorts of extremely light and strong bridges adapted to be most easily carried . . . I have methods for destroying every turret or fortress. . . . I will make covered chariots, safe and unassailable. . . . In case of need I will make big guns, mortars, and light ordnance of fine and useful forms out of the common type." And then he added, almost as an afterthought, "In times of peace I believe I can give perfect satisfaction and to the equal of any other in architecture . . . can carry out sculpture . . . and also I can do in painting whatever may be done."
The *Mona Lisa*, for example.

The Master Student

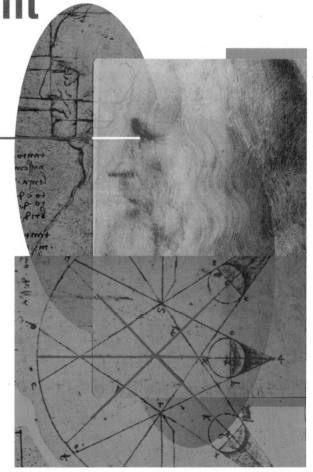

THIS BOOK IS about something that cannot be taught. It's about becoming a master student.

Mastery means attaining a level of skill that goes beyond technique. For a master, methods and procedures are automatic responses to the needs of the task. Work is effortless; struggle evaporates. The master carpenter is so familiar with her tools that they are part of her. To a master chef, utensils are old friends. Because these masters don't have to think about the details of the process, they bring more of themselves to their work.

Mastery can lead to flashy results—an incredible painting, for example, or a gem of a short story. In basketball, mastery might result in an unbelievable shot at the buzzer. For a musician, it might be the performance of a lifetime—the moment when everything comes together.

Psychologist Mihaly Csikszentmihalyi describes mastery as the experience of *flow*. During this experience, our attention is completely focused: "Self-consciousness disappears, yet one feels stronger than usual. The sense of time is distorted: hours seem to pass by in minutes . . . whatever one does becomes worth doing for its own sake; living becomes its own justification."[5]

When the master student is in such a state, she makes learning look easy. She works hard without seeming to make any effort. She's relaxed *and* alert, disciplined *and* spontaneous, focused *and* fun-loving.

You might say that those statements don't make sense. Mastery, in fact, doesn't make sense. It cannot be captured with words. It defies analysis. Mastery cannot be taught. It can only be learned and experienced.

Examine the following list of characteristics of master students in light of your own experience. The list is not complete. It merely points in a direction. Look in that direction and you'll begin to see the endless diversity of master students. These people are old and young, male and female. They exist in every period of history. And they come from every culture, race, and ethnic group.

Also remember to look to yourself. No one can teach us to be master students; we already are master students. We are natural learners by design. As students, we can discover that every day.

Following are some traits shared by master students.

Inquisitive. The master student is curious about everything. By posing questions, she can generate interest in the most mundane, humdrum situations. When she is bored during a biology lecture, she thinks to herself, "I always get bored when I listen to this instructor. Why is that? Maybe it's because he reminds me of my boring Uncle Ralph, who always tells those endless fishing stories. He even looks like Uncle Ralph. Amazing! Boredom is certainly interesting." Then she asks herself, "What can I do to get value out of this lecture, even though it seems boring?" And she finds an answer.

Able to focus attention. Watch a 2-year-old at play. Pay attention to his eyes. The wide-eyed look reveals an energy and a capacity for amazement that keep his attention absolutely focused in the here and now. The master student's focused attention has a childlike quality. The world, to a child, is always new. Because the master student can focus attention, to him the world is always new, too.

Willing to change. The unknown does not frighten the master student. In fact, she welcomes it—even the unknown in herself. We all have pictures of who we think we are, and these pictures can be useful. However, they also can prevent learning and growth. The master student is open to changes in her environment and in herself.

Able to organize and sort. The master student can take a large body of information and sift through it to discover relationships. He can play with information, organizing data by size, color, function, timeliness, and hundreds of other categories.

Competent. Mastery of skills is important to the master student. When she learns mathematical formulas, she studies them until they become second nature. She practices until she knows them cold, then puts in a few extra minutes. She also is able to apply what she learns to new and different situations.

Positive. The master student doesn't give in to negative thoughts or feelings. He is able to cope and deal with problems of daily life.

Able to suspend judgment. The master student has opinions and positions, and she is able to let go of them when appropriate. She realizes she is more than her thoughts. She can quiet her internal dialogue and listen to an opposing viewpoint. She doesn't let judgment get in the way of learning. Rather than approaching discussions with a "Prove it to me and then I'll believe it" attitude, she asks herself, "What if this is true?" and explores possibilities.

Energetic. Notice the student with a spring in his step—the one who is enthusiastic and involved in class. When he reads, he often sits on the very edge of his chair, and he plays with the same intensity. He is a master student.

Well. Health is important to the master student, though not necessarily in the sense of being free of illness. Rather, she values her body and treats it with respect. She tends to her emotional and spiritual health, as well as her physical health.

Self-aware. The master student is willing to evaluate himself and his behavior. He regularly tells the truth about his strengths and those aspects that could be improved.

Responsible. There is a difference between responsibility and blame, and the master student knows it well. She is willing to take responsibility for everything in her life—even for events that most people would blame on others.

For example, if a master student takes a required class that most students consider boring, she chooses to take responsibility for her interest level. She looks for ways to link the class to one of her goals. She sees the class as an opportunity to experiment with new study techniques that will enhance her performance in any course. She remembers that by choosing her thoughts and behaviors, she can create interesting classes, enjoyable relationships, fulfilling work experiences, or just about anything else she wants.

Willing to take risks. The master student often takes on projects with no guarantee of success. He participates in class dialogues at the risk of looking foolish. He tackles difficult subjects in term papers. He welcomes the risk of a challenging course.

Willing to participate. Don't look for the master student on the sidelines. She's in the game. She is a player who can be counted on. She is willing to make a commitment and to follow through on it.

A generalist. The master student is interested in everything around him. He has a broad base of knowledge in many fields and can apply it to his specialties.

Willing to accept paradox. The word *paradox* comes from two Greek words, *para* ("beyond") and *doxen* ("opinion"). A paradox is something that is beyond opinion or, more accurately, something that might seem contradictory or absurd yet might actually have meaning.

For example, the master student can be committed to managing money and reaching her financial goals. At the same time, she can be totally detached from money, knowing that her real worth is independent of how much money she has. The master student recognizes the limitations of the mind and is at home with paradox. She can accept that ambiguity.

Courageous. The master student admits his fear and fully experiences it. For example, he will approach a tough exam as an opportunity to explore feelings of anxiety and tension related to the pressure to perform. He does not deny fear; he embraces it.

Self-directed. Rewards or punishments provided by others do not motivate the master student. Her motivation to learn comes from within.

Spontaneous. The master student is truly in the here and now. He is able to respond to the moment in fresh, surprising, and unplanned ways.

Relaxed about grades. Grades make the master student neither depressed nor euphoric. She recognizes that sometimes grades are important. At the same time, grades are not the only reason she studies. She does not measure her worth as a human being by the grades she receives.

Intuitive. The master student has an inner sense that cannot be explained by logic. He has learned to trust his feelings, and he works to develop this intuitive sense.

Creative. Where others see dull details and trivia, the master student sees opportunities to create. She can gather pieces of knowledge from a wide range of subjects and put them together in new ways. The master student is creative in every aspect of her life.

Willing to be uncomfortable. The master student does not place comfort first. When discomfort is necessary to reach a goal, he is willing to experience it. He can endure personal hardships and can look at unpleasant things with detachment.

Optimistic. The master student sees setbacks as temporary and isolated, knowing that she can choose her response to any circumstance.

Willing to laugh. The master student might laugh at any moment, and his sense of humor includes the ability to laugh at himself.

Going to school is a big investment. The stakes are high. It's OK to be serious about that, but the master student knows he doesn't have to go to school on the deferred-fun program. He celebrates learning, and understands one of the best ways to do that is to have a laugh now and then.

Hungry. Human beings begin life with a natural appetite for knowledge. In some people it soon gets dulled. The master student has tapped that hunger, and it gives her a desire to learn for the sake of learning.

Willing to work. Once inspired, the master student is willing to follow through with sweat. He knows that genius and creativity are the results of persistence and work. When in high gear, the master student works with the intensity of a child at play.

Caring. A master student cares about knowledge and has a passion for ideas. She also cares about people and appreciates learning from others. She flourishes in a community that values win/win outcomes, cooperation, and love.

The master student in you. The master student is in all of us. By design, human beings are learning machines. We have an innate ability to learn, and all of us have room to grow and improve.

It is important to understand the difference between learning and being taught. Human beings can resist being taught anything. Psychologist Carl Rogers goes so far as to say that anything that can be taught to a human being is either inconsequential or just plain harmful.[6] What is important in education, Rogers asserts, is learning. And everyone has the ability to learn.

Unfortunately, people also learn to hide that ability. As they experience the pain that sometimes accompanies learning, they shut down. If a child experiences embarrassment in front of a group of people, he may learn to avoid similar situations. In doing so, he restricts his possibilities.

Some children "learn" that they are slow learners. If they learn it well enough, their behavior starts to match that label.

As people grow older, they sometimes accumulate a growing list of ideas to defend—a catalog of familiar experiences that discourages them from learning anything new.

Still, the master student within survives. To tap that resource, you don't need to acquire anything. You already have everything you need. Every day you can rediscover the natural learner within you. ✳

olly/Shutterstock

Motivation—getting beyond "I'm just not in the mood"

THERE ARE at least two ways to think about motivation. One way is to use the terms *self-discipline, willpower,* and *motivation* to describe something missing in ourselves. We use these words to explain another person's success—or our own shortcomings: "If I were more motivated, I'd get more involved in school." "Of course she got an A. She has self-discipline." "If I had more willpower, I'd lose weight." It seems that certain people are born with lots of motivation, while others miss out on it.

A second approach to thinking about motivation is to stop assuming that motivation is mysterious, determined at birth, or hard to come by. Perhaps there's nothing in you that's missing. What we call motivation could be something that you already possess—the ability to do a task even when you don't feel like it. This is a habit that you can develop with practice. The following suggestions offer ways to do that.

Promise it. Motivation can come simply from being clear about your goals and acting on them. Say that you want to start a study group. You can commit yourself to inviting people and setting a time and place to meet. Promise your classmates that you'll do this, and ask them to hold you accountable. Self-discipline, willpower, motivation—none of these mysterious characteristics needs to get in your way. Just make a promise and keep your word.

Befriend your discomfort. Begin by investigating the discomfort. Notice the thoughts running through your head, and speak them out loud: "I'd rather walk on a bed of coals than do this." "This is the last thing I want to do right now."

Also observe what's happening with your body. For example, are you breathing faster or slower than usual?

Is your breathing shallow or deep? Are your shoulders tight? Do you feel any tension in your stomach?

Once you're in contact with your mind and body, stay with the discomfort a few minutes longer. Don't judge it as good or bad. Accepting the thoughts and body sensations robs them of power. They might still be there, but in time they can stop being a barrier for you.

Discomfort can be a gift—an opportunity to do valuable work on yourself. On the other side of discomfort lies mastery.

Change your mind—and your body. You can also get past discomfort by planting new thoughts in your mind or changing your physical stance. For example, instead of slumping in a chair, sit up straight or stand up. You can also get physically active by taking a short walk. Notice what happens to your discomfort.

Work with your thoughts, also. Replace "I can't stand this" with "I'll feel great when this is done" or "Doing this will help me get something I want."

Sweeten the task. Sometimes it's just one aspect of a task that holds you back. You can stop procrastinating merely by changing that aspect. If distaste for your physical environment keeps you from studying, you can change that environment. Reading about social psychology might seem like a yawner when you're alone in a dark corner of the house. Moving to a cheery, well-lit library can sweeten the task.

Talk about how bad it is. One way to get past negative attitudes is to take them to an extreme. When faced with an unpleasant task, launch into a no-holds-barred gripe session. Pull out all the stops: "There's no way I can start my income taxes now. This is terrible beyond words—an absolute disaster. This is a

Galina Barskaya/Shutterstock

catastrophe of global proportions!" Griping taken this far can restore perspective. It shows how self-talk can turn inconveniences into crises.

Turn up the pressure. Sometimes motivation is a luxury. Pretend that the due date for your project has been moved up one day, one week, or one month. Raising the stress level slightly can spur you into action. Then the issue of motivation seems beside the point, and meeting the due date moves to the forefront.

Turn down the pressure. The mere thought of starting a huge task can induce anxiety. To get past this feeling, turn down the pressure by taking "baby steps." Divide a large project into small tasks. In 30 minutes or less, you could preview a book, create a rough outline for a paper, or solve two or three math problems. Careful planning can help you discover many such steps to make a big job doable.

Ask for support. Other people can become your allies in overcoming procrastination. For example, form a support group and declare what you intend to accomplish before each meeting. Then ask members to hold you accountable. If you want to begin exercising regularly, ask another person to walk with you three times weekly. People in support groups ranging from Alcoholics Anonymous to Weight Watchers know the power of this strategy.

Adopt a model. One strategy for succeeding at any task is to hang around the masters. Find someone you consider successful, and spend time with her. Observe this person and use her as a model for your own behavior. You can "try on" this person's actions and attitudes. Look for tools that feel right for you. This person can become a mentor to you.

Compare the payoffs to the costs. All behaviors have payoffs and costs. Even unwanted behaviors such as cramming for exams or neglecting exercise have

payoffs. Cramming might give you more time that's free of commitments. Neglecting exercise can give you more time to sleep.

We can openly acknowledge the payoffs and then follow up with the next step—determining the costs. For example, skipping a reading assignment can give you time to go to the movies. However, you might be unprepared for class and have twice as much to read the following week.

Maybe there is another way to get the payoff (going to the movies) without paying the cost (skipping the reading assignment). With some thoughtful weekly planning, you might choose to give up a few hours of television and end up with enough time to read the assignment *and* go to the movies.

Comparing the costs and benefits of any behavior can fuel our motivation. We can choose new behaviors because they align with what we want most.

Do it later. At times, it's effective to save a task for later. For example, writing a résumé can wait until you've taken the time to analyze your job skills and map out your career goals. Putting it off does not show a lack of motivation—it shows planning.

Heed the message. Sometimes lack of motivation carries a message that's worth heeding. For example, consider the student who majors in accounting but seizes every chance to be with children. His chronic reluctance to read accounting textbooks might not be a problem. Instead, it might reveal his desire to major in elementary education. His original career choice might have come from the belief that "real men don't teach kindergarten." In such cases, an apparent lack of motivation signals a deeper wisdom trying to get through. ✳

Ways to change a habit

CONSIDER A NEW WAY to think about the word *habit*. Imagine for a moment that many of our most troublesome problems and even our most basic traits are just habits.

The expanding waistline that your friend is blaming on her spouse's cooking—maybe that's just a habit called overeating.

The fit of rage that a student blames on a teacher—maybe that's just the student's habit of closing the door to new ideas.

Procrastination, stress, and money shortages might just be names that we give to collections of habits—scores of simple, small, repeated behaviors that combine to create a huge result. The same goes for health, wealth, love, and many of the other things that we want from life.

One way to change your thinking about success and failure is to focus on habits. Behaviors such as failing to complete reading assignments or skipping class might be habits leading to outcomes that "could not" be avoided, including dropping out of school. In the same way, behaviors such as completing assignments and attending class might lead to the outcome of getting an "A."

When you confront a behavior that undermines your goals or creates a circumstance that you don't want, consider a new attitude: That behavior is just a habit. And it can be changed.

Thinking about ourselves as creatures of habit actually gives us power. Then we are not faced with the monumental task of changing our very nature. Rather, we can take on the doable job of changing our habits. One change in behavior that seems insignificant at first can have effects that ripple throughout your life.

Tell the truth. Telling the truth about any habit—from chewing our fingernails to cheating on tests—frees us. Without taking this step, our efforts to change might be as ineffective as rearranging the deck chairs on the *Titanic.* Telling the truth allows us to see what's actually sinking the ship.

When we admit what's really going on in our lives, our defenses come down. We become open to accepting help from others. The support we need to change a habit has an opportunity to make an impact.

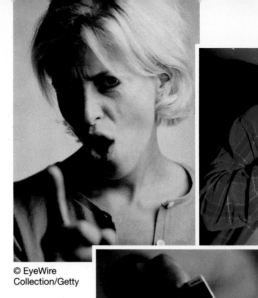

© EyeWire Collection/Getty

© Ryan McV

© Daniel Allan/Getty

Choose and commit to a new behavior. It often helps to choose a new habit to replace an old one. First, make a commitment to practice the new habit. Tell key people in your life about your decision to change. Set up a plan for when and how. Answer questions such as these: When will I apply the new habit? Where will I be? Who will be with me? What will I be seeing, hearing, touching, saying, or doing? Exactly how will I think, speak, or act differently?

For example, consider the student who always snacks when he studies. Each time he sits down to read, he positions a bag of potato chips within easy reach. For him, opening a book is a cue to start chewing. Snacking is especially easy, given the place he chooses to study: the kitchen. He decides to change this habit by studying at a desk in his bedroom instead of at the kitchen table. And every time he feels the urge to bite into a potato chip, he drinks from a glass of water instead.

Richard Malott, a psychologist who specializes in helping people overcome procrastination, lists three key steps in committing to a new behavior.[7] First, *specify* your goal in numerical terms whenever possible. For example, commit to reading 30 pages per day, Monday through Friday. Second, *observe* your behavior and record the results—in this case, the number of pages that you actually read every day. Finally, set up a small *consequence* for failing to keep your commitment. For instance, pay a friend one quarter for each day that you read less than 30 pages.

Affirm your intention. You can pave the way for a new behavior by clearing a mental path for it. Before you apply the new behavior, rehearse it in your mind. Mentally picture what actions you will take and in what order.

Say that you plan to improve your handwriting when taking notes. Imagine yourself in class with a blank notebook poised before you. See yourself taking up a finely crafted pen. Notice how comfortable it feels in your hand. See yourself writing clearly and legibly. You can even picture how you will make individual letters: the *e*'s, *i*'s, and *r*'s. Then, when class is over, see yourself reviewing your notes and taking pleasure in how easy they are to read.

Start with a small change. You can sometimes rearrange a whole pattern of behaviors by changing one small habit. If you have a habit of always being late for classes, then be on time for one class. As soon as you change the old pattern by getting ready and going on time to one class, you might find yourself arriving at all of your classes on time. You might even start arriving everywhere else on time, too. The joy of this process is watching one small change of habit ripple through your whole life.

Get feedback and support. Getting feedback and support is a crucial step in adopting a new behavior. It is also a point at which many plans for change break down. It's easy to practice your new behavior with great enthusiasm for a few days. After the initial rush of excitement, though, things can get a little tougher. You begin to find excuses for slipping back into old habits: "One more cigarette won't hurt." "I can get back to my diet tomorrow." "It's been a tough day. I deserve this beer."

One way to get feedback is to bring other people into the picture. Ask others to remind you that you are changing your habit if they see you backsliding. If you want to stop an old behavior, such as cramming for tests, then tell everyone about your goal. When you want to start a new behavior, though, consider telling only a few people—those who truly support your efforts.

Starting new habits might call for the more focused, long-lasting support that close friends or family members can give. Support from others can be as simple as a quick phone call: "Hi. Have you started that outline for your research paper yet?" Or it can be as formal as a support group that meets once a week to review everyone's goals and action plans.

You can also be an effective source of feedback. You know yourself better than anyone else does and can design a system to monitor your behavior. Create your own charts to track your behavior, or write about your progress in your journal. Figure out a way to monitor your progress.

Practice, practice, practice—without self-judgment. Psychologist B. F. Skinner defines learning as a stable change in behavior that comes as a result of practice.[8] This widely accepted idea is key to changing habits. Act on your intention over and over again. If you fail or forget, let go of any self-judgment. Just keep practicing the new habit. Allow whatever time it takes to make a change.

Accept the feelings of discomfort that might come with a new habit. Keep practicing the new behavior, even if it feels unnatural. Trust the process. Grow into the new behavior. However, if this new habit doesn't work, simply note what happened (without guilt or blame), select a new behavior, and begin this cycle of steps over again.

Making mistakes as you practice doesn't mean that you've failed. Even when you don't get the results you want from a new behavior, you learn something valuable in the process. Once you understand ways to change one habit, you will be able to change almost any habit. ✱

© EyeWire Collection/Getty

© Stockbyte

© Jules Frazier/Getty

Master Student Profiles

Each chapter of this text includes a Master Student Profile of a person who embodies one or more qualities of a master student. As you read about these people and others like them, ask yourself: "How can I apply this?" Look for the timeless qualities in the people you read about. Many of the master students used tools that you can use today.

The people profiled in this book were chosen because they demonstrate unusual and effective ways to learn. Remember that these are just 12 examples of master students (one for each chapter). You can read more about these master students and others in the Master Student Hall of Fame on the Web site.

As you read the Master Student Profiles, ask yourself questions based on each mode of learning: Why is this person considered a master student? What attitudes or behaviors helped to create her mastery? How can I develop those qualities? What if I could use his example to create positive new results in my own life?

Also reflect on other master students you've read about or know personally. Focus on people who excel at learning. The master student is not a vague or remote ideal. Rather, master students move freely among us.

In fact, there's one living inside your skin.

6 critical thinking exercise
Demonstrating mastery

Review the article "The Master Student" in this chapter. Then skim the Master Student Profiles on the last page of each chapter in this book. Choose one of the people profiled, and describe in the space below how this person embodies qualities of a master student.

 Complete this exercise online.

Ideas Are Tools

There are many ideas in this book. When you first encounter them, don't believe any of them. Instead, think of the ideas as tools.

For example, you use a hammer for a purpose—to drive a nail. You don't try to figure out whether the hammer is "right." You just use it. If it works, you use it again. If it doesn't work, you get a different hammer.

People have plenty of room in their lives for different kinds of hammers, but they tend to limit their openness for different kinds of ideas. A new idea, at some level, is a threat to their very being—unlike a new hammer, which is simply a new hammer.

Most of us have a built-in desire to be right. Our ideas, we often think, represent ourselves.

Some ideas are worth believing. But please note: This book does not contain any of those ideas. The ideas on these pages are strictly "hammers."

Imagine someone defending a hammer. Picture this person holding up a hammer and declaring, "I hold this hammer to be self-evident. Give me this hammer or give me death. Those other hammers are flawed. There are only two kinds of people in this world: people who believe in this hammer and people who don't."

That ridiculous picture makes a point. This book is not a manifesto or set of beliefs. It's a toolbox, and tools are meant to be used.

If you read about a tool in this book that doesn't sound "right" or one that sounds a little goofy, remember that the ideas here are for using, not necessarily for believing. Suspend your judgment. Test the idea for yourself. If it works, use it. If it doesn't, don't use it.

Any tool—whether it's a hammer, a computer program, or a study technique—is designed to do a specific job. A master mechanic carries a variety of tools, because no single tool works for all jobs. If you throw a tool away because it doesn't work in one situation, you won't be able to pull it out later when it's just what you need. So if an idea doesn't work for you and you are satisfied that you gave it a fair chance, don't throw it away. File it away instead. The idea might come in handy soon.

And remember, this book is not about figuring out the "right" way. Even the "ideas-are-tools" approach is not "right."

It's a hammer . . . (or maybe a saw).

(www) Complete this exercise online.

Edmond Van Hoorick/Digital Vision/Getty Images

Career Application

Shortly after graduating with an A.A. degree in Business Administration, Sylvia Lopez was thrilled to land a job as a staff accountant at a market research firm. After one week, she wanted to quit. She didn't think she would ever learn to deal with her coworkers. Their personalities just seemed too different.

For example, there was the account coordinator, Ed Washington. He spent hours a day on the phone calling prospective customers who responded to the corporate Web site. Since Ed's office door was always open and he had a loud voice, people inevitably overheard his calls. It seemed to Sylvia that he spent a lot of time socializing with clients—asking about their hobbies and family lives. Even though Ed was regarded as a skilled salesperson, Sylvia wondered when he actually got any work done.

Sylvia also felt uncomfortable with Linda Martinez, the firm's accounting analyst and her direct supervisor. Linda kept her office door closed most of the time. In contrast to Ed, Linda hardly ever stopped to chat informally. Instead of taking lunch breaks, she typically packed a bag lunch and ate it while checking e-mail or updating the company databases. Linda had a reputation as a top-notch employee. Yet the only time people saw her was at scheduled staff meetings. Linda led those meetings and distributed a detailed agenda in advance. Although Ed was on a first-name basis with everyone in the office, Linda made it clear that she wished to be addressed as "Ms. Martinez."

After worrying for several days about how to deal with the differences among her coworkers, Sylvia scheduled times to meet with Ed and Linda individually about her concerns. Before each meeting, she carefully prepared her opening remarks, writing them out. For Ed, her notes included this comment: "Since I'm new on the job and feel pressed for time, I'd like to get your help in making the most efficient use of our meeting time." And for Linda she wrote: "I'd like to make sure my performance is up to par. Is there any way I can get regular feedback from you about how I'm doing?"

Andrew Taylor/Shutterstock

Reflecting on this scenario

List at least two strategies from this chapter that would be useful to Sylvia in this situation. Briefly describe how she could apply each one.

_____

_____

_____

_____

_____

_____

_____

_____

_____

_____

_____

chapter 1

Quiz

■ Career Application
◀ ◀ ◀ ◀ ◀
■ Transferable Skills
■ Master Student Profile

Name_____   Date____/____/____

1. Take the following statement and rewrite it as a more effective First Step: "I am terrible at managing money."

2. Define the term *mastery* as it is used in this chapter.

3. The First Step technique refers only to telling the truth about your areas for improvement. True or false? Explain your answer.

4. The four modes of learning are associated with certain questions. Give the appropriate question for each mode.

5. Give two examples of ways that you can accommodate people with different learning styles.

6. According to the text, thinking of ourselves as creatures of habit can actually empower us. True or false? Explain your answer.

7. List three types of intelligence defined by Howard Gardner. Then describe one learning strategy related to each type of intelligence that you listed.

8. According to the Power Process: "Ideas Are Tools." If you want the ideas in this book to work, you must believe in them. True or false? Explain your answer.

9. Define the word *metacognition.*

10. This chapter presents two views of the nature of motivation. Briefly explain the difference between them.

Focus on Transferable Skills

The Discovery Wheel in this chapter includes a section labeled *Self-discovery*. For the next 10 to 15 minutes, go beyond your initial responses to that exercise by completing the following statements. Take a snapshot of your current transferable skills related to self-discovery. Then focus on a new skill that you'd like to develop, or an existing skill that you can take to a deeper level.

Before completing the following items, you might find it useful to jump ahead to Chapter 2 to review the articles "Jumpstart Your Education with Transferable Skills" on page 58 and "101 Transferable Skills" on page 60.

SELF-AWARENESS

Three things I do well as a student are . . .

Three ways that I excel as an employee are . . .

STYLES

If asked to describe my learning style in one sentence, I would say that I am . . .

To become a more flexible learner, I could . . .

FLEXIBILITY

When I disagree with what someone else says about me, my first response is usually to . . .

In these situations, I could be more effective by . . .

NEXT ACTION

The transferable skill related to self-awareness, styles, or flexibility that I'd most like to develop is . . .

To develop that skill, the most important thing I can do next is to . . .

chapter 1
....

▪ Career Application
▪ Quiz
▪ Transferable Skills

◄ ◄ ◄ ◄ ◄

Master Student PROFILE

Jerry Yang
. . . is inquisitive

© TAO CHUAN YEH/Getty Images

In 1994, David Filo and Jerry Yang were in typical start-up mode—working 20 hours a day, sleeping in the office, juiced on the idea that people were discovering their concept and plugging in. There was only one difference between them and most new entrepreneurs: They weren't making any money. We're not talking about an absence of profitability. We're talking about an absence of revenue. There were no sales. None. And, the fact is, the Yahoo! founders didn't care. Filo and Yang were working like maniacs for the sheer joy of it.

Their mission? Bringing order to the terrible, tangled World Wide Web. Back then—in the pre-history of the Internet—plenty of interesting Websites existed. But the forum wasn't organized; there was no system that enabled people to find the sites they wanted in an easy, orderly way . . .

. . . By 1995, the service had become so popular, the partners were able to raise $1 million in venture capital to expand the business. There was no trail to follow, however; back then, Internet commerce was still in its infancy. But the partners knew they had a tiger by the tail. "What we did took 20 hours a day," says Yang, 29. "But we were one of the first to [try to organize the Web], and we did it better than anyone."

Yang, born in Taiwan and raised in San Jose, California, was named Chief Executive Officer of Yahoo! on June 18, 2007. Yang reflected on his vision and the future of the company on Yahoo's! blog, Yodel Anecdotal™:

The title of Chief Yahoo takes on new meaning today. I have the great honor of stepping into the role of Yahoo!'s Chief Executive Officer. Yahoo! has an incredibly bright future and I make this move with deep conviction and enthusiasm. I've partnered closely with our executive teams for 12 years to steer our strategy and direction and today I'm ready for this challenge.

What is [my] vision? A Yahoo! that executes with speed, clarity and discipline. A Yahoo! that increases its focus on differentiating its products and investing in creativity and innovation. A Yahoo! that better monetizes its audience. A Yahoo! whose great talent is galvanized to address its challenges. And a Yahoo! that is better focused on what's important to its users, customers, and employees.

. . . We have incredible assets. This company has massive potential, drive, determination and skills, and we won't be satisfied until the external perception of Yahoo! accurately reflects that reality.

I have absolute conviction about Yahoo!'s potential for long-term success as an Internet leader. Yahoo! is a company that started with a vision and a dream and, make no mistake, that dream is very much alive. I'm committed to doing whatever it takes to transform Yahoo! into an even greater success in the future.

The time for me is right. The time is now. The Internet is still young, the opportunities ahead are tremendous, and I'm ready to rally our nearly 12,000 Yahoos around the world to help seize them.

Adapted from "Unconventional Thinking," *Entrepreneur Magazine*, September, 1997; and Jerry Yang, "Yodel Anecdotal™", June 18th, 2007, yodel.yahoo.com/2007/06/18/my-new-job. Reproduced with permission of Yahoo! Inc.® 2007 by Yahoo! Inc. Yahoo! and the Yahoo! logo are trademarks of Yahoo! Inc.

(1968–) Founder and CEO of Yahoo!

Learn more about Jerry Yang and other master students at the Master Student Hall of Fame.

3 Time

Master Student Map

as you read, ask yourself

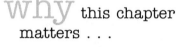

what if . . .

I could meet my goals with time to spare?

why this chapter matters . . .

Procrastination and lack of planning can quickly undermine your success in school and at work.

what is included . . .

how you can use this chapter . . .

- Discover the details about how you currently use time.
- Set goals that make a difference in the quality of your life.
- Know exactly what to do today, this week, and this month to achieve your goals.
- Eliminate procrastination.

MASTER EMPLOYEE in *action*

In my college classes I would get syllabi from professors that laid out the whole year. Assignments were never mentioned again and it was up to me to do them on time. At work, I have a whole series of tasks to complete on my own from week to week. And I now know how/when to do those things without being asked.

—KARLIS BRYAN, ASSISTANT MEDIA BUYER

Photo courtesy of Karlis Bryan

You've got the time

THE WORDS *time management* may call forth images of restriction and control. You might visualize a prune-faced Scrooge hunched over your shoulder, stopwatch in hand, telling you what to do every minute. The whole situation is bad news.

Here's the good news: You do have enough time for the things you want to do. All it takes is thinking about the possibilities and making conscious choices.

Time is an equal opportunity resource. All of us, regardless of gender, race, creed, or national origin, have exactly the same number of hours in a week. No matter how famous we are, no matter how rich or poor, we get 168 hours to spend each week—no more, no less.

Time is also an unusual commodity. It cannot be saved. You can't stockpile time like wood for the stove or food for the winter. It can't be seen, heard, touched, tasted, or smelled. You can't sense time directly. Even scientists and philosophers find it hard to describe. Because time is so elusive, it is easy to ignore. That doesn't bother time at all. Time is perfectly content to remain hidden until you are nearly out of it. And when you are out of it, you are completely out of it.

Time is a nonrenewable resource. If you're out of wood, you can chop some more. If you're out of money, you can earn a little extra. If you're out of love, there is still hope. If you're out of health, it can often be restored. But when you're out of time, that's it. When this minute is gone, it's gone.

Time seems to pass at varying speeds. Sometimes it crawls. On Friday afternoons, classroom clocks can creep. After you've worked a 10-hour day, reading the last few pages of an economics assignment can turn minutes into hours. A year in school can stretch out to an eternity.

At the other end of the spectrum, time flies. There are moments when you are so absorbed in what you're doing that hours disappear like magic.

Approach time as if you are in control. Sometimes it seems that your friends control your time, that your boss controls your time, that your teachers or your parents or your kids or somebody else controls your time. Maybe that is not true, though. When you say you don't have enough time, you might really be saying that you are not spending the time you *do* have in the way that you want.

Everything written about time management boils down to two topics. One involves knowing exactly *what* you want. The other involves knowing *how* to get what you want. State your wants as written goals. Then choose activities that will help you meet those goals.

You should spend your most valuable resource in the way you choose. Start by observing how you use time. Critical Thinking Exercise 14: "The Time Monitor/Time Plan Process" gives you this opportunity. ✳

journal entry ⑧

Discovery/Intention Statement

Create value from this chapter

Think back to a time during the past year when you rushed to finish a project or when you did not find time for an activity that was important to you. List one thing you might have done that created this outcome.

I discovered that I . . .

_____

_____

_____

_____

_____

Now take a few minutes to skim this chapter. Find five techniques that you intend to use. List them below, along with their associated page numbers.

Strategy	Page Number
_____	_____
_____	_____
_____	_____
_____	_____
_____	_____

critical thinking exercise

14 The Time Monitor/Time Plan process

The purpose of this exercise is to transform time into a knowable and predictable resource. Complete this exercise over a two-week period:

- During the first week, you *monitor* your activities to get detailed information about how you actually spend your time.
- After you analyze your first week in Journal Entry 9, you *plan* the second week.
- During the second week, you *monitor* your activity again and compare it with your plan.
- Based on everything you've learned, you *plan* again.

For this exercise, monitor your time in 15-minute intervals, 24 hours a day, for seven days. Record how much time you spend sleeping, eating, studying, attending lectures, traveling to and from class, working, watching television, listening to music, taking care of the kids, running errands—everything.

If this sounds crazy, hang on for a minute. This exercise is not about keeping track of the rest of your life in 15-minute intervals. It is an opportunity to become conscious of how you spend your time—your life. Use the Time Monitor/Time Plan process only for as long as it helps you do that.

When you know exactly how you spend your time, you can make choices with open eyes. You can spend more time on the things that are most important to you and less time on the unimportant. Monitoring your time puts you in control of your life.

Here's an eye opener for many students. If you think you already have a good idea of how you manage time, predict how many hours you will spend in a week on each category of activity listed in the form on page 90 (Four categories are already provided; you can add more at any time.) Make your predictions before your first week of monitoring. Write them in the margin to the left of each category. After monitoring your time for one week, see how accurate your predictions were.

The following charts are used for monitoring and planning, and include instructions for using them. Some students choose other materials, such as 3 x 5 cards, calendars, campus planners, or time management software. You might even develop your own way to monitor your time.

(www) Do this exercise online.

1. **Get to know the Time Monitor/Time Plan.** Look at the sample Time Monitor/Time Plan on page 89. Note that each day has two columns—one labeled "Monitor" and the other labeled "Plan." During the first week, you will use only the "Monitor" column, just like this student did.

On Monday, the student in this example got up at 6:45 a.m., showered, and got dressed. He finished this activity and began breakfast at 7:15. He put this new activity in at the time he began and drew a line just above it. He ate from 7:15 to 7:45. It took him 15 minutes to walk to class (7:45 to 8:00), and he attended classes from 8:00 to 11:00.

When you begin an activity, write it down next to the time you begin. Round off to the nearest 15 minutes. If, for example, you begin eating at 8:06, enter your starting time as 8:00. Over time, it will probably even out. In any case, you will be close enough to realize the benefits of this exercise.

Keep your Time Monitor/Time Plan with you every minute you are awake for one week. Take a few moments every two or three hours to record what you've done. Or enter a note each time you change activities.

2. **Remember to use your Time Monitor/Time Plan.** It might be easy to forget to fill out your Time Monitor/Time Plan. One way to remember is to create a visual reminder for yourself. You can use this technique for any activity you want to remember.

Relax for a moment, close your eyes, and imagine that you see your Time Monitor/Time Plan. Imagine that it has arms and legs and is as big as a person. Picture the form sitting at your desk at home, in your car, in one of your classrooms, or in your favorite chair. Visualize it sitting wherever you're likely to sit. When you sit down, the Time Monitor/Time Plan will get squashed unless you pick it up and use it.

You can make this image more effective by adding sound effects. The Time Monitor/Time Plan might scream, "Get off me!" Or since time can be related to money, you might associate the Time Monitor/Time Plan with the sound of an old-fashioned cash register. Imagine that every time you sit down, a cash register rings to remind you it's there.

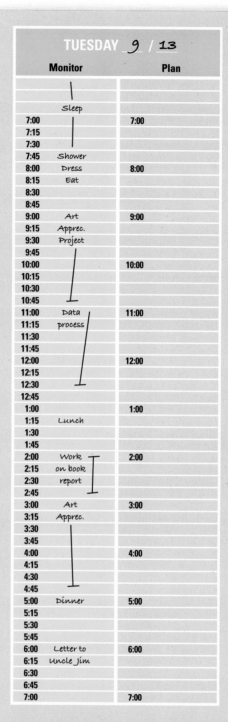

MONDAY _9_ / _12_	
Monitor	**Plan**
Get up	
Shower	
7:00 ————	7:00
7:15 Breakfast	
7:30 _⊥_	
7:45 Walk to class	
8:00 Econ 1	8:00
8:15	
8:30	
8:45	
9:00	9:00
9:15	
9:30	
9:45	
10:00 Bío 1	10:00
10:15	
10:30	
10:45 _⊥_	
11:00	11:00
11:15 Study	
11:30	
11:45	
12:00	12:00
12:15 Lunch	
12:30	
12:45	
1:00	1:00
1:15 Eng. Lit	
1:30	
1:45	
2:00	2:00
2:15 Coffeehouse	
2:30	
2:45	
3:00	3:00
3:15	
3:30	
3:45	
4:00 _⊥_	4:00
4:15 Study	
4:30	
4:45	
5:00	5:00
5:15 Dinner	
5:30	
5:45	
6:00	6:00
6:15	
6:30 Babysit	
6:45	
7:00	7:00

TUESDAY _9_ / _13_	
Monitor	**Plan**
Sleep	
7:00	7:00
7:15	
7:30	
7:45 Shower	
8:00 Dress	8:00
8:15 Eat	
8:30	
8:45	
9:00 Art	9:00
9:15 Apprec.	
9:30 Project	
9:45	
10:00	10:00
10:15	
10:30	
10:45	
11:00 Data	11:00
11:15 process	
11:30	
11:45	
12:00	12:00
12:15	
12:30	
12:45	
1:00	1:00
1:15 Lunch	
1:30	
1:45	
2:00 Work	2:00
2:15 on book	
2:30 report	
2:45	
3:00 Art	3:00
3:15 Apprec.	
3:30	
3:45	
4:00	4:00
4:15	
4:30	
4:45	
5:00 Dinner	5:00
5:15	
5:30	
5:45	
6:00 Letter to	6:00
6:15 Uncle Jim	
6:30	
6:45	
7:00	7:00

3. **Evaluate the Time Monitor/Time Plan.** After you've monitored your time for one week, group your activities together by categories. The form on page 90 lists the categories "Sleep," "Class," "Study," and "Meals." Think of other categories you could add. "Grooming" might include showering, putting on makeup, brushing teeth, and getting dressed. "Travel" could include walking, driving, taking the bus, and riding your bike. Other categories might be "Exercise," "Entertainment," "Work," "Television," "Domestic," and "Children."

Write in the categories that work for you, and then do the following:

- Guess how many hours you *think* you spent on each category of activity. List these hours in the "Estimated" column.

- List the *actual* number of hours you spent on each activity, adding up the figures from your daily time monitoring. List these hours in the "Monitored" column. Make sure that the grand total of all categories is 168 hours.

- Now take a minute and let these numbers sink in. Compare the totals in the "Estimated" and "Monitored" columns.

Notice your reactions. You might be surprised. You might feel disappointed or even angry about where your time goes.

Use those feelings as motivation to plan your time differently. Go to the "Planned" column and choose how much time you *want* to spend on various categories during the coming week. As you do this, allow yourself to have fun. Approach planning in the spirit of adventure. Think of yourself as an artist who's creating a new life.

In several months you might want to take another detailed look at how you spend your life. Fill in the "Monitor" and "Plan" columns on pages 91–92 simultaneously. Use a continuous cycle of monitoring and planning to get the full benefits of this exercise for the rest of your life. Let time management become more than a technique. Transform it into a habit—a constant awareness of how you spend your lifetime.

WEEK OF ___ / ___ / ___ /			
Category	Estimated	Monitored	Planned
Sleep			
Class			
Study			
Meals			

MONDAY ___ / ___ / ___ /	
Monitor	**Plan**
7:00	7:00
7:15	
7:30	
7:45	
8:00	8:00
8:15	
8:30	
8:45	
9:00	9:00
9:15	
9:30	
9:45	
10:00	10:00
10:15	
10:30	
10:45	
11:00	11:00
11:15	
11:30	
11:45	
12:00	12:00
12:15	
12:30	
12:45	
1:00	1:00
1:15	
1:30	
1:45	
2:00	2:00
2:15	
2:30	
2:45	
3:00	3:00
3:15	
3:30	
3:45	
4:00	4:00
4:15	
4:30	
4:45	
5:00	5:00
5:15	
5:30	
5:45	
6:00	6:00
6:15	
6:30	
6:45	
7:00	7:00
7:15	
7:30	
7:45	
8:00	8:00
8:15	
8:30	
8:45	
9:00	9:00
9:15	
9:30	
9:45	
10:00	10:00
10:15	
10:30	
10:45	
11:00	11:00
11:15	
11:30	
11:45	
12:00	12:00

TUESDAY ___ / ___ / ___ /	
Monitor	**Plan**
7:00	7:00
7:15	
7:30	
7:45	
8:00	8:00
8:15	
8:30	
8:45	
9:00	9:00
9:15	
9:30	
9:45	
10:00	10:00
10:15	
10:30	
10:45	
11:00	11:00
11:15	
11:30	
11:45	
12:00	12:00
12:15	
12:30	
12:45	
1:00	1:00
1:15	
1:30	
1:45	
2:00	2:00
2:15	
2:30	
2:45	
3:00	3:00
3:15	
3:30	
3:45	
4:00	4:00
4:15	
4:30	
4:45	
5:00	5:00
5:15	
5:30	
5:45	
6:00	6:00
6:15	
6:30	
6:45	
7:00	7:00
7:15	
7:30	
7:45	
8:00	8:00
8:15	
8:30	
8:45	
9:00	9:00
9:15	
9:30	
9:45	
10:00	10:00
10:15	
10:30	
10:45	
11:00	11:00
11:15	
11:30	
11:45	
12:00	12:00

WEDNESDAY ___ / __ / ___ /	
Monitor	**Plan**
7:00	7:00
7:15	
7:30	
7:45	
8:00	8:00
8:15	
8:30	
8:45	
9:00	9:00
9:15	
9:30	
9:45	
10:00	10:00
10:15	
10:30	
10:45	
11:00	11:00
11:15	
11:30	
11:45	
12:00	12:00
12:15	
12:30	
12:45	
1:00	1:00
1:15	
1:30	
1:45	
2:00	2:00
2:15	
2:30	
2:45	
3:00	3:00
3:15	
3:30	
3:45	
4:00	4:00
4:15	
4:30	
4:45	
5:00	5:00
5:15	
5:30	
5:45	
6:00	6:00
6:15	
6:30	
6:45	
7:00	7:00
7:15	
7:30	
7:45	
8:00	8:00
8:15	
8:30	
8:45	
9:00	9:00
9:15	
9:30	
9:45	
10:00	10:00
10:15	
10:30	
10:45	
11:00	11:00
11:15	
11:30	
11:45	
12:00	12:00

THURSDAY ___ / ___ / ___ /

Monitor	Plan
7:00	7:00
7:15	
7:30	
7:45	
8:00	8:00
8:15	
8:30	
8:45	
9:00	9:00
9:15	
9:30	
9:45	
10:00	10:00
10:15	
10:30	
10:45	
11:00	11:00
11:15	
11:30	
11:45	
12:00	12:00
12:15	
12:30	
12:45	
1:00	1:00
1:15	
1:30	
1:45	
2:00	2:00
2:15	
2:30	
2:45	
3:00	3:00
3:15	
3:30	
3:45	
4:00	4:00
4:15	
4:30	
4:45	
5:00	5:00
5:15	
5:30	
5:45	
6:00	6:00
6:15	
6:30	
6:45	
7:00	7:00
7:15	
7:30	
7:45	
8:00	8:00
8:15	
8:30	
8:45	
9:00	9:00
9:15	
9:30	
9:45	
10:00	10:00
10:15	
10:30	
10:45	
11:00	11:00
11:15	
11:30	
11:45	
12:00	12:00

FRIDAY ___ / ___ / ___ /

Monitor	Plan
7:00	7:00
7:15	
7:30	
7:45	
8:00	8:00
8:15	
8:30	
8:45	
9:00	9:00
9:15	
9:30	
9:45	
10:00	10:00
10:15	
10:30	
10:45	
11:00	11:00
11:15	
11:30	
11:45	
12:00	12:00
12:15	
12:30	
12:45	
1:00	1:00
1:15	
1:30	
1:45	
2:00	2:00
2:15	
2:30	
2:45	
3:00	3:00
3:15	
3:30	
3:45	
4:00	4:00
4:15	
4:30	
4:45	
5:00	5:00
5:15	
5:30	
5:45	
6:00	6:00
6:15	
6:30	
6:45	
7:00	7:00
7:15	
7:30	
7:45	
8:00	8:00
8:15	
8:30	
8:45	
9:00	9:00
9:15	
9:30	
9:45	
10:00	10:00
10:15	
10:30	
10:45	
11:00	11:00
11:15	
11:30	
11:45	
12:00	12:00

SATURDAY ___ / ___ / ___ /

Monitor	Plan

SUNDAY ___ / ___ / ___ /

Monitor	Plan

Discovery Statement

Reflecting on how you spend the time of your life

Now that you have monitored one week, reflect on how you spend the time of your life:

After one week of monitoring my time, I discovered that . . .

_____

_____

_____

_____

_____

_____

_____

_____

_____

I want to spend more time on . . .

_____

_____

_____

_____

_____

_____

_____

_____

I want to spend less time on . . .

_____

_____

_____

_____

_____

_____

_____

_____

_____

_____

I was surprised that I spent so much time on . . .

_____

_____

_____

_____

_____

_____

_____

_____

_____

I was surprised that I spent so little time on . . .

_____

_____

_____

_____

_____

_____

_____

_____

3

TIME

Setting and achieving goals

Many of us have vague, idealized notions of what we want out of life. These notions float among the clouds in our heads. They are wonderful, fuzzy, safe thoughts such as "I want to be a good person," "I want to be financially secure," or "I want to be happy."

Jon Feingersh/Blend Images/Getty

SUCH OUTCOMES ARE great possible goals. When we keep these goals in a generalized form, however, we may become confused about ways to actually achieve them. If you really want to meet a goal, translate it into specific, concrete behaviors. Find out what that goal looks like. Listen to what it sounds like. Pick it up and feel how heavy that goal is. Inspect the switches, valves, joints, cogs, and fastenings of the goal. Make your goal as real as a chain saw. There is nothing vague or fuzzy about chain saws. You can see them, feel them, and hear them. They have a clear function. Goals can be every bit as real and useful.

Writing down your goals exponentially increases your chances of meeting them. Writing exposes undefined terms, unrealistic time frames, and other symptoms of fuzzy thinking. If you've been completing Intention Statements as explained in the Introduction to this book, then you've already had experience writing goals. Both goals and Intention Statements address changes you want to make in your behavior, your values, or your circumstances—or in all of these areas. To keep track of your goals, write each one on a separate 3 x 5 card, or key them all into a word-processing file on your computer.

There are many useful methods for setting goals. You're about to learn one of them. This method is based on writing specific goals that relate to several time frames and areas of your life. Experiment with this method and modify it as you see fit. Also, reflect regularly on your goals. The keywords to remember are *specific, time, areas,* and *reflect.* Combine the first letter of each word and you get *STAR.* Use this acronym to remember the suggestions that follow.

Write specific goals. In writing, state your goals as observable actions or measurable results. Think in detail about how things will be different once your goals are attained. List the changes in what you'd see, feel, touch, taste, hear, be, do, or have.

Suppose that one of your goals is to become a better student by studying harder. You're headed in a powerful direction; now translate that goal into a concrete action, such as "I will study two hours for every hour I'm in class." Specific goals make clear what actions are needed or what results are expected. Consider these examples:

Vague goal	Specific goal
Get a good education.	Graduate with B.S. degree in engineering, with honors, by 2014.
Enhance my spiritual life.	Meditate for 15 minutes daily.
Improve my appearance.	Lose 6 pounds during the next 6 months.
Get a good job.	Work as a computer security specialist at a mid-sized company where I can continue to learn and advance to higher positions.
Get more friends.	Introduce myself to at least one new person each week.
Be debt-free.	Pay off at least 50 percent of the total balance on my credit card each month.
Be happy.	Learn simple and effective ways to release negative emotions in the moment that they occur.

When stated specifically, a goal might look different to you. If you examine it closely, a goal you once thought you wanted might not be something you want after all. Or you might discover that you want to choose a new path to achieve a goal that you are sure you want.

Write goals in several time frames. To get a comprehensive vision of your future, write down the following:

- *Long-term goals.* Long-term goals represent major targets in your life. These goals can take 5 to 20 years to achieve. In some cases, they will take a lifetime. They can include goals in education, careers, personal relationships, travel, financial security—whatever is important to you. Consider the answers to the following questions as you create your long-term goals: What do you want to accomplish in your life? Do you want your life to make a statement? If so, what is that statement?

- *Mid-term goals.* Mid-term goals are objectives you can accomplish in one to five years. They include goals such as completing a course of education, paying off a car loan, or achieving a specific career level. These goals usually support your long-term goals.

- *Short-term goals.* Short-term goals are the ones you can accomplish in a year or less. These goals are specific achievements, such as completing a particular course or group of courses, hiking down the Appalachian Trail, or organizing a family reunion. A short-term financial goal would probably include an exact dollar amount. Whatever your short-term goals are, they will require action now or in the near future.

Write goals in several areas of life. People who set goals in only one area of life—such as their career—may find that their personal growth becomes one-sided.

They might experience success at work while neglecting their health or relationships with family members and friends.

To avoid this outcome, set goals in a variety of categories. Consider what you want to experience in your:

- Education
- Career
- Financial life
- Family life
- Social life
- Spiritual life
- Level of health

Add goals in other areas as they occur to you.

Reflect on your goals. Each week, take a few minutes to think about your goals. You can perform the following spot checks:

- *Check in with your feelings.* Think about how the process of setting your goals felt. Consider the satisfaction you'll gain in attaining your objectives. If you don't feel a significant emotional connection with a written goal, consider letting it go or filing it away to review later.

- *Check for alignment.* Look for connections among your goals. Do your short-term goals align with your mid-term goals? Will your mid-term goals help you achieve your long-term goals? Look for a fit between all of your goals and your purpose for taking part in higher education, as well as your overall purpose in life.

- *Check for obstacles.* All kinds of things can come between you and your goals, such as constraints on time and money. Anticipate obstacles, and start looking now for workable solutions.

- *Check for immediate steps.* Here's a way to link goal setting to time management. Create a list of small, achievable steps you can take right away to accomplish each of your short-term goals. Ask yourself: What is the physical action that I could take to achieve my goal? Add these actions to your to-do list on an appropriate day. If you want to take one of these actions on a certain date, then enter it into a calendar that you consult daily. Over the coming weeks, review your to-do list and calendar. Take note of your progress, and celebrate your successes. ✳

Huntstock/Getty

15 critical thinking exercise
Get real with your goals

One way to make goals effective is to examine them up close. That's what this exercise is about. Using a process of brainstorming and evaluation, you can break a long-term goal into smaller segments until you have taken it completely apart. When you analyze a goal to this level of detail, you're well on the way to meeting it. For this exercise, you will use a pen, extra paper, and a watch with a second hand. (A digital watch with a built-in stopwatch feature is even better.) Timing is an important part of the brainstorming process, so follow the stated time limits. This entire exercise takes about an hour.

Part 1: Long-term goals

Brainstorm. Begin with an eight-minute brainstorm. Use a separate sheet of paper for this part of the exercise. For eight minutes, write down everything you think you want in your life. Write as fast as you can, and write whatever comes into your head. Leave no thought out. Don't worry about accuracy. The object of a brainstorm is to generate as many ideas as possible.

Evaluate. After you have finished brainstorming, spend the next six minutes looking over your list. Analyze what you wrote. Read the list out loud. If something is missing, add it. Look for common themes or relationships among your goals. Then select three long-term goals that are important to you—goals that will take many years to achieve. Write these goals in the following space provided.

_____

_____

_____

Before you continue, take a minute to reflect on the process you've used so far. What criteria did you use to select your top three goals?

Part 2: Mid-term goals

Brainstorm. Read out loud the three long-term goals you selected in Part 1. Choose one of them. Then brainstorm a list of goals you might achieve in the next one to five years that would lead to the accomplishment of that one long-term goal. These are mid-term goals. Spend eight minutes on this brainstorm. Go for quantity.

Evaluate. Analyze your brainstorm of mid-term goals. Then select three that you determine to be important in meeting the long-term goal you picked. Allow yourself six minutes for this part of the exercise. Write your selections in the following space provided.

_____

_____

_____

Again, pause for reflection before going on to the next part of this exercise. Why do you see these three goals as more important than the other mid-term goals you generated? On a separate sheet of paper, write about your reasons for selecting these three goals.

Part 3: Short-term goals

Brainstorm. Review your list of mid-term goals, and select one. In another eight-minute brainstorm, generate a list of short-term goals—those you can accomplish in a year or less that will lead to the attainment of that mid-term goal. Write down everything that comes to mind. Do not evaluate or judge these ideas yet. For now, the more ideas you write down, the better.

Evaluate. Analyze your list of short-term goals. The most effective brainstorms are conducted by suspending judgment, so you might find some bizarre ideas on your list. That's fine. Now is the time to cross them out. Next, evaluate your remaining short-term goals, and select three that you are willing and able to accomplish. Allow yourself six minutes for this part of the exercise. Then write your selections in the following space provided.

_____

_____

_____

The more you practice, the more effective you can be at choosing goals that have meaning for you. You can repeat this exercise, employing the other long-term goals you generated or creating new ones.

 Complete this exercise online.

One of the most effective ways to stay on track and actually get things done is to use a daily to-do list. While the Time Monitor/Time Plan gives you a general picture of the week, your daily to-do list shows specific tasks you want to complete within the next 24 hours.

The ABC daily to-do list

© Deborah Jaffe/Getty

ONE ADVANTAGE OF keeping a daily to-do list is that you don't have to remember what to do next. It's on the list. A typical day in the life of a student is full of separate, often unrelated tasks—reading, attending lectures, reviewing notes, working at a job, writing papers, researching special projects, running errands. It's easy to forget an important task on a busy day. When that task is written down, you don't have to rely on your memory.

The following steps present one method for creating and using to-do lists. This method involves ranking each item on your list according to three levels of importance—A, B, and C. Experiment with these steps, modify them as you see fit, and invent new techniques that work for you.

Step 1. Brainstorm tasks

To get started, list all of the tasks you want to get done tomorrow. Each task will become an item on a to-do list. Don't worry about putting the entries in order or scheduling them yet. Just list everything you want to accomplish on a sheet of paper or planning calendar, or in a special notebook. You can also use 3 x 5 cards, writing one task on each card. Cards work well because you can slip them into your pocket or rearrange them, and you never have to copy to-do items from one list to another.

Step 2. Estimate time

For each task you wrote down in Step 1, estimate how long it will take you to complete it. This can be tricky. If

you allow too little time, you end up feeling rushed. If you allow too much time, you become less productive. For now, give it your best guess. If you are unsure, overestimate rather than underestimate how long it will take for each task. Overestimating has two benefits: (1) it avoids a schedule that is too tight, missed deadlines, and the resulting feelings of frustration and failure; and (2) it allows time for the unexpected things that come up every day—the spontaneous to-dos. Now pull out your calendar or Time Monitor/Time Plan. You've probably scheduled some hours for activities such as classes or work. This leaves the unscheduled hours for tackling your to-do lists.

Add up the time needed to complete all your to-do items. Also add up the number of unscheduled hours in your day. Then compare the two totals. The power of this step is that you can spot overload in advance. If you have eight hours' worth of to-do items but only four unscheduled hours, that's a potential problem. To solve it, proceed to Step 3.

Step 3. Rate each task by priority

To prevent overscheduling, decide which to-do items are the most important, given the time you have available. One suggestion for making this decision comes from the book *How to Get Control of Your Time and Your Life* by Alan Lakein: Simply label each task A, B, or C.[1]

The A's on your list are those things that are the most critical. They include assignments that are coming due or jobs that need to be done immediately. Also included are activities that lead directly to your short-term goals.

The B's on your list are important, but less so than the A's. Although B's might someday become A's, for the present these tasks are not as urgent as A's. They can be postponed, if necessary, for another day.

The C's do not require immediate attention. C priorities include activities such as "shop for a new blender" and "research genealogy on the Internet." C's are often small, easy jobs with no set timeline. They, too, can be postponed.

Once you've labeled the items on your to-do list, schedule time for all of the A's. The B's and C's can be done randomly during the day when you are in-between tasks and are not yet ready to start the next A.

Step 4. Cross off tasks

Keep your to-do list with you at all times. Cross off activities when you finish them, and add new ones when you think of them. If you're using 3 x 5 cards, you can toss away or recycle the cards with completed items. Crossing off tasks and releasing cards can be fun—a visible reward for your diligence. This step fosters a sense of accomplishment.

When using the ABC priority method, you might experience an ailment common to students: C fever. Symptoms include the uncontrollable urge to drop that A task and begin crossing C's off your to-do list. If your history paper is due tomorrow, you might feel compelled to vacuum the rug, call your third cousin in Tulsa, and make a trip to the store for shoelaces. The

reason C fever is so common is that A tasks are usually more difficult or time-consuming to achieve, with a higher risk of failure.

If you notice symptoms of C fever, ask yourself, "Does this job really need to be done now? Do I really need to alphabetize my DVD collection, or might I better use this time to study for tomorrow's data-processing exam?" Use your to-do list to keep yourself on task, working on your A's. But don't panic or berate yourself when you realize that in the last six hours, you have completed 11 C's and not a single A. Just calmly return to the A's.

Step 5. Evaluate

At the end of the day, evaluate your performance. Look for A priorities you didn't complete. Look for items that repeatedly turn up as B's or C's on your list and never seem to get done. Consider changing them to A's or dropping them altogether. Similarly, you might consider changing an A that didn't get done to a B or C priority. When you're done evaluating, start on tomorrow's to-do list. Be willing to admit mistakes. You might at first rank some items as A's only to realize later that they are actually C's. And some of the C's that lurk at the bottom of your list day after day might really be A's. When you keep a daily to-do list, you can adjust these priorities *before* they become problems.

In any case, make starting your own to-do list an A priority. ✳

16 critical thinking exercise
Choose strategies to manage time and tasks

After reading the article "The ABC Daily To-Do List," choose one technique to apply—preferably within the next 24 hours. In the following space, summarize that technique in one sentence:

_____

_____

_____

After using the technique for at least one week and observing the results, use the following space to describe how well it worked for you. If the technique worked well, consider making it a habit. If it did *not* work well, list a way to modify the strategy so that it becomes a better fit for you:

_____

_____

_____

Stop procrastination NOW

CONSIDER A BOLD idea: To stop procrastinating, just stop procrastinating. Now. Giving up procrastination is actually a simple choice. People just *tell* themselves that it takes months or even years to give up this habit.

Test this idea for yourself. Think of something that you've been putting off. Choose a small, specific task—one that you can complete in five minutes or less. Then do that task today.

Tomorrow, choose another task and do it. Repeat this strategy each day for one week. Notice what happens to your habit of procrastination. In addition, experiment with the following ideas.

Discover the costs. Find out if procrastination keeps you from getting what you want. Clearly seeing the side effects of procrastination can help you kick the habit.

Discover your procrastination style.
Psychologist Linda Sapadin identifies different styles of procrastination.[2] For example, *dreamers* have big goals that they seldom translate into specific plans. *Worriers* focus on the worst-case scenario and are likely to talk more about problems than about solutions. *Defiers* resist new tasks or promise to do them and then don't follow through. *Overdoers* create extra work for themselves by refusing to delegate tasks and neglecting to set priorities. And *perfectionists* put off tasks for fear of making a mistake.

Awareness of your procrastination style is a key to changing your behavior. If you exhibit the characteristics of an overdoer, for example, then say no to new projects. Also ask for help in completing your current projects.

To discover your procrastination style, observe your behavior. Avoid judgments. Just be a scientist: Record the facts. Write Discovery Statements about specific ways you procrastinate. Follow up with Intention Statements about what to do differently.

Trick yourself into getting started. If you have a 50-page chapter to read, then grab the book and say to yourself, "I'm not really going to read this chapter right now. I'm just going to flip through the pages and scan the headings for 10 minutes." Tricks like these can get you started on a task you've been dreading.

Let feelings follow action. If you put off exercising until you feel energetic, you might wait for months. Instead, get moving now. Then watch your feelings change. After five minutes of brisk walking, you might be in the mood for a 20-minute run. This principle—action generates motivation—can apply to any task that you've put on the back burner.

Choose to work under pressure. Sometimes people thrive under pressure. As one writer puts it, "I don't do my *best* work under deadline. I do my *only* work under deadline." Used selectively, this strategy might also work for you. Put yourself in control. If you choose to work with a due date staring you right in the face, then schedule a big block of time during the preceding week. Until then, enjoy!

Think ahead. Use the monthly calendar on page 109 or the long-term planner on pages 111–112 to list due dates for assignments in all your courses. Using these tools, you can anticipate heavy demands on your time and take action to prevent last-minute crunches. Make *From Master Student to Master Employee* your home base—the first place to turn in taking control of your schedule.

Give up "someday." Procrastination rests on this vague notion: *I'll do it someday.* Other people reinforce this notion by telling you that your life will *really* start when you. . . . (Fill in the blank with phrases like *graduate from college, get married, have kids, get promoted,* or *retire.*) Using this logic, you could wait your whole life to start living. Avoid this fate. Take action today.

Create goals that draw you forward. A goal that grabs you by the heartstrings is an inspiration to act now. If you're procrastinating, then set some goals that excite you. Then you might wake up one day and discover that procrastination is part of your past. ✳

 Find more strategies for ending procrastination.

25 ways to get the most out of now

The following techniques are about getting the most from study time. They're listed in four categories:

- When to study.
- Where to study.
- Ways to handle the rest of the world.
- Things to ask yourself if you get stuck.

Don't feel pressured to use all of the techniques or to tackle them in order. As you read, note the suggestions you think will be helpful. Pick one technique to use now. When it becomes a habit, come back to this article and select another one. Repeat this cycle, and enjoy the results as they unfold in your life.

Ferenc Szelepcsenyi/Shutterstock

When to study

Study difficult (or boring) subjects first. If your chemistry problems put you to sleep, get to them first, while you are fresh. We tend to give top priority to what we enjoy studying, yet the courses that we find most difficult often require the most creative energy. Save your favorite subjects for later. If you find yourself avoiding a particular subject, get up an hour earlier to study it before breakfast. With that chore out of the way, the rest of the day can be a breeze.

Be aware of your best time of day. Many people learn best in daylight hours. If this is true for you, schedule study time for your most difficult subjects before nightfall.

Unless you grew up on a farm, the idea of being conscious at 5 a.m. might seem ridiculous. Yet many successful businesspeople begin the day at 5 a.m. or earlier. Athletes and yoga practitioners use the early morning, too. Some writers complete their best work before 9 a.m.

Others experience the same benefits by staying up late. They flourish after midnight. If you aren't convinced, then experiment. When you're in a time crunch, get up early or stay up late. You might even see a sunrise.

Use waiting time. Five minutes waiting for a subway, 20 minutes waiting for the dentist, 10 minutes in-between classes—waiting time adds up fast. Have short study tasks ready to do during these periods. For example, you can carry 3 x 5 cards with facts, formulas, or definitions and pull them out anywhere.

A CD or mp3 player can help you use commuting time to your advantage. Use your computer to make a recording of yourself reading your notes. Then transfer that recording onto a CD or mp3 player. Play it as you drive, or listen through headphones as you ride on the bus or subway.

Study two hours for every hour you're in class. Students in higher education are regularly advised to allow two hours of study time for every hour spent in class. If you are taking 15 credit hours, then plan to spend 30 hours a week studying. The benefits of following this advice will be apparent at exam time.

Keep in mind that the "two hours for one" rule doesn't distinguish between focused time and unfocused time. In one four-hour block of study time, it's possible to use up two of those hours with phone calls, breaks, daydreaming, and doodling. With study time, quality counts as much as quantity.

Avoid marathon study sessions. When possible, study in shorter sessions. Three 3-hour sessions are usually more productive than one 9-hour session. If you must study in a large block of time, work on several subjects, and avoid studying similar topics one after the other.

Where to study

Use a regular study area. Your body and your mind know where you are. Using the same place to study, day after day, helps train your responses. When you arrive at that particular place, you can focus your attention more quickly.

Study where you'll be alert. In bed, your body gets a signal. For most students, that signal is more likely to be "Time to sleep!" than "Time to study!" Just as you train your body to be alert at your desk, you also train it to slow down near your bed. For that reason, don't study where you sleep.

Easy chairs and sofas are also dangerous places to study. Learning requires energy. Give your body a message that energy is needed. Put yourself in a situation that supports this message. For example, some schools offer empty classrooms as places to study. Many students report that they find themselves studying effectively in a classroom setting.

Use a library. Libraries are designed for learning. The lighting is perfect. The noise level is low. A wealth of material is available. Entering a library is a signal to focus the mind and get to work. Many students can get more done in a shorter time frame at the library than anywhere else. Experiment for yourself.

Ways to handle the rest of the world

Pay attention to your attention. Breaks in concentration are often caused by internal interruptions. Your own thoughts jump in to divert you from your studies. When this happens, notice these thoughts and then let them go. Perhaps the thought of getting something else done is distracting you. One option is to handle that other task now and study later. You can also write yourself a note about it, or schedule a specific time to do it.

Agree with living mates about study time. This agreement includes roommates, spouses, and children. Make the rules about study time clear, and be sure to follow them yourself. Explicit agreements—even written contracts—work well. One student always wears a colorful hat when he wants to study. When his wife and children see the hat, they respect his wish to be left alone.

Get off the phone. The phone is the ultimate interrupter. People who wouldn't think of distracting you in person might call or text you at the worst times because they can't see that you are studying. You don't have to be a victim of your cell phone. If a simple "I can't talk; I'm studying" doesn't work, use dead silence.

Keep on going?

Some people keep on going, even when they get stuck or fail again and again. To such people belongs the world. Consider the hapless politician who compiled this record:

- Failed in business, 1831.
- Defeated for legislature, 1832.
- Failed in business a second time, 1833.
- Suffered a nervous breakdown, 1836.
- Defeated for speaker of the house, 1838.
- Defeated for elector, 1840.
- Defeated for Congress, 1843.
- Defeated for Senate, 1855.
- Defeated for vice president, 1856.
- Defeated for Senate, 1858.
- Elected president, 1860.

Who was the fool who kept on going in spite of so many failures?

Answer: The fool was Abraham Lincoln.

It's a conversation killer. Another idea is to short-circuit the whole problem: Turn off your phone or silence it.

Learn to say no. Saying no is a time-saver and a valuable life skill for everyone. Some people feel it is rude to refuse a request. However, you can say no effectively and courteously. Others want you to succeed as a student. When you tell them that you can't do what they ask because you are busy educating yourself, most people will understand.

Hang a "do not disturb" sign on your door. Many hotels will give you a free "do not disturb" sign for the advertising. You can also create a sign yourself. They work. Using signs can relieve you of making a decision about cutting off each interruption—a time-saver in itself.

Get ready the night before. Completing a few simple tasks just before you go to bed can help you get in gear the next day. If you need to make some phone calls first thing in the morning, look up those numbers, write them on 3 x 5 cards, and set them near the phone. If you need to drive to a new location, make a note of the address and check the directions online, then put them next to your car keys. If you plan to spend the next afternoon writing a paper, get your materials together: dictionary, notes, outline, paper, pencil, flash drive, laptop—whatever you need. Pack your lunch or put gas in the car. Organize the baby's diaper bag and your briefcase or backpack.

Remember cultural differences

There are as many different styles for managing time as there are people. These styles vary across cultures.

In the United States and England, for example, business meetings typically start on time. That's also true in Scandinavian countries such as Norway and Sweden. However, travelers to Panama might find that meetings start about a half-hour late. Furthermore, people who complain about late meetings while doing business in Mexico might be considered rude.

When you study or work with people of different races and ethnic backgrounds, look for differences in their approach to time. A behavior that you might view as rude or careless—such as showing up late for appointments—could simply result from seeing the world in a different way.

Call ahead. We often think of talking on the telephone as a prime time-waster. Used wisely, though, the telephone can actually help manage time. Before you go shopping, call the store to see if it carries the items you're looking for. If you're driving, call for directions to your destination (or look them up online). A few seconds on the phone or computer can save hours in wasted trips and wrong turns.

Avoid noise distractions. To promote concentration, avoid studying in front of the television, and turn off the radio. Many students insist that they study better with background noise, and it might be true. Some students report good results with carefully selected and controlled music. For many others, silence is the best form of music to study by.

At times noise levels might be out of your control. A neighbor or roommate might decide to find out how far she can turn up her music before the walls crumble. Meanwhile, your ability to concentrate on the principles of sociology goes down the drain. To avoid this scenario, schedule study sessions during periods when your living environment is usually quiet. If you live in a residence hall, ask if study rooms are available. Otherwise, go somewhere else where it's quiet, such as the library. Some students have even found refuge in quiet coffee shops, self-service laundries, and places of worship.

Manage interruptions. Notice how others misuse your time. Be aware of repeat offenders. Ask yourself if there are certain friends or relatives who consistently interrupt your study time.

If avoiding the interrupter is impractical, send a clear message. Sometimes others don't realize that they are breaking your concentration. You can give them a gentle, yet firm, reminder: "What you're saying is important. Can we schedule a time to talk about it when I can give you my full attention?" If this strategy doesn't work, there are other ways to make your message more effective. For more ideas, see Chapter 9: "Communicating."

See if you can "firewall" yourself for selected study periods each week. Find a place where you can count on being alone and working without interruption.

However, sometimes interruptions still happen. Therefore, create a system for dealing with them. One option is to take an index card and write a quick note about what you're doing the moment an interruption occurs. As soon as possible, return to the card and pick up the task where you left off.

Things to ask yourself if you get stuck

Ask: "What is one task I can accomplish toward achieving my goal?" This technique is helpful when you face a big, imposing job. Pick out one small accomplishment, preferably one you can complete in about five minutes; then do it. The satisfaction of getting one thing done can spur you on to get one more thing done. Meanwhile, the job gets smaller.

Ask: "Am I being too hard on myself?" If you are feeling frustrated with a reading assignment, if your attention wanders repeatedly, or if you've fallen behind on math problems that are due tomorrow, take a minute to listen to the messages you are giving yourself. Are you scolding yourself too harshly? Lighten up. Allow yourself to feel a little foolish, and then get on with the task at hand. Don't add to the problem by berating yourself.

Worrying about the future is another way people beat themselves up: "How will I ever get all this done?" "What if every paper I'm assigned turns out to be this hard?" "If I can't do the simple calculations now, how will I ever pass the final?" Instead of promoting learning, such questions fuel anxiety.

Labeling and generalizing weaknesses are other ways people are hard on themselves. Being objective and specific in the messages you send yourself will help eliminate this form of self-punishment and will likely generate new possibilities. An alternative to saying "I'm terrible in algebra" is to say "I don't understand factoring equations." This rewording suggests a plan to improve.

You might be able to lighten the load by discovering how your learning styles affect your behavior. For example, you may have a bias toward concrete experience rather than abstract thinking. If so, after setting a goal, you might want to move directly into action.

In large part, the ability to learn through concrete experience is a valuable trait. After all, action is necessary to achieve goals. At the same time, you might find it helpful to allow extra time to plan. Careful planning can help you avoid unnecessary activity. Instead of using a planner that shows a day at a time, experiment with a calendar that displays a week or month at a glance. The expanded format can help you look farther into the future and stay on track as you set out to meet long-term goals.

Ask: "Is this a piano?" Carpenters who construct rough frames for buildings have a saying they use when they bend a nail or accidentally hack a chunk out of a two-by-four: "Well, this ain't no piano." It means that perfection is not necessary. Ask yourself if what you are doing needs to be perfect. Perhaps you don't have to apply the same standards of grammar to lecture notes that you would apply to a term paper. If you can complete a job 95 percent perfectly in two hours and 100 percent perfectly in four hours, ask yourself whether the additional 5 percent improvement is worth doubling the amount of time you spend.

Sometimes, though, it *is* a piano. A tiny miscalculation can ruin an entire lab experiment. A misstep in solving a complex math problem can negate hours of work. Computers are notorious for turning little errors into nightmares. Accept lower standards only when appropriate.

A related suggestion is to weed out low-priority tasks. The to-do list for a large project can include dozens of items, not all of which are equally important. Some can be done later, while others can be skipped altogether, if time is short.

Apply this idea when you study. In a long reading assignment, look for pages you can skim or skip. When it's appropriate, read chapter summaries or article abstracts. As you review your notes, look for material that might not be covered on a test, and decide whether you want to study it.

Ask: "Would I pay myself for what I'm doing right now?" If you were employed as a student, would you be earning your wages? Ask yourself this question when you notice that you've taken your third snack break in 30 minutes. Then remember that you are, in fact, employed as a student. You are investing in your own productivity and are paying a big price for the privilege of being a student. Doing a mediocre job now might result in fewer opportunities in the future.

Ask: "Can I do just one more thing?" Ask yourself this question at the end of a long day. Almost always you will have enough energy to do just one more short task. The overall increase in your productivity might surprise you.

Ask: "Am I making time for things that are important but not urgent?" If we spend most of our time putting out fires, we can feel drained and frustrated. According to Stephen R. Covey, this chain of events occurs when we forget to take time for things that are not urgent but are truly important.[3] Examples of truly important activities include exercising regularly, reading, praying or meditating, spending quality time alone or with family members and friends, traveling, and cooking nutritious meals. Each of these activities can contribute directly to a long-term goal or life mission. Yet when schedules get tight, we often forgo these things, waiting for that elusive day when we'll "finally have more time."

That day won't come until we choose to make time for what's truly important. Knowing this, we can use some of the suggestions in this chapter to free up more time.

Ask: "Can I delegate this?" Instead of slogging through complicated tasks alone, you can draw on the talents and energy of other people. Busy executives know the value of delegating tasks to coworkers. Without delegation, many projects would flounder or die.

You can apply the same principle in your life. Instead of doing all the housework or cooking by yourself, for example, you can assign some of the tasks to family members or roommates. Rather than making a trip to the library to look up a simple fact, you can call and ask a library assistant to research it for you. Instead of driving across town to deliver a package, you can hire a delivery service to do so. All of these tactics can free up extra hours for studying.

It's not practical to delegate certain study tasks, such as writing term papers or completing reading assignments. However, you can still draw on the ideas of others in completing such tasks. For instance, form a writing group to edit and critique papers, brainstorm topics or titles, and develop lists of sources.

If you're absent from a class, find a classmate to summarize the lecture, discussion, and any upcoming assignments. Presidents depend on briefings. You can use the same technique.

Ask: "How did I just waste time?" Notice when time passes and you haven't accomplished what you had planned to do. Take a minute to review your actions, and note the specific ways you wasted time. We tend to operate by habit, wasting time in the same ways over and over again. When you are aware of things you do that drain your time, you are more likely to catch yourself in the act next time. Observing one small quirk might save you hours. But keep this in mind: Asking you to notice how you waste time is not intended to make you feel guilty. The point is to increase your skill by getting specific information about how you use time.

Ask: "Could I find the time if I really wanted to?" The next time you're tempted to say, "I just don't have time," pause for a minute. Question the truth of this statement. Could you find four more hours this week for studying? Suppose that someone offered to pay you $10,000 to find those four hours. Suppose, too, that

Commuter students: Manage the demands on your time

Some commuter students talk about the "3 C" problem—going from the *car* to *class* and straight back to the *car*. These students feel isolated from campus life. You can avoid that fate and still honor your current commitments:

Focus on a few high-priority activities. Reflect on the main commitments in your life. See if you can reduce them to three or four major activities, such as work, family, and school. Tackle other major projects, such as finding a new job, after you get your degree.

Join a study group. In addition to boosting your test scores, study groups can help you meet people and feel more connected to school.

Meet with your instructors. Once each week or two, set aside an extra 15 minutes to chat with one of your instructors before or after class. Also schedule regular times to meet with instructors during their office hours.

Attend a weekend event on campus. Invite your family and friends to attend concerts, plays, speakers, and other school-related events.

Ask about programs for commuter students. Your school might have a lounge with lockers, desks, and computers that commuter students can use. Search out these spaces and look for notices of special events and services for commuter students.

you will get paid only if you don't lose sleep, call in sick for work, or sacrifice anything important to you. Could you find the time if vast sums of money were involved?

Remember that when it comes to school, vast sums of money *are* involved.

Ask: "Am I willing to promise it?" This time-management idea might be the most powerful of all: If you want to find time for a task, promise yourself—and others—that you'll get it done.

One way to accomplish big things in life is to make big promises. There's little reward in promising what's safe or predictable. No athlete promises to place seventh at the Olympics. Chances are that if you're not making big promises, you're not stretching yourself.

The point of making a promise is not to chain yourself to a rigid schedule or impossible expectations.

You can promise to reach goals without unbearable stress. You can keep schedules flexible and carry out your plans with ease, joy, and satisfaction.

At times, though, you might go too far. Some promises may be truly beyond you, and you might break them. However, failing to keep a promise is just that—failing to keep a promise. A broken promise is not the end of the world.

Promises can work magic. When your word is on the line, it's possible to discover reserves of time and energy you didn't know existed. Promises can push you to exceed your expectations. ✳

 Discover even more ways to get the most out of now.

The 7-day antiprocrastination plan

Listed here are seven strategies you can use to reduce or eliminate many sources of procrastination. The suggestions are tied to the days of the week to help you remember them. Use this list to remind yourself that each day of your life presents an opportunity to stop the cycle of procrastination.

MONDAY Make it Meaningful What is important about the task you've been putting off? List all the benefits of completing that task. Look at it in relation to your short-, mid-, or long-term goals. Be specific about the rewards for getting it done, including how you will feel when the task is completed. To remember this strategy, keep in mind that it starts with the letter ***M,*** as in the word ***Monday.***

TUESDAY Take it Apart Break big jobs into a series of small ones you can do in 15 minutes or less. If a long reading assignment intimidates you, divide it into two- or three-page sections. Make a list of the sections, and cross them off as you complete them so you can see your progress. Even the biggest projects can be broken down into a series of small tasks. This strategy starts with the letter ***T,*** so mentally tie it to ***Tuesday.***

WEDNESDAY Write an Intention Statement If you can't get started on a term paper, you might write, "I intend to write a list of at least ten possible topics by 9 p.m. I will reward myself with an hour of guilt-free recreational reading." Write your intention on a 3x5 card. Carry it with you or post it in your study area, where you can see it often. In your memory, file the first word in this strategy—***write***—with ***Wednesday.***

THURSDAY Tell Everyone Publicly announce your intention to get a task done. Tell a friend that you intend to learn ten irregular French verbs by Saturday. Tell your spouse, roommate, parents, and children. Include anyone who will ask whether you've completed the assignment or who will suggest ways to get it done. Make the world your support group. Associate ***tell*** with ***Thursday.***

FRIDAY Find a Reward Construct rewards to yourself carefully. Be willing to withhold them if you do not complete the task. Don't pick a movie as a reward for studying biology if you plan to go to the movie anyway. And when you legitimately reap your reward, notice how it feels. Remember that ***Friday*** is a fine day to ***find*** a reward. (Of course, you can find a reward on any day of the week. Rhyming ***Friday*** with ***fine*** day is just a memory trick.)

SATURDAY Settle it Now Do it now. The minute you notice yourself procrastinating, plunge into the task. Imagine yourself at a cold mountain lake, poised to dive. Gradual immersion would be slow torture. It's often less painful to leap. Then be sure to savor the feeling of having the task behind you. Link ***settle*** with ***Saturday.***

SUNDAY Say No When you keep pushing a task into a low-priority category, reexamine your purpose for doing that task at all. If you realize that you really don't intend to do something, quit telling yourself that you will. That's procrastinating. Just say no. Then you're not procrastinating. You don't have to carry around the baggage of an undone task. ***Sunday***—the last day of this 7-day plan—is a great day to finally let go and just ***say*** no.

Image Source/Alamy

Organizing time and tasks at work

TO SUCCEED AT getting organized, think in terms of two broad strategies. First, get the big picture—what you intend to accomplish this month, this quarter, this year, and beyond. Second, set priorities for your day-to-day, hour-to-hour tasks.

Get real with project due dates. The more complicated the project, the more you can benefit from getting organized. This is especially true with projects that extend well into the future. Start by scheduling a long-term goal—for example, the due date for the final product. Next, set interim due dates for the work you'll produce at key points leading up to that final date. These interim dates function as mid-term goals. In turn, each mid-term goal can lead you to more immediate, short-term goals.

For example, say that you're a computer technician and your team plans to complete a major hardware and software upgrade for your company in one year (long-term goal). As a team, set goals for finishing major parts of this project, such as due dates for installing new computers in individual departments (mid-term goals). You could also set up meetings with each department head over the next month to update them on your plans (short-term goals).

You may end up juggling several major projects at once. To plan effectively, enter all the relevant due dates in a monthly calendar so that you can see several of them at a glance.

Monitor work time and tasks. Another way to get a big picture of your work life is to look for broad patterns in how you currently spend your work time. Use the Time Monitor/Time Plan explained earlier in this chapter to do this analysis. Find out which tasks burn up most of your hours on the job.

With this data in hand, you can make immediate choices to minimize downtime and boost your productivity. Start by looking for low-value activities to eliminate. Also note your peak periods of energy during the workday. Schedule your most challenging tasks for these times.

Schedule fixed blocks of time first. Start with recurring meetings, for instance. These time periods are usually determined in advance and occur at regular times each week or month. Be realistic about how much time you need for such events. Then schedule other tasks around them.

Set clear starting and stopping times. Tasks often expand to fill the time we allot for them. "It always takes me two hours just to deal with my e-mails each day" might become a self-fulfilling prophecy. As an alternative, schedule a certain amount of time for reading and responding to e-mail. Set a timer and stick to it. People often find that they can gradually decrease such time by forcing themselves to work a little more efficiently. This can usually be done without sacrificing the quality of your work.

Clean your desk. For starters, purge your cubicle and files of everything you don't need. Start tossing junk mail the moment that it arrives. Next, start a "to read" file for documents that you can review at any time. Pack this folder for your next plane trip or bus ride. Finally, avoid the habit of writing reminder notes on random scraps of paper. Store all your to-do items in a unified system, such as a stack of 3 x 5 cards or a single file on your computer. Having an uncluttered desk makes it easier for you to find things. And that saves time. ✳

BananaStock/Alamy

Beyond time management:
Staying focused on what matters

Ask some people about managing time, and a dreaded image appears in their minds.

THEY SEE A person with a 100-item to-do list clutching a calendar chock full of appointments. They imagine a robot who values cold efficiency, compulsively accounts for every minute, and has no time for people.

It might help you to think beyond time management to the larger concept of *planning*. The point of planning is not to load your schedule with obligations. Instead, planning is about getting the important things done and still having time to be human. An effective planner is productive and relaxed at the same time.

Discover your style. If you find it hard to work from a conventional to-do list, you can try plotting your day on a mind map. (Mind maps are explained in Chapter 6: "Notes.") Doing so might feel especially comfortable if you're blessed with a natural visual intelligence, as explained in the discussion of Howard Gardner's theory of multiple intelligences in Chapter 1: "First Steps."

Another approach might be to write to-do items, one per 3 x 5 card, in any order in which tasks occur to you. Later you can edit, sort, and rank the cards, choosing which items to do. This method will probably appeal to you if you learn best through active experimentation and using your kinesthetic intelligence, which involves movement and the sense of touch.

Do less. Planning is as much about dropping worthless activities as about adding new ones. See if you can reduce or eliminate activities that contribute little to your values. When you add a new item to your calendar or to-do list, consider dropping a current one.

Buy less. Before you purchase an item, estimate how much time it will take to locate, assemble, use, repair, and maintain it. You might be able to free up hours by doing without.

Slow down. Sometimes it's useful to hurry, such as when you're late for a meeting or about to miss a plane. At other times, haste is a choice that serves no real purpose. If you're speeding through the day like a launched missile, consider what would happen if you got to your next destination a few minutes later than planned. Rushing might not be worth the added strain.

Handle it now. A long to-do list can result from postponing decisions and procrastinating. An alternative is to handle a task or decision immediately. Answer that letter now. Make that phone call as soon as it occurs to you. Then you don't have to add the task to your calendar or to-do list.

Remember people. Few people on their deathbeds ever say, "I wish I'd spent more time at the office." They're more likely to say, "I wish I'd spent more time with my family and friends." The pace of daily life can lead us to neglect the people we cherish.

Efficiency is a concept that applies to things—not people. When it comes to maintaining and nurturing relationships, we can often benefit from loosening up our schedules. We can allow extra time for spontaneous visits and free-ranging conversations.

Forget about time. Take time away from time. Schedule downtime—a space in your day when you ignore to-do lists, appointments, and accomplishments. This period is when you're accountable to no one else and have nothing to accomplish. Even a few minutes spent in this way can yield a sense of renewal. One way to manage time is periodically to forget about it.

Strictly speaking, time cannot be managed. The minutes, hours, days, and years simply march ahead. What we can do is manage *ourselves* with respect to time. A few basic principles can help us do that just as effectively as a truckload of cold-blooded techniques. ✳

17 critical thinking exercise
Master monthly calendar

This exercise will give you an opportunity to step back from the details of your daily schedule and get a bigger picture of your life. The more difficult it is for you to plan beyond the current day or week, the greater the benefit of this exercise.

Your basic tool is a one-month calendar. Use it to block out specific times for upcoming events such as study group meetings, due dates for assignments, review periods before tests, and other time-sensitive tasks.

To get started, you might want to copy the blank monthly calendar on page 109 onto both sides of a sheet of paper. You can also make several copies of these pages and tape them together so that you can see several months at a glance.

Be creative. Experiment with a variety of uses for your monthly calendar. For instance, you can note day-to-day changes in your health or moods, list the places you visit while you are on vacation, or circle each day that you practice a new habit. For examples of filled-in monthly calendars, see the following example.

 Find printable copies of this monthly calendar online.

MONDAY	TUESDAY	WEDNESDAY	THURSDAY	FRIDAY	SATURDAY	SUNDAY

Name _____

Month _____

TIME

3

Gearing up:
Using a long-term planner

Planning a day, a week, or a month ahead is a powerful practice. Using a long-term planner—one that displays an entire quarter, semester, or year at a glance—can yield even more benefits.

WITH A LONG-TERM planner, you can eliminate a lot of unpleasant surprises. Long-term planning allows you to avoid scheduling conflicts—the kind that obligate you to be in two places at the same time three weeks from now. You can also anticipate busy periods, and start preparing for them now. Say good-bye to all-night cram sessions; say hello to serenity.

Find a long-term planner, or make your own. Many office supply stores carry academic planners in paper form that cover an entire school year. Computer software for time management offers the same features. You can also be creative and make your own long-term planner. A big roll of newsprint pinned to a bulletin board or taped to a wall will do nicely.

Enter scheduled dates that extend into the future. Use your long-term planner to list commitments that extend beyond the current month. Enter test dates, lab sessions, days that classes will be canceled, and other events that will take place over this term and next term.

Create a master assignment list. Find the syllabus for each course you're currently taking. Then, in your long-term planner, enter the due dates for all of the assignments in all of your courses.

The purpose of this technique is not to make you feel overwhelmed. Rather, its aim is to help you take a First Step toward recognizing the demands on your time. Armed with the truth about how you use your time, you can make more accurate plans.

Include nonacademic events. In addition to tracking academic commitments, you can use your long-term planner to mark significant events in your life outside school. Include birthdays, doctors' appointments, concert dates, credit card payment due dates, and car maintenance schedules.

Use your long-term planner to divide and conquer. Big assignments such as term papers or major presentations pose a special risk. When you have three months to do a project, you might say to yourself, "That looks like a lot of work, but I've got plenty of time. No problem." But two months, three weeks, and six days from now, it could suddenly be a huge problem.

For some people, academic life is a series of last-minute crises punctuated by periods of exhaustion. You can avoid that fate. The trick is to set due dates *before* the final due date.

When planning to write a term paper, for instance, enter the final due date in your long-term planner. Then set individual due dates for each milestone in the writing process—creating an outline, completing your research, finishing a first draft, editing the draft, and preparing the final copy. By meeting these interim due dates, you make steady progress on the assignment throughout the term. ✳

 Find printable copies of this long-term planner online.

Week of	Monday	Tuesday	Wednesday	Thursday	Friday	Saturday	Sunday
9 / 5							
9 / 12		English quiz					
9 / 19			English paper due		Speech #1		
9 / 26	Chemistry test					Skiing at the lake	
10 / 3		English quiz			Speech #2		
10 / 10				Geography project due			
10 / 17				--- No classes ---			

LONG-TERM PLANNER ___ / ___ / ___ to ___ / ___ / ___

Week of	Monday	Tuesday	Wednesday	Thursday	Friday	Saturday	Sunday
__ / __							
__ / __							
__ / __							
__ / __							
__ / __							
__ / __							
__ / __							
__ / __							
__ / __							
__ / __							
__ / __							
__ / __							
__ / __							
__ / __							
__ / __							
__ / __							
__ / __							
__ / __							
__ / __							
__ / __							
__ / __							
__ / __							
__ / __							
__ / __							
__ / __							
__ / __							
__ / __							
__ / __							
__ / __							
__ / __							
__ / __							

TIME

3

LONG-TERM PLANNER ___ / ___ / ___ to ___ / ___ / ___

Week of	Monday	Tuesday	Wednesday	Thursday	Friday	Saturday	Sunday
___ / ___							
___ / ___							
___ / ___							
___ / ___							
___ / ___							
___ / ___							
___ / ___							
___ / ___							
___ / ___							
___ / ___							
___ / ___							
___ / ___							
___ / ___							
___ / ___							
___ / ___							
___ / ___							
___ / ___							
___ / ___							
___ / ___							
___ / ___							
___ / ___							
___ / ___							
___ / ___							
___ / ___							
___ / ___							
___ / ___							
___ / ___							
___ / ___							
___ / ___							
___ / ___							
___ / ___							
___ / ___							

TIME

3

Be Here Now

Being right here, right now is such a simple idea. It seems obvious. Where else can you be but where you are? When else can you be there but when you are there?

The answer is that you can be somewhere else at any time—in your head. It's common for our thoughts to distract us from where we've chosen to be. When we let this happen, we lose the benefits of focusing our attention on what's important to us in the present moment.

To "be here now" means to do what you're doing when you're doing it. It means to be where you are when you're there. Students consistently report that focusing attention on the here and now is one of the most powerful tools in this book.

We all have a voice in our head that hardly ever shuts up. If you don't believe it, conduct this experiment: Close your eyes for 10 seconds, and pay attention to what is going on in your head. Please do this right now.

Notice something? Perhaps a voice in your head was saying, "Forget it. I'm in a hurry." Another might have said, "I wonder when 10 seconds is up." Another could have been saying, "What little voice? I don't hear any little voice."

That's the voice.

This voice can take you anywhere at any time—especially when you are studying. When the voice takes you away, you might appear to be studying, but your brain is at the beach.

All of us have experienced this voice, as well as the absence of it.

When our inner voices are silent, time no longer seems to exist. We forget worries, aches, pains, reasons, excuses, and justifications. We fully experience the here and now. Life is magic.

Do not expect to be rid of daydreams entirely. That is neither possible nor desirable. Inner voices serve a purpose. They enable us to analyze, predict, classify, and understand events out there in the "real" world. The trick is to consciously choose when to be with your inner voice and when to let it go.

Instead of trying to force a stray thought out of your head—a futile enterprise—simply notice it. Accept it. Tell yourself, "There's that thought again." Then gently return your attention to the task at hand. That thought, or another, will come back. Your mind will drift. Simply notice again where your thoughts take you, and gently bring yourself back to the here and now.

The idea behind this Power Process is simple. When you plan for the future, plan for the future. When you listen to a lecture, listen to a lecture. When you read this book, read this book. And when you choose to daydream, daydream. Do what you're doing when you're doing it.

Be where you are when you're there. Be here now . . . and now . . . and now.

 Learn more about this Power Process online.

© Luca Tettoni/Corbis

Career Application

Steve Carlson is a technical writer for DCS, a company that makes products for multimedia teleconferencing: digital video cameras, large-screen televisions, and software. He joined DCS two years ago, after graduating with a B.A. in Technical Communications. This is his first full-time, professional job.

Steve works in a five-person documentation department. The department creates sales brochures, user manuals, and other documents about DCS products. Working with his manager, Louise Chao, Steve helps decide which documents are needed for each DCS product. He then writes documents, edits documents written by others, and works closely with a graphic designer who oversees document production.

On a Friday afternoon, Louise knocks on the door of Steve's office. She wants Steve to handle a rush project—a new product brochure to be researched, written, designed, and printed in two weeks. Louise is on the way to another meeting and only has five minutes to talk.

Steve's schedule is already full of projects. For the last month, he has been working Saturdays to stay on top of his workload. As Louise describes the project, Steve listens without comment. When Louise is finished, Steve points to a large wallboard in his office.

This wallboard is a chart that shows all of Steve's active projects. This chart includes a visual time line for each project that shows due dates for researching, outlining, drafting, and revising each document. Steve has negotiated these dates with the product development teams. Each time line is color-coded—red for urgent projects, green for other active projects, and yellow for planned projects that are not yet active. Steve uses the wallboard to plan his day-to-day tasks and visually represent his workload.

"I estimate that it would take me at least three full days to research and write the document you're talking about," Steve says. "In addition, meetings with my designer would take up another two days. So doing the brochure means that I'd need to free up at least one week of my time."

Steve then points to the projects shown in red on his wallboard. "Louise, I know this new product brochure is important to you," he says. "Can we schedule a time to choose which of these urgent projects I could delay for a week to meet your request?"

Asia Images Group/Getty

Reflecting on this scenario

List at least two strategies from this chapter that would be useful to Steve in this situation. Briefly describe how he could apply each one.

_____

_____

_____

_____

_____

_____

_____

_____

_____

_____

Quiz

Name _____   Date ____/____/____

1. Briefly explain how making promises can help you manage time.

2. Rewrite the statement "study harder" so that it becomes a specific goal.

3. The text suggests that you set long-term goals. Write one example of a long-term goal.

4. Write a mid-term and short-term goal that can help you achieve the long-term goal that you listed for Question 3.

5. Describe three strategies for managing time and tasks at work.

6. In time management terms, what is meant by "This ain't no piano"?

7. Define *C fever* as it applies to the ABC priority method.

8. Describe three strategies for overcoming procrastination.

9. According to the text, overcoming procrastination is a complex process that can take months or even years. True or false? Explain your answer.

10. Describe three ways to get the most value from using a long-term planner.

Focus on Transferable Skills

The Discovery Wheel in Chapter 1: "First Steps" includes a section labeled "Time." For the next 10 to 15 minutes, go beyond your initial responses to that exercise. Take a snapshot of your current transferable skills related to time management and goal setting. Then focus on a skill that you'd like to develop next.

You might want to prepare for this exercise by reviewing the articles "Jumpstart Your Education with Transferable Skills" on page 58 and "101 Transferable Skills" on page 60.

GOALS

I would describe my ability to set specific goals as . . .

The most important goal for me to achieve during this school year is . . .

DAILY PLANNING

When setting priorities for what to do each day, the first thing I consider is . . .

I keep track of my daily to-do items by . . .

PROCRASTINATION

The kinds of tasks on which I tend to procrastinate include . . .

My strategies for overcoming procrastination currently include . . .

BALANCE

My ability to balance recreation with working and studying can be described as . . .

If I sense that I'm not making enough time for family and friends, I respond by . . .

NEXT ACTION

The transferable skill related to time that I would most like to develop is . . .

To develop that skill, the most important thing I can do next is to . . .

Master Student PROFILE

Richard Anderson
. . . is responsible

Mark Wilson/RM/
Getty Images News

**(1955–) CEO of
Delta Airlines**

Q. What was the most important leadership lesson you learned?

A. I've learned to be patient and not lose my temper. And the reason that's important is everything you do is an example, and people look at everything you do and take a signal from everything you do. And when you lose your temper, it really squelches debate and sends the wrong signal about how you want your organization to run. . . .

Q. Are there other things that you've learned to do more of, or less?

A. You've got to be thankful to the people who get the work done, and you've got to be thankful to your customers. So, I find myself, more and more, writing hand-written notes to people. I must write a half a dozen a day.

Q. Looking back over your career, even to the early years, do you recall an insight that set you on a different trajectory?

A. Yes, and it was actually at my first job while I went to night law school at South Texas College of Law. And I had a good full-time job as the administrative assistant to the D.A. And what you understood was you really needed to be a problem-solver, not a problem-creator. You know, don't bring a Rubik's cube to the table, unless you have an idea on how you're going to try to get an answer. And always try to be a leader that comes up with the creative answers to the hard problems.

Q. And what about advice on your career?

A. If you just focus on getting your job done and being a good colleague and a team player in an organization, and not focused about being overly ambitious and wanting pay raises and promotions and the like, and just doing your job and being a part of a team, the rest of it all takes care of itself.

Q. Did somebody give you that advice, or was that something that you came to understand yourself?

A. My mother and father died from cancer when I was 20, and so I was working full time, and I was pretty fortunate to be around a lot of good people that had that kind of culture and approach to things. It was just by osmosis that I came to those kinds of conclusions. . . .

Q. And is there any change in the kind of qualities you're looking for [in job candidates] compared with 5, 10 years ago?

A. I think this communication point is getting more and more important. People really have to be able to handle the written and spoken word. And when I say written word, I don't mean PowerPoints. I don't think PowerPoints help people think as clearly as they should because you don't have to put a complete thought in place. You can just put a phrase with a bullet in front of it. And it doesn't have a subject, a verb and an object, so you aren't expressing complete thoughts. . . .

Q. What about time management?

A. Only touch paper once. No. 2, always have your homework done. No. 3, return your calls very promptly. No. 4, stick to your schedule. I keep my watch about 10 minutes ahead. It's important to run on time, particularly at an airline. And use your time wisely. And then, once a month, take the rest of the calendar year, or the next six months and re-review how you are using your time and reprioritize what you're doing.

Learn more about Richard Anderson and other master students at the Master Student Hall of Fame.

6 Notes

Master Student Map

as you read, ask yourself

what if . . .

I could take notes that remain useful for weeks, months, or even years to come?

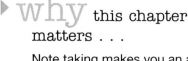

why this chapter matters . . .

Note taking makes you an active learner, enhances memory, and influences how well you do on tests and other evaluations.

how

you can use this chapter . . .

- Experiment with several formats for note taking.
- Create a note-taking format that works especially well for you.
- Take effective notes in special situations—while reading, when speakers talk fast, and during meetings.

what is included . . .

MASTER EMPLOYEE *in action*

It is essential that I am meticulous about the information I record on the various documents that pass through my hand each day. Thankfully in college I was introduced to various note taking strategies. After trying out several, I was able to come up with a system that is now second nature to me.

—JOANN ADAMS, COURT CLERK

Photo courtesy of Joann Adams

The note-taking process flows

ONE WAY TO understand note taking is to realize that taking notes is just one part of the process. Effective note taking consists of three parts: observing, recording, and reviewing. First, you observe an "event"—a statement by an instructor, a lab experiment, a slide show of an artist's works, or a chapter of required reading. Then you record your observations of that event; that is, you "take notes." Finally, you review what you have recorded.

Each part of the note-taking process is essential, and each depends on the others. Your observations determine what you record. What you record determines what you review. And the quality of your review can determine how effective your next observations will be. For example, if you review your notes on the Sino-Japanese War of 1894, the next day's lecture on the Boxer Rebellion of 1900 will make more sense.

Legible and speedy handwriting is also useful in taking notes. Knowledge about outlining is handy, too. A nifty pen, a new notebook, and a laptop computer are all great note-taking devices. However, they're all worthless—unless you participate as an energetic observer *in* class and regularly review your notes *after* class. If you take those two steps, you can turn even the most disorganized chicken scratches into a powerful tool.

Sometimes note taking looks like a passive affair, especially in large lecture classes. One person at the front of the room does most of the talking. Everyone else is seated and silent, taking notes. The lecturer seems to be doing all of the work.

Don't be deceived. Observe more closely, and you'll see some students taking notes in a way that radiates energy. They're awake and alert, poised on the edge of their seats. They're writing—a physical activity that expresses mental engagement. These students listen for levels of ideas and information, make choices about what to record, and compile materials to review.

In higher education, you might spend hundreds of hours taking notes. Making them more effective is a direct investment in your success. Think of your notes as a textbook that *you* create—one that's more current and more in tune with your learning preferences than any textbook you could buy. ✳

journal entry 12

Discovery/Intention Statement

Get what you want from this chapter

Think about the possible benefits of improving your skills at note taking. Recall a recent incident in which you had difficulty taking notes. Perhaps you were listening to an instructor who talked fast, or you got confused and stopped taking notes altogether. Describe the incident in the following space.

_____

_____

_____

_____

Now preview this chapter to find at least five strategies that you can use right away to help you take better notes. Sum up each of those strategies in a few words, and then note page numbers where you can find out more about each suggestion.

Strategy	Page number

Reflect on your intention to experiment actively with this chapter. Describe a specific situation in which you promise to apply the strategies you previously listed. If possible, choose a situation that will occur within the next 24 hours.

I intend to . . .

_____

_____

_____

6

NOTES

OBSERVE
The note-taking process flows

SHERLOCK HOLMES, a fictional master detective and student of the obvious, could track down a villain by observing the fold of his scarf and the mud on his shoes. In real life, a doctor can save a life by observing a mole—one a patient has always had—that undergoes a rapid change.

An accountant can save a client thousands of dollars by observing the details of a spreadsheet. A student can save hours of study time by observing that she gets twice as much done at a particular time of day.

Keen observers see facts and relationships. They know ways to focus their attention on the details and then tap their creative energy to discover patterns. To sharpen your classroom observation skills, experiment with the following techniques, and continue to use those that you find most valuable. Many of these strategies can be adapted to the notes you take while reading.

Set the stage

Complete outside assignments. Nothing is more discouraging (or boring) than sitting through a lecture about the relationship of Le Chatelier's principle to the study of kinetics if you've never heard of Henri Louis Le Chatelier or kinetics. The more familiar you are with a subject, the more easily you can absorb important information during class lectures. Instructors usually assume that students will complete assignments, and they construct their lectures accordingly.

Bring materials. A good pen does not make you a good observer, but the lack of a pen or notebook can be distracting enough to take the fine edge off your concentration. Make sure you have a pen, pencil, notebook, or any other materials you need. Bring your textbook to class, especially if the lectures relate closely to the text.

If you are consistently unprepared for a class, that might suggest something about your intentions concerning the course. Find out if it does. The next time you're in a frantic scramble to borrow pen and paper 37 seconds before the class begins, notice the cost. Use the borrowed pen and paper to write a Discovery Statement about your lack of preparation. Consider whether you intend to be successful in the course.

Sit front and center. Students who get as close as possible to the front and center of the classroom often

(woman) ballyscanlon/Getty, (frame) mike.irwin/Shutterstock

do better on tests for several reasons. The closer you sit to the lecturer, the harder it is to fall asleep. The closer you sit to the front, the fewer interesting or distracting classmates are situated between you and the instructor. Material on the board is easier to read from up front. Also, the instructor can see you more easily when you have a question.

Instructors are usually not trained to perform. Some can project their energy to a large audience, but some cannot. A professor who sounds boring from the back of the room might sound more interesting up close.

Sitting up front enables you to become a constructive force in the classroom. By returning the positive energy that an engaged teacher gives out, you can reinforce the teacher's enthusiasm and enhance your experience of the class.

In addition, sound waves from the human voice begin to degrade at a distance of 8 to 12 feet. If you sit more than 15 feet from the speaker, your ability to hear and take effective notes might be compromised. Get close to the source of the sound. Get close to the energy.

Sitting close to the front is a way to commit yourself to getting what you want out of school. One reason students gravitate to the back of the classroom is that they think the instructor is less likely to call on them. Sitting in back can signal a lack of commitment. When you sit up front, you are declaring your willingness to take a risk and participate.

Conduct a short preclass review. Arrive early, and then put your brain in gear by reviewing your notes

What to do when you miss a class

For most courses, you'll benefit by attending every class session. If you miss a class, catch up as quickly as possible. Following are some way to do that:

Clarify policies on missed classes   On the first day of classes, find out about your instructors' policies on absences. See if you will be allowed to make up assignments, quizzes, and tests. You should also inquire about doing extra-credit assignments.

Contact a classmate   Early in the semester, identify a student in each class who seems responsible and dependable. Exchange e-mail addresses and phone numbers. If you know you won't be in class, contact this student ahead of time. When you notice that your classmate is absent, pick up extra copies of handouts, make assignment lists, and offer copies of your notes.

Contact your instructor   If you miss a class, e-mail, phone, or fax your instructor, or put a note in his mailbox. Ask if he has another section of the same course that you can attend so you won't miss the lecture information. Also ask about getting handouts you might need before the next class meeting.

Consider technology   If there is a Web site for your class, check it for assignments and the availability of handouts you missed. Free online services such as NoteMesh allow students to share notes with one another. These services use wiki software, which allows you to create and edit Web pages using any browser. Before using such tools, however, check with your instructors for their policies on note sharing.

---

from the previous class. Scan your reading assignment. Look at the sections you have underlined or highlighted. Review assigned problems and exercises. Note questions you intend to ask.

Clarify your intentions. Take a 3×5 card to class with you. On that card, write a short Intention Statement about what you plan to get from the class. Describe your intended level of participation or the quality of attention you will bring to the subject. Be specific. If you found your previous class notes to be inadequate, write down what you intend to do to make your notes from this class session more useful.

"Be here now" in class

Accept your wandering mind. The techniques in Chapter 3's Power Process: "Be Here Now" can be especially useful when your head soars into the clouds. Don't fight daydreaming. When you notice your mind wandering during class, look at it as an opportunity to refocus your attention. Accept the fact that you are in class listening to a lecture and not somewhere else. If thermodynamics is losing out to beach parties, let go of the beach.

Notice your writing. When you discover yourself slipping into a fantasyland, feel the weight of your pen in your hand. Notice how your notes look. Paying attention to the act of writing can bring you back to the here and now.

You also can use writing in a more direct way to clear your mind of distracting thoughts. Pause for a few seconds, and write those thoughts down. If you're distracted by thoughts of errands you need to run after class, list them on a 3×5 card that you will stick in your pocket. You can also simply put a symbol, such as an arrow or asterisk, in your notes to mark the

places where your mind started to wander. Once your distractions are out of your mind and safely stored on paper, you can gently return your attention to taking notes.

Be with the instructor. In your mind, put yourself right up front with the instructor. Imagine that you and the instructor are the only ones in the room and that the lecture is a personal conversation between the two of you. Pay attention to the instructor's body language and facial expressions. Look the instructor in the eye.

Remember that the power of this suggestion is immediately reduced by digital distractions—Web surfing, e-mail checking, or text messaging. Taking notes is a way to stay focused. The physical act of taking notes signals your mind to stay in the same room as the instructor.

Notice your environment. When you become aware of yourself daydreaming, bring yourself back to class by paying attention to the temperature in the room, the feel of your chair, or the quality of light coming through the window. Run your hand along the surface of your desk. Listen to the chalk on the blackboard or the sound of the teacher's voice. Be in that environment. Once your attention is back in the room, you can focus on what's happening in class.

Postpone debate. When you hear something you disagree with, note your disagreement and let it go. Don't allow your internal dialogue to drown out subsequent material. If your disagreement is persistent and strong, make note of it and then move on. Internal debate can prevent you from absorbing new information. It is OK to absorb information you don't agree with. Just absorb it with the mental tag "My instructor says . . . , and I don't agree with it."

Let go of judgments about lecture styles.
Human beings are judgment machines. We evaluate everything, especially other people. If another person's eyebrows are too close together (or too far apart), if she walks a certain way, or if she speaks with an unusual accent, we instantly make up a story about her. We do this so quickly that the process is usually not a conscious one.

Don't let your attitude about an instructor's lecture style, habits, or appearance get in the way of your education. You can decrease the power of your judgments if you pay attention to them and let them go.

You can even let go of judgments about rambling, unorganized lectures. Turn them to your advantage. Take the initiative, and organize the material yourself. While taking notes, separate the key points from the examples and supporting evidence. Note the places where you got confused, and make a list of questions to ask.

Participate in class activities. Ask questions. Volunteer for demonstrations. Join in class discussions. Be willing to take a risk or look foolish, if that's what it takes for you to learn. Chances are, the question you think is dumb is also on the minds of several of your classmates.

Relate the class to your goals. If you have trouble staying awake in a particular class, write at the top of your notes how that class relates to a specific goal. Identify the reward or payoff for reaching that goal.

Think critically about what you hear. This suggestion might seem contrary to the previously mentioned technique "postpone debate." It's not. You might choose not to think critically about the instructor's ideas during the lecture. That's fine. Do it later, as you review and edit your notes. This is the time to list questions or write down your agreements and disagreements.

Watch for clues

Be alert to repetition. When an instructor repeats a phrase or an idea, make a note of it. Repetition is a signal that the instructor thinks the information is important.

Listen for introductory, concluding, and transition words and phrases. Introductory, concluding, and transition words and phrases include phrases such as *the following three factors, in conclusion, the most important consideration, in addition to,* and *on the other hand.* These phrases and others signal relationships, definitions, new subjects, conclusions, cause and effect, and examples. They reveal the structure of the lecture. You can use these phrases to organize your notes.

Watch the board or PowerPoint presentation.
If an instructor takes the time to write something down on the board or show it in a PowerPoint presentation, consider the material to be important. Copy all diagrams and drawings, equations, names, places, dates, statistics, and definitions.

Watch the instructor's eyes. If an instructor glances at his notes and then makes a point, it is probably a signal that the information is especially important. Anything he reads from his notes is a potential test question.

Highlight the obvious clues. Instructors often hint strongly or tell students point-blank that certain information is likely to appear on an exam. Make stars or other special marks in your notes next to this information. Instructors are not trying to hide what's important.

Notice the instructor's interest level. If the instructor is excited about a topic, it is more likely to appear on an exam. Pay attention when she seems more animated than usual. ✳

 Find more strategies for observing online.

journal entry

Discovery/Intention Statement

Create more value from lectures

Think back on the last few lectures you have attended. How do you currently observe (listen to) lectures? What specific behaviors do you have as you sit and listen? Briefly describe your responses in the following space.

I discovered that I . . .

_____

_____

_____

_____

Now write an Intention Statement about any changes you want to make in the way you respond to lectures.

I intend to . . .

_____

_____

_____

_____

RECORD
The note-taking process flows

THE FORMAT AND STRUCTURE of your notes are more important than how fast you write or the elegance of your handwriting. The following techniques can improve the effectiveness of your notes.

General techniques for note taking

Use keywords. An easy way to sort the extraneous material from the important points is to take notes using keywords. Keywords contain the essence of communication. The two main kinds of keywords are:

- Concepts, technical terms, names, and numbers.
- Linking words, including those that describe action, relationship, and degree (for example, *most, least,* and *faster*).

Keywords evoke images and associations with other words and ideas. They trigger your memory. That characteristic makes them powerful review tools. One keyword can initiate the recall of a whole cluster of ideas. A few keywords can form a chain from which you can reconstruct an entire lecture.

To see how keywords work, take yourself to an imaginary classroom. You are now in the middle of an anatomy lecture. Picture what the room looks like, what it feels like, how it smells. You hear the instructor say:

OK, what happens when we look directly over our heads and see a piano falling out of the sky? How do we take that signal and translate it into the action of getting out of the way? The first thing that happens is that a stimulus is generated in the neurons—receptor neurons—of the eye. Light reflected from the piano reaches our eyes. In other words, we see the piano.

The receptor neurons in the eye transmit that sensory signal—the sight of the piano—to the body's nervous system. That's all they can do—pass on information. So we've got a sensory signal coming into the nervous system. But the neurons that initiate movement in our legs are effector neurons. The information from the sensory neurons must be transmitted to effector neurons or we will get squashed by the piano. There must be some kind of interconnection between receptor and effector neurons. What happens between the two? What is the connection?

Keywords you might note in this example include *stimulus, generated, receptor neurons, transmit, sensory*

signals, nervous system, effector neurons, and *connection.* You can reduce the instructor's 163 words to these 12 keywords. With a few transitional words, your notes might look like this:

> Stimulus (piano) generated in receptor neurons (eye)
>
> Sensory signals transmitted by nervous system to effector neurons (legs)
>
> What connects receptor to effector?

Note the last keyword of the previous lecture: *connection.* This word is part of the instructor's question and leads to the next point in the lecture. Be on the lookout for questions like this. They can help you organize your notes and are often clues for test questions.

Use pictures and diagrams. Make relationships visual. Copy all diagrams from the board, and invent your own.

A drawing of a piano falling on someone who is looking up, for example, might be used to demonstrate the relationship of receptor neurons to effector neurons. Label the eyes "receptor" and the feet "effector." This picture implies that the sight of the piano must be translated into a motor response. By connecting the explanation of the process with the unusual picture of the piano falling, you can link the elements of process together.

Write notes in paragraphs. When it is difficult to follow the organization of a lecture or put information into outline form, create a series of informal paragraphs. These paragraphs should contain few complete sentences. Reserve complete sentences for precise definitions, direct quotations, and important points that the instructor emphasizes by repetition or other signals—such as the phrase "This is an important point."

(woman) ballyscanlon/Getty, (hands/camera) tezzstock/Shutterstock, (frame) Jenson/Shutterstock

Copy material from the board and a PowerPoint presentation. Record all formulas, diagrams, and problems that the teacher presents on the board or in a PowerPoint presentation. Copy dates, numbers, names, places, and other facts. If it's presented visually in class, put it in your notes. You can even use your own signals or codes to flag that material.

Use a three-ring binder. Three-ring binders have several advantages over other kinds of notebooks. First, pages can be removed and spread out when you review. This way, you can get a complete picture of a lecture. Second, the three-ring-binder format allows you to insert handouts right into your notes. Third, you can insert your own out-of-class notes in the correct order.

Use only one side of a piece of paper. When you use one side of a page, you can review and organize all your notes by spreading them out side by side. Most students find the benefit well worth the cost of the paper. Perhaps you're concerned about the environmental impact of consuming more paper. If so, you can use the blank side of old notes and use recycled paper.

Use 3×5 cards. As an alternative to using notebook paper, use 3×5 cards to take lecture notes. Copy each new concept onto a separate 3×5 card.

Keep your own thoughts separate. For the most part, avoid making editorial comments in your lecture notes. The danger is that when you return to your notes, you might mistake your own ideas for those of the instructor. If you want to make a comment, clearly label it as your own.

Use an "I'm lost" signal. No matter how attentive and alert you are during a lecture, you might get lost or confused at some point. If it is inappropriate to

interrupt the instructor to ask a question, record in your notes that you were lost. Invent your own signal—for example, a circled question mark. When you write down your code for "I'm lost," leave space for the explanation or clarification that you will get it later. The space will also be a signal that you missed something. Later, you can speak to your instructor or ask to see a fellow student's notes.

Label, number, and date all notes. Develop the habit of labeling and dating your notes at the beginning of each class. Number the page, too. Sometimes the sequence of material in a lecture is important. Write your name and phone number in each notebook in case you lose it.

Use standard abbreviations. Be consistent with your abbreviations. If you make up your own abbreviations or symbols, write a key explaining them in your notes. Avoid vague abbreviations. When you use an abbreviation such as *comm.* for *committee,* you run the risk of not being able to remember whether you meant *committee, commission, common,* or *commit.* One way to abbreviate is to leave out vowels. For example, *talk* becomes *tlk, said* becomes *sd, American* becomes *Amrcn.*

Leave blank space. Notes tightly crammed into every corner of the page are hard to read and difficult to use for review. Give your eyes a break by leaving plenty of space.

Later, when you review, you can use the blank spaces in your notes to clarify points, write questions, and add other material.

Take notes in different colors. You can use colors as highly visible organizers. For example, you can signal important points with red or use one color of ink for notes about the text and another color for lecture notes.

Use graphic signals. The following ideas can be used with any note-taking format:

- Use brackets, parentheses, circles, and squares to group information that belongs together.
- Use stars, arrows, and underlining to indicate important points. Flag the most important points with double stars, double arrows, or double underlines.
- Use arrows and connecting lines to link related groups.
- Use equal signs, greater-than signs, and less-than signs to indicate compared quantities.

To avoid creating confusion with graphic symbols, use them carefully and consistently. Write a "dictionary" of your symbols in the front of your notebooks; an example is on the next page.

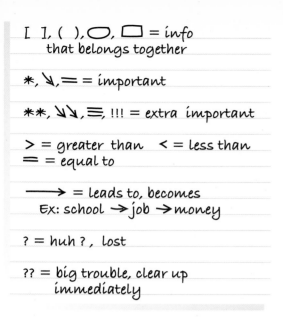

$[\ ], (\ ), \bigcirc, \Box$	= info that belongs together

$*, \searrow, =$ = important

$**, \searrow\searrow, \equiv, !!!$ = extra important

$>$ = greater than $<$ = less than
$=$ = equal to

$\longrightarrow$ = leads to, becomes
Ex: school $\rightarrow$ job $\rightarrow$ money

$?$ = huh?, lost

$??$ = big trouble, clear up immediately

Use recorders effectively. Some students record lectures with audio recorders, but there are persuasive arguments against doing so. When you record a lecture, there is a strong temptation to daydream. After all, you can always listen to the lecture again later on. Unfortunately, if you let the recorder do all of the work, you are skipping a valuable part of the learning process.

There are other potential problems as well. Listening to recorded lectures can take a lot of time—more time than reviewing written notes. Recorders can't answer the questions you didn't ask in class. Also, recording devices malfunction. In fact, the unscientific Hypothesis of Recording Glitches states that the tendency of recorders to malfunction is directly proportional to the importance of the material.

With those warnings in mind, you can use a recorder effectively if you choose. For example, you can use recordings as backups to written notes. (Check with your instructor first. Some prefer not to be recorded.) Turn the recorder on; then take notes as if it weren't there. Recordings can be especially useful if an instructor speaks fast.

The Cornell method

A note-taking system that has worked for students around the world is the *Cornell method*.[1] Originally developed by Walter Pauk at Cornell University during the 1950s, this approach continues to be taught across the United States and in other countries as well.

The cornerstone of this method is what Pauk calls the *cue column*—a wide margin on the left-hand side of the paper. The cue column is the key to the Cornell method's many benefits. Here's how to use it.

Format your paper. On each sheet of your notepaper, draw a vertical line, top to bottom, about two inches from the left edge of the paper. This line

creates the cue column—the space to the left of the line. You can also find Web sites that allow you to print out pages in this format. Just do an Internet search using the keywords *cornell method pdf*.

Take notes, leaving the cue column blank. As you read an assignment or listen to a lecture, take notes on the right-hand side of the paper. Fill up this column with sentences, paragraphs, outlines, charts, or drawings. Do not write in the cue column. You'll use this space later, as you do the next steps.

Condense your notes in the cue column. Think of the notes you took on the right-hand side of the paper as a set of answers. In the cue column, list potential test questions that correspond to your notes. Write one question for each major term or point.

As an alternative to questions, you can list keywords from your notes. Yet another option is to pretend that your notes are a series of articles on different topics. In the cue column, write a newspaper-style headline for each "article." In any case, be brief. If you cram the cue column full of words, you defeat its purpose of reducing the number of words and length of your notes.

Write a summary. Pauk recommends that you reduce your notes even more by writing a brief summary at the bottom of each page. This step offers you another way to engage actively with the material.

Cue column	Notes
What are the 3 phases of Muscle Reading?	Phase 1: Before you read Phase 2: While you read Phase 3: After you read
What are the steps in phase 1?	1. Preview 2. Outline 3. Question
What are the steps in phase 2?	4. Read 5. Underline 6. Answer
What are the steps in phase 3?	7. Recite 8. Review 9. Review again
What is an acronym for Muscle Reading?	Pry = preview Out = outline Questions = question Root = read Up = underline Answers = answer Recite Review Review again

Summary
Muscle Reading includes 3 phases: before, during, and after reading. Each phase includes 3 steps. Use the acronym to recall all the steps.

Use the cue column to recite. Cover the right-hand side of your notes with a blank sheet of paper. Leave only the cue column showing. Then look at each item you wrote in the cue column and talk about it. If you wrote questions, answer each question. If you wrote keywords, define each word and talk about why it's important. If you wrote headlines in the cue column, explain what each one means and offer supporting details. After reciting, uncover your notes and look for any important points you missed.

Mind mapping

Mind mapping, a system developed by Tony Buzan,[2] can be used in conjunction with the Cornell method to take notes. In some circumstances, you might want to use mind maps exclusively.

To understand mind maps, first review the features of traditional note taking. Outlines (explained in the next section) divide major topics into minor topics, which, in turn, are subdivided further. They organize information in a sequential, linear way.

The traditional outline reflects only a limited range of brain function—a point that is often made in discussions about "left-brain" and "right-brain" activities. People often use the term *right brain* when referring to creative, pattern-making, visual, intuitive brain activity. They use the term *left brain* when talking about orderly, logical, step-by-step characteristics of thought. Writing teacher Gabrielle Rico uses another metaphor. She refers to the left-brain mode as our "sign mind" (concerned with words) and the right-brain mode as our "design mind" (concerned with visuals).[3] A mind map uses both kinds of brain functions. Mind maps can contain lists and sequences and show relationships. They can also provide a picture of a subject. They work on both verbal and nonverbal levels.

One benefit of mind maps is that they quickly, vividly, and accurately show the relationships between ideas. Also, mind mapping helps you think from general to specific. By choosing a main topic, you focus first on the big picture, then zero in on subordinate details. By using only keywords, you can condense a large subject into a small area on a mind map. You can review more quickly by looking at the keywords on a mind map than by reading notes word for word.

Give yourself plenty of room. To create a mind map, use blank paper that measures at least 11 by 17 inches. If that's not available, turn regular notebook paper on its side so that you can take notes in a horizontal (instead of vertical) format. If you use a computer to take notes in class, consider investing in software that allows you to create digital mind maps that can include graphics, photos, and URL links.

Determine the main concept of the lecture, article, or chapter. As you listen to a lecture or read from your text, figure out the main concept. Write it in the center of the paper and circle it, underline it, or highlight it with color. You can also write the concept in large letters. Record concepts related to the main concept on lines that radiate outward from the center. An alternative is to circle or box in these concepts.

Use keywords only. Whenever possible, reduce each concept to a single word per line, circle, or box in your mind map. Although this reduction might seem awkward at first, it prompts you to summarize and condense ideas to their essence. That results in fewer words for you to write now and fewer to review when it's time to prepare for tests. (Using shorthand symbols and abbreviations can help.) Keywords are usually nouns and verbs that communicate the bulk of the speaker's ideas. Choose words that are rich in associations and that can help you recreate the lecture.

Create links. A single mind map doesn't have to include all of the ideas contained in a lecture, book, or article. Instead, you can link mind maps. For example, draw a mind map that sums up the five key points in a chapter, and then make a separate, more detailed mind map for each of those key points. Within each mind map, include references to the other mind maps. This technique helps explain and reinforce the relationships among many ideas. Some students pin several mind maps next to one another on a bulletin board or tape them to a wall. This allows for a dramatic—and effective—look at the big picture.

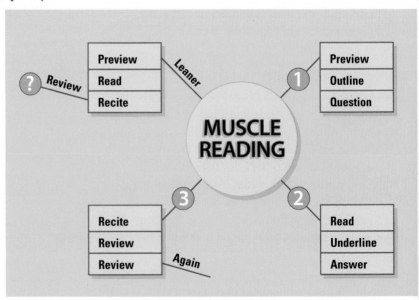

Outlining

A traditional outline shows the relationships among major points and supporting ideas. One benefit of taking notes in the outline format is that doing so can totally occupy your attention. You are recording ideas and also organizing them. This process can be an advantage if the material has been presented in a disorganized way. By playing with variations, you can discover the power of outlining to reveal relationships among ideas. Technically, each word, phrase, or sentence that appears in an outline is called a *heading*. Headings are arranged in different levels:

- In the first, or top, level of headings, note the major topics presented in a lecture or reading assignment.

- In the second level of headings, record the key points that relate to each topic in the first-level headings.

- In the third level of headings, record specific facts and details that support or explain each of your second-level headings. Each additional level of subordinate heading supports the ideas in the previous level of heading.

Roman numerals offer one way to illustrate the difference between levels of headings. See the following examples below and to the right.

Distinguish levels with indentations only:

Muscle Reading includes 3 phases
 Phase 1: Before you read
  Preview

Distinguish levels with bullets and dashes:

MUSCLE READING INCLUDES 3 PHASES
 • Phase 1: Before you read
  – Preview

Distinguish headings by size:

MUSCLE READING INCLUDES 3 PHASES
Phase 1: Before you read
Preview

First-level heading

Second-level heading

Third-level heading

I. Muscle Reading includes 3 phases.
 A. Phase 1: Before you read
  1. Preview
  2. Outline
  3. Question
 B. Phase 2: While you read
  4. Read
  5. Underline
  6. Answer
 C. Phase 3: After you read
  7. Recite
  8. Review
  9. Review again

Combining formats

Feel free to use different note-taking systems for different subjects and to combine formats. Do what works for you.

For example, combine mind maps with the Cornell method. You can modify the Cornell format by dividing your notepaper in half. Reserve one half for mind maps and the other for linear information such as lists, graphs, and outlines, as well as equations, long

explanations, and word-for-word definitions. You can incorporate a mind map into your paragraph-style notes whenever you feel one is appropriate. Mind maps are also useful for summarizing notes taken in the Cornell format.

John Sperry, a teacher at Utah Valley State College, developed a note-taking system that can include all of the formats discussed in this article:

- Fill up a three-ring binder with fresh paper. Open your notebook so that you see two blank pages—one on the left and one on the right. Plan to take notes across this entire two-page spread.

- During class or while reading, write your notes only on the left-hand page. Place a large dash next to each main topic or point. If your instructor skips a step or switches topics unexpectedly, just keep writing.

- Later, use the right-hand page to review and elaborate on the notes that you took earlier. Use this page for anything you want. For example, add visuals such as mind maps. Write review questions, headlines, possible test questions, summaries, outlines, mnemonics, or analogies that link new concepts to your current knowledge.

- To keep ideas in sequence, place appropriate numbers on top of the dashes in your notes on the left-hand page. Even if concepts are presented out of order during class, they'll still be numbered correctly in your notes. ✳

 See more examples of notes in various formats online.

NOTES

6

REVIEW
The note-taking process flows

(woman) ballyscanlon/Getty, (frames) Vladimir Wrangel/Shutterstock

THINK OF REVIEWING as an integral part of note taking rather than an added task. To make new information useful, encode it in a way that connects that information to your long-term memory. The key is reviewing.

Review within 24 hours. In Chapter 5: "Reading," when you read the suggestion to review what you've read within 24 hours, you were asked to sound the trumpet. If you have one, get it out and sound it again. This note-taking technique might be the most powerful one you can use. In fact, it might save you hours of review time later in the term.

Many students are surprised that they can remember the content of a lecture in the minutes and hours after class. They are even more surprised by how well they can read the sloppiest of notes at that time. Unfortunately, short-term memory deteriorates quickly. The good news is that if you review your notes soon enough, you can move that information from short-term to long-term memory. Best of all, you can do it in just a few minutes—often 10 minutes or less.

The sooner you review your notes, the better, especially if the content is difficult. In fact, you can start reviewing during class. When your instructor pauses to set up the overhead display or erase the board, scan your notes. Dot the *i*'s, cross the *t*'s, and write out unclear abbreviations. Another way to use this technique is to get to your next class as quickly as you can. Then use the four or five minutes before the lecture begins to review the notes you just took in the previous class. If you do not get to your notes immediately after class, you can still benefit by reviewing them later in the day. A review right before you go to sleep can also be valuable.

Think of the day's unreviewed notes as leaky faucets, constantly dripping and losing precious information until you shut them off with a quick review. Remember, it's possible to forget most of the material within 24 hours—unless you review.

Edit your notes. During your first review, fix words that are illegible. Write out abbreviated words that might be unclear to you later. Make sure you can read everything. If you can't read something or don't understand something you *can* read, mark it and make a note to ask your instructor or another student about it. Check to see that your notes are labeled with the date and class and that the pages are numbered.

Fill in keywords in the left-hand column. This task is important if you are to get the full benefit of using the Cornell method. Using the keyword principles described earlier in this chapter, go through your notes and write keywords or phrases in the left-hand column.

These keywords will speed up the review process later.

Use your keywords as cues to recite. Cover your notes with a blank sheet of paper so that you can see only the keywords in the left-hand margin. Take each keyword in order, and recite as much as you can about the point. Then uncover your notes and look for any important points you missed.

Conduct short weekly review periods. Once a week, review all of your notes again. These review sessions don't need to take a lot of time. Even a 20-minute weekly review period is valuable. Some students find that a weekend review—say, on Sunday afternoon—helps them stay in continuous touch with the material. Scheduling regular review sessions on your calendar helps develop the habit.

As you review, step back to see the larger picture. In addition to reciting or repeating the material to yourself, ask questions about it: Does this relate to my goals? How does this compare to information I already know, in this field or another? Will I be tested on this material? What will I do with this material? How can I associate it with something that deeply interests me?

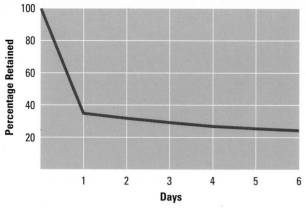

To study the process of memory and forgetting, Hermann Ebbinghaus devised a method for testing memory. The results, shown here in what has come to be known as the Ebbinghaus forgetting curve, demonstrate that forgetting occurs most rapidly shortly after learning and then gradually declines over time.

Consider typing your notes. Some students type up their handwritten notes on the computer. The argument for doing so is threefold. First, typed notes are easier to read. Second, they take up less space. Third, the process of typing them forces you to review the material.

Another alternative is to bypass handwriting altogether and take notes in class on a laptop. This solution has a potential drawback, though: Computer errors can wipe out your notes files. If you like using this method of taking notes, save your files frequently, and back up your work onto a jump drive or other portable drive.

Create summaries. Mind mapping is an excellent way to summarize large sections of your course notes or reading assignments. Create one map that shows all the main topics you want to remember. Then create another map about each main topic. After drawing your maps, look at your original notes and fill in anything you missed. This system is fun and quick.

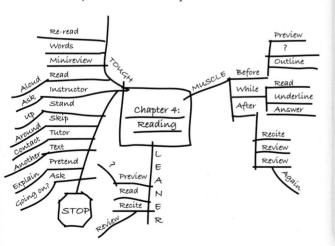

Another option is to create a "cheat sheet." There's only one guideline: Fit all your review notes on a single sheet of paper. Use any note-taking format that you want—mind map, outline, Cornell method, or a combination of all of them. The beauty of this technique is that it forces you to pick out main ideas and key details. There's not enough room for anything else!

If you're feeling adventurous, create your cheat sheet on a single index card. Start with the larger sizes (5×7 or 4×6) and then work down to a 3×5 card.

Some instructors might let you use a summary sheet during an exam. But even if you can't use it, you'll benefit from creating one while you study for the test. Summarizing is a powerful way to review. ✳

journal entry 14

Discovery Statement

Reflect on your review habits

Think about the way you have conducted reviews of your notes in the past. Respond to the following statements by checking "Always," "Often," "Sometimes," "Seldom," or "Never" after each.

1. I review my notes immediately after class.

_____ Always _____ Often __✓__ Sometimes

_____ Seldom _____ Never

2. I conduct weekly reviews of my notes.

_____ Always _____ Often _____ Sometimes

__✓__ Seldom _____ Never

3. I make summary sheets of my notes.

_____ Always __✓__ Often _____ Sometimes

_____ Seldom _____ Never

4. I edit my notes within 24 hours.

_____ Always _____ Often __✓__ Sometimes

_____ Seldom _____ Never

5. Before class, I conduct a brief review of the notes I took in the previous class.

_____ Always _____ Often _____ Sometimes

_____ Seldom __✓__ Never

Observe, record, and review at work

TAKING NOTES AT WORK allows you to apply many of the transferable skills covered in this book—listening, remembering, writing, and critical thinking. Remember that the ability to take clear and concise notes is one way to make yourself valuable to an employer. It might even help you get promoted.

Be prepared

Before meetings, complete background reading on the topics to be discussed, including minutes from relevant meetings in the past. Doing this sets the stage for taking better notes in upcoming meetings. It's easier to make sense of what people say when you already know something about the meeting topics.

Experiment with formats

During meetings, experiment with Cornell format notes, mind mapping, outlining, concept mapping, or some combination of these. Feel free to add boldface headings, charts, tables, graphs, and other visuals that make the main ideas stand out. If you're taking notes to distribute to coworkers, they will appreciate it if you get to the point and keep paragraphs short.

Your employer may have specific guidelines for taking meeting notes. Ask your supervisor about this. Note that in some cases—such as minutes taken during a board of directors meeting—notes may function as legal documents reviewed by the IRS or another independent auditor.

Keep up with speakers

When taking notes during fast-paced meetings and conference calls, use suggestions from the article "When a Speaker Talks *Fast*" in this chapter. Immediately after the call or meeting, review and edit your notes.

Notice your handwriting

Colleagues may read your handwriting often. If your penmanship creates communication problems or does not convey a positive image, simply notice this fact. Then

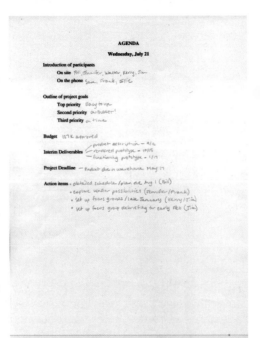

pay conscious attention to your handwriting as you take notes.

Remember the "four A's"

Consider adding the following topics to your notes:

- *Attendance.* In many organizations, people expect meeting notes to include a list of attendees. For large meetings, see if you can get an advance list of the people who are expected to attend. Bring this to the meeting and check off peoples' names as they enter the room. Along with your list of attendees, include the name of your department, the date, the time, and the name of the person who led the meeting.

- *Agenda.* Think of the agenda as a road map—a way to keep the discussion on track. Skilled planners often put an agenda in writing and distribute it in advance of a meeting. Use this agenda while you take notes.

- *Agreements.* The purpose of most meetings is to reach an agreement about something—a policy, project, or plan. Focus on capturing the details about each agreement.

- *Actions.* During meetings, people often commit to take some type of action in the future. Record each follow-up action and who agreed to do it.

Follow-up action is often a make-or-break point for project teams. One mark of exceptional teams is that people make agreements about what they will do—and then keep those agreements.

You can set a powerful example. Ask whether any of the points you included in your notes call for follow-up action on your part. Highlight such items in your notes. Then add them to your calendar or to-do list and follow through.

Review

After meetings, review the notes you took. Edit or rewrite your notes for clarity and accuracy. If you took handwritten notes, consider entering the important points into a computer file. ✳

Get to the bones of your book with concept maps

CONCEPT MAPPING, pioneered by Joseph Novak and D. Bob Gowin, is a tool to make major ideas in a book leap off the page.[4] In creating a concept map, you reduce an author's message to its essence—its bare bones. Concept maps can also be used to display the organization of lectures and discussions.

Concepts and links are the building blocks of knowledge. A *concept* is a name for a group of related things or ideas. *Links* are words or phrases that describe the relationship between concepts. Consider the following paragraph:

> Muscle Reading consists of three phases. Phase 1 includes tasks to complete before reading. Phase 2 tasks take place during reading. Finally, Phase 3 includes tasks to complete after reading.

In this paragraph, examples of concepts are *Muscle Reading, reading, phases, tasks, Phase 1, Phase 2,* and *Phase 3*. Links include *consists of, includes, before, during,* and *after*.

To create a concept map, list concepts and then arrange them in a meaningful order from general to specific. Then fill in the links between concepts, forming meaningful statements.

Concept mapping promotes critical thinking. It alerts you to missing concepts or faulty links between concepts. In addition, concept mapping mirrors the way that your brain learns—that is, by linking new concepts to concepts that you already know.

To create a concept map, use the following steps:

1. **List the key concepts in the text.** Aim to express each concept in three words or less. Most concept words are nouns, including terms and proper names. At this point, you can list the concepts in any order.

2. **Rank the concepts so that they flow from general to specific.** On a large sheet of paper, write the main concept at the top of the page. Place the most specific concepts near the bottom. Arrange the rest of the concepts in appropriate positions throughout the middle of the page. Circle each concept.

3. **Draw lines that connect the concepts.** On these connecting lines, add words that describe the relationship between the concepts. Again, limit yourself to the fewest words needed to make an accurate link—three words or less. Linking words are often verbs, verb phrases, or prepositions.

4. **Finally, review your map.** Look for any concepts that are repeated in several places on the map. You can avoid these repetitions by adding more links between concepts. ✳

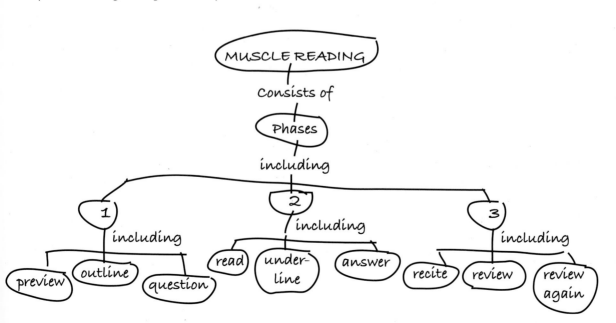

Taking notes while reading

TAKING NOTES WHILE READING requires the same skills that apply to taking class notes: observing, recording, and reviewing. Use these skills to take notes for review and for research.

Review notes

Take review notes when you want more detailed notes than writing in the margin of your text allows. You might want to single out a particularly difficult section of a text and make separate notes. You can also make summaries of overlapping lecture and text material. Since you can't underline or make notes in library books, these sources will require separate notes, too.

To take more effective review notes, follow these suggestions:

- *Use a variety of formats.* Translate text into Cornell notes, mind maps, or outlines. Combine these formats to create your own. Translate diagrams, charts, and other visual elements into words. Then reverse the process by translating straight text into visual elements.

- *However, don't let the creation of formats get in your way.* Even a simple list of key points and examples can become a powerful review tool.

- *Condense a passage to key quotes.* Authors embed their essential ideas in key sentences. As you read, continually ask yourself, "What's the point?" Then see if you can point to a specific sentence on the page to answer your question. Look especially at headings, subheadings, and topic sentences of paragraphs. Write these key sentences word for word in your notes, and put them within quotation marks. Copy as few sentences as you can and still retain the core meaning of the passage.

- *Condense by paraphrasing.* Pretend that you have to summarize a chapter, article, or book on a postcard. Limit yourself to a single paragraph—or a single sentence—and use your own words. This is a great way to test your understanding of the material.

- *Take a cue from the table of contents.* Look at the table of contents in your book. Write each major heading on a piece of paper, or key those headings into a word-processing file on your computer. Include page numbers. Next, see if you can improve on the table of contents. Substitute your own headings for those that appear in the book. Turn

single words or phrases into complete sentences, and use words that are meaningful to you.

- *Note special concepts in math and science.* When you read mathematical, scientific, or other technical materials, copy important formulas or equations. Recreate important diagrams, and draw your own visual representations of concepts. Also write down data that might appear on an exam.

Research notes

Take research notes when preparing to write a paper or deliver a speech. One traditional method of research is to take notes on index cards. You write one idea, fact, or quotation per card. The advantage of limiting each card to one item of information is that you can easily arrange cards according to the sequence of your outline—and ongoing changes in your outline.

Taking notes on a computer offers the same flexibility as index cards. In addition, you can take advantage of software features that help you create tables of contents, indexes, graphics, and other elements you might want to use in your project later on.

No matter which method you use, your research notes will fall into two main categories.

The first category includes information about your sources. For example, a source card for a book will show the author, title, date and place of publication, and publisher. You'll need such information later in the writing process as you create a formal list of your sources—especially sources of quotes or paraphrased material that is included in the body of your paper or presentation. By keeping track of your sources as you conduct research, you create a working bibliography. Ask your instructor about what source information to record (and also see the sidebar to this article). When recording your own ideas, simply note the source as "me."

The second category of research notes includes the actual ideas and facts that you will use to create the content of your paper or presentation. Again, if you're using index cards, write only *one* piece of information on each information card—a single quotation, fact, or concept. Doing so makes it easier for you to sort cards later.

Be sure to avoid plagiarism. When people take words or images from a source and present them as their own, they are committing plagiarism. Even when plagiarism is accidental, the consequences can be harsh. For essential information on this topic, see the "Avoiding Plagiarism" sidebar in Chapter 8 on page 238.

If you're taking notes on a computer and using Internet sources, be especially careful to avoid plagiarism. When you copy text or images from a Web site, separate those notes from your own ideas. Use a different font for copied material, or enclose it in quotation marks.

Schedule time to review all the information and ideas that your research has produced. By allowing time for rereading and reflecting on all the notes you've taken, you create the conditions for genuine understanding.

Start by summarizing major points of view on your topic. Note points of agreement and disagreement among your sources.

Also see if you can find direct answers to the questions that you had when you started researching. These answers could become headings in your paper.

Look for connections between the ideas, facts, and examples that appear in your resource materials. Also look for connections between your research and your life—ideas that you can verify based on personal experience.

Adapt to special cases. The style of your notes can vary according to the nature of the reading material. For example, if you are assigned a short story or poem, read the entire work once without taking any notes. On your first reading, simply enjoy the piece. When you finish, write down your immediate impressions. Then go over the piece and make brief notes on characters, images, symbols, settings, plot, point of view, or other aspects of the work. ✳

 Find examples of effective research and review notes online.

Note this information about your sources

The following text features checklists of the information to record about various types of sources. Whenever possible, print out or make photocopies of each source. For books, include a copy of the title page and copyright page, both of which are found in the front matter. For magazines and scholarly journals, copy the table of contents.

For each book you consult, record the following:
- ☐ Author
- ☐ Editor (if listed)
- ☐ Translator (if listed)
- ☐ Edition number (if listed)
- ☐ Full title, including the subtitle
- ☐ Name and location of the publisher
- ☐ Copyright date
- ☐ Page numbers for passages that you quote, summarize, or paraphrase

For each article you consult, record the following:
- ☐ Author
- ☐ Editor (if listed)
- ☐ Translator (if listed)
- ☐ Full title, including the subtitle
- ☐ Name of the periodical
- ☐ Volume number
- ☐ Issue number
- ☐ Issue date
- ☐ Page numbers for passages that you quote, summarize, or paraphrase

For each computer-based source you consult (CD-ROMs and Internet documents), record the following:
- ☐ Author
- ☐ Editor (if listed)
- ☐ Translator (if listed)
- ☐ Full title of the page or article, including the subtitle
- ☐ Name of the organization that posted the site or published the CD-ROM
- ☐ Dates when the page or other document was published and revised
- ☐ Date when you accessed the source
- ☐ URL for Web pages (the uniform resource locator, or Web site address, which often starts with http://)
- ☐ Version number (for CD-ROMs)
- ☐ Volume, issue number, and date for online journals

Note: Computer-based sources may not list all the above information. For Web pages, at a minimum, record the date you accessed the source and the URL.

For each interview you conduct, record the following:
- ☐ Name of the person you interviewed
- ☐ Professional title of the person you interviewed
- ☐ Contact information for the person you interviewed—mailing address, phone number, e-mail address
- ☐ Date of the interview

NOTES

6

Enroll your instructor in your education

Thinkstock/Getty

FACED WITH AN instructor you don't like, you have two basic choices. One is to label the instructor a "dud" and let it go at that. When you make this choice, you get to endure class and complain to other students. This choice puts you at the mercy of circumstance. It gives your instructor sole responsibility for the quality of your education and the value of your tuition payments.

There is another option. Don't give away your power. Instead, take responsibility for your education.

Show interest in class. Students give teachers moment-by-moment feedback in class. That feedback comes through posture, eye contact, responses to questions, and participation in class discussions. If you find a class boring, recreate the instructor through a massive display of interest. Ask lots of questions. Sit up straight, make eye contact, and take detailed notes. Your enthusiasm might enliven your instructor. If not, you are still creating a more enjoyable class for yourself.

Release judgments. Maybe your instructor reminds you of someone you don't like—your annoying Aunt Edna, a rude store clerk, or the fifth-grade teacher who kept you after school. Your attitudes are in your own head and beyond the instructor's control. Likewise, an instructor's beliefs about politics or religion are not related to teaching ability. Being aware of such things can help you let go of negative judgments.

Get to know the instructor. Meet with your instructor during office hours. Teachers who seem boring in class can be fascinating in person.

Students who do well in higher education often get to know at least one instructor outside of class. In some cases, these instructors become mentors and informal advisors.

Open up to diversity. Sometimes students can create their instructors by letting go of pictures about different races and ethnic groups. According to one picture, a Hispanic person cannot teach English literature. According to other pictures, a white teacher cannot have anything valid to say about African music, a teacher in a wheelchair cannot command the attention of a hundred people in a lecture hall, and a male instructor cannot

speak credibly about feminism. All of those pictures can clash with reality. Releasing them can open up new opportunities for understanding and appreciation.

Separate liking from learning. You don't have to like an instructor to learn from one. See if you can focus on the instructor's content instead of form. *Form* is the way something is organized or presented. If you are irritated at the sound of an instructor's voice, you're focusing on form. When you put aside your concern about her voice and turn your attention to the points she's making, you're focusing on *content*.

Seek alternatives. You might feel more comfortable with another teacher's style or method of organizing course materials. Consider changing teachers, asking another teacher for help outside class, or attending an additional section taught by a different instructor. You can also learn from other students, courses, tutors, study groups, books, and DVDs. Be a master student, even when you have teachers you don't like. Your education is your own creation.

Avoid excuses. Instructors know every excuse. Most teachers can see a snow job coming before the first flake hits the ground. Accept responsibility for your own mistakes, and avoid thinking that you can fool the teacher.

Submit professional work. Prepare papers and projects as if you were submitting them to an employer. Imagine that your work will determine whether you get a promotion and pay raise. Instructors often grade hundreds of papers during a term. Your neat, orderly, well-organized paper can stand out and lift a teacher's spirits. ✳

 Discover more ways to create positive relationships with instructors online.

When a speaker talks *fast*

Take more time to prepare for class. Familiarity with a subject increases your ability to pick up on key points. If an instructor lectures quickly or is difficult to understand, conduct a thorough preview of the material to be covered.

Be willing to make choices. When an instructor talks fast, focus your attention on key points. Instead of trying to write everything down, choose what you think is important. Occasionally, you will make a wrong choice and neglect an important point. Worse things could happen. Stay with the lecture, write down keywords, and revise your notes immediately after class.

Exchange photocopies of notes with classmates. Your fellow students might write down something you missed. At the same time, your notes might help them. Exchanging photocopies can fill in the gaps.

Leave large empty spaces in your notes. Leave plenty of room for filling in information you missed. Use a symbol that signals you've missed something, so you can remember to come back to it.

See the instructor after class. Take your class notes with you, and show the instructor what you missed.

Use an audio recorder. Recording a lecture gives you a chance to hear it again whenever you choose. Some audio recording software allows you to vary the speed of the recording. With this feature, you can perform magic and actually slow down the instructor's speech.

Before class, take notes on your reading assignment. You can take detailed notes on the text before class. Leave plenty of blank space. Take these notes with you to class, and simply add your lecture notes to them.

Go to the lecture again. Many classes are taught in multiple sections. That gives you the chance to hear a lecture at least twice—once in your regular class and again in another section of the class.

Learn shorthand. Some note-taking systems, known as shorthand, are specifically designed for getting ideas down fast. Books and courses are available to help you learn these systems. You can also devise your own shorthand method by inventing one- or two-letter symbols for common words and phrases.

Ask questions—even if you're totally lost. Many instructors allow a question session. This is the time to ask about the points you missed.

At times you might feel so lost that you can't even formulate a question. That's OK. One option is to report this fact to the instructor. He can often guide you to a clear question. Another option is to ask a related question. Doing so might lead you to the question you really wanted to ask.

Ask the instructor to slow down. This solution is the most obvious. If asking the instructor to slow down doesn't work, ask her to repeat what you missed. ✳

Meeting with your instructor

Meeting with an instructor outside class can save hours of study time and help your grade. To get the most from these meetings, consider doing the following:

- Schedule a meeting time during the instructor's office hours.
- If you need to cancel or reschedule, let your instructor know well in advance.
- Ask about ways to prepare for upcoming exams.
- If the course is in a subject area that interests you, ask about the possibilities of declaring a major in that area and the possible careers that are associated with that major.
- Avoid questions that might offend your instructor—for example, "I missed class on Monday. Did we do anything important?"
- When the meeting is over, thank your instructor for making time for you.

Discovery/Intention Statement

Reflect on notes from school and work

Choose a set of notes that you've taken in class recently. Next to it, place notes that you took during a meeting at work.

Now compare the two sets of notes. Look past their content and consider their format. What visual differences do you see between the notes from work and the notes from class?

I discovered that . . .

_____

_____

_____

_____

_____

Also think about the *process* of taking notes in these two settings. Did you find it easier or more difficult to take notes at work than in class?

I discovered that . . .

_____

_____

_____

_____

_____

_____

_____

_____

After comparing these two sets of notes, reflect on what you can do differently in the future to take more effective notes at work.

I intend to . . .

_____

_____

_____

_____

_____

_____

_____

_____

critical thinking exercise
Television note taking

You can use evening news broadcasts to practice listening for keywords, writing quickly, focusing your attention, and reviewing. The more you practice, the better you become.

The next time you watch the news, use pen and paper to jot down keywords and information. During the commercials, review and revise your notes. At the end of the broadcast, spend five minutes reviewing all of your notes. Create a mind map of a few news stories, then sum up the news of the day for a friend.

This exercise will help you develop an ear for keywords. Since you can't ask questions or request that the speaker slow down, you train yourself to stay totally in the moment.

If you get behind, relax, leave a space, and return your attention to the broadcast.

Don't be discouraged if you miss a lot the first time around. Do this exercise several times, and observe how your mind works.

If you find it too difficult to take notes during a fast-paced television news show, check your local broadcast schedule for a news documentary. Documentaries are often slower paced. Another option is to record a program and then take notes. You can stop the recording at any point to review your notes. You can also ask a classmate to do the same exercise, and then compare notes the next day.

I Create It All

This article describes a powerful tool for times of trouble. In a crisis, "I create it all" can lead the way to solutions. "I create it all" means treating experiences, events, and circumstances in your life *as if* you created them.

"I create it all" is one of the most unusual and bizarre suggestions in this book. It certainly is not a belief. Use it when it works. Don't when it doesn't.

Keeping that in mind, consider how powerful this Power Process can be. It is really about the difference between two distinct positions in life: being a victim or being responsible.

A victim of circumstances is controlled by outside forces. We've all felt like victims at one time or another. Sometimes we felt helpless.

In contrast, we can take responsibility. Responsibility is "response-ability"—the ability to choose a *response* to any event. You can choose your *response* to any event, even when the event itself is beyond your control.

Many students approach grades from the position of being victims. When the student who sees the world this way gets an F, she reacts something like this:

"Another F! That teacher couldn't teach her way out of a wet paper bag. She can't teach English for anything. And that textbook—what a bore!"

The problem with this viewpoint is that in looking for excuses, the student is robbing herself of the power to get any grade other than an F. She's giving all of her power to a bad teacher and a boring textbook.

There is another way; it is called *taking responsibility*. You can recognize that you choose your grades by choosing your actions. Then you are the source, rather than the result, of the grades you get. The student who got an F could react like this:

"Another F! Oh, shoot! Well, hmmm. . . . What did I do to create it?"

Now, that's power. By asking, "How did I contribute to this outcome?" you are no longer the victim. This student might continue by saying, "Well, let's see. I didn't review my notes after class. That might have done it." Or "I went out with my friends the night before the test. Well, that probably helped me fulfill some of the requirements for getting an F."

The point is this: When the F is the result of your friends, the book, or the teacher, you probably can't do anything about it. However, if you *chose* the F, you can choose a different grade next time. You are in charge.

Learn more about using this Power Process online.

Career Application

Hanae Niigata is a part-time receptionist at a large cardiovascular clinic. Her responsibilities include handling incoming calls, scheduling patient visits, maintaining medical records, and completing other tasks assigned by her office manager.

sozaijiten/Datacraft/Getty

Hanae's career focus is health care. She has worked as a home health aide and is currently enrolled in school. Her goal is to complete an Associate in Science degree in nursing and work as a registered nurse.

Hanae has a reputation as a hard worker. Even in a noisy environment with frequent interruptions, she completes tasks that require attention to detail and sustained concentration. She catches errors on medical records that her coworkers tend to miss. In addition, Hanae is often the first person in the office to whom people turn when they have a problem to solve. Even in the most difficult circumstances, she can generate a list of options—including solutions that occur to no one else.

Today, the office manager asked Hanae to attend a two-hour course on a new telephone system soon to be installed in her office. She was told to take good notes so she could teach the other five receptionists. Hanae was shocked that the old system was being replaced. In her opinion, it was user-friendly.

As the training session began, Hanae diligently attempted to write down almost everything the instructor said. While doing so, she repeatedly found herself distracted by the thought that her manager was replacing a perfectly good phone system with some "sure-to-be-a-nightmare, high-tech garbage."

After completing the course, Hanae sat down with her manager to fill him in on the new system. As she thumbed through her notes, she realized they didn't make much sense to her, even though she had just finished writing them. She couldn't recall much of the course from memory either, leaving her with little information to share with her manager.

Reflecting on this scenario

List two or three suggestions for Hanae that could make her note taking more effective. Be specific.

_____

_____

_____

_____

_____

_____

_____

_____

_____

_____

_____

_____

Quiz

Name _____   Date ____/____/____

1. What are the three major steps of effective note taking as explained in this chapter? Summarize each step in one sentence.

2. According to the text, neat handwriting and a knowledge of outlining are the only requirements for taking effective notes. True or false? Explain your answer.

3. What are some advantages of sitting in the front and center of the classroom?

4. Instructors sometimes give clues that the material they are presenting is important. List three of these clues.

5. Postponing debate while taking notes means that you have to agree with everything that the instructor says. True or false? Explain your answer.

6. Graphic signals include which of the following?
   (a) Brackets and parentheses
   (b) Stars and arrows
   (c) Underlining and connecting lines
   (d) Equal signs, greater-than signs, and less-than signs
   (e) All of the above

7. Describe the two main types of keywords. Then write down at least five keywords from this chapter.

8. Describe a way to apply the Power Process: "Be Here Now" to the job of taking notes in class.

9. Describe three strategies for reviewing notes.

10. Briefly define the word *responsibility* as it is used in the Power Process: "I Create It All."

Focus on Transferable Skills

The Discovery Wheel in Chapter 1 includes a section labeled "Notes." Take a few minutes right now to go beyond your initial responses to that exercise. Take a snapshot of your skills as they exist today, after reading and doing this chapter. Then choose a new skill to develop—one that you can use in school and at work.

You might want to prepare for this exercise by reviewing the articles "Jumpstart Your Education with Transferable Skills" on page 58 and "101 Transferable Skills" on page 60.

OBSERVING

If my attention wanders while taking notes, I refocus by . . .

When I strongly disagree with the opinion of a speaker or author, I respond by . . .

RECORDING

The formats I usually use to take notes are . . .

A note-taking format that I'd like to experiment with is . . .

REVIEWING

If asked to rate the overall quality of the notes that I've taken in the last week, I would say that . . .

In general, I find my notes to be most useful when they . . .

NEXT ACTION

The biggest change I'd like to make in the way I take notes is . . .

To make this change, I intend to . . .

Master Student PROFILE

Faye Wattleton

. . . is willing to participate

© Maiman Rick/CORBIS SYGMA

I don't ever recall not wanting to be a nurse, or not saying I wanted to be a nurse. This was, in part, certainly my mother's influence. She wanted me to be a missionary nurse. It wasn't sufficient just to be a nurse, I had to commit to a religious cause as well. Missionary nurses work in church hospitals, in Africa and all over the world. I suspect this was suggested to me before I even understood the power of suggestion, and I always grew up saying I was going to be a nurse. I earned two degrees in nursing, but never practiced as a nurse. In the broadest sense of the word, you can say I have nursed all the time, but not in the technical sense. After undergraduate school, I taught nursing for two years. Then I went to graduate school at Columbia University and earned my master's degree. Following that I moved to Dayton, Ohio, to work in a public health department. There, I was asked to join the board of the local Planned Parenthood. Two years later, I became executive director of the local chapter. Then, seven years later, I became the national president of the organization.

I'm sure the suggestion to become a nurse was colored by the limitation on women's options in those years. Women were nurses, social workers, or teachers. I don't ever remember being explicitly told, "Oh, you can't be that because you're a girl." It just was. . . . It was never conveyed to me there were any limitations on what I could do and what my work could be, although I'm sure the idea that I be a nurse, as opposed to a doctor or something else, was due to the limitations on the role of women at that time.

Even though we lived in a working class community, there wasn't as much integration, so blacks of all economic levels lived in the black community. My father was a laborer, and my mother was a seamstress, but I went to nursing school with our doctor's son. The doctor's family lived a few blocks from us. This was before the Civil Rights movement, and before blacks moved into white or integrated neighborhoods. That experience also played a very important role in my sense of who I am ethnically, as well as what the possibilities were for me. We lived next door to professionals, as well as the housepainter who had the most beautiful house on the block because he painted and decorated it beautifully.

I try to find the best people I can in various specialties so I can learn from them. I want people who are better than me in their specialties, maybe not better than me in running the whole shebang, but better than me in the communications field or legal field. Stitching everything together to make it work as a [piece of] machinery is, for me, the challenge and the excitement.

I try very hard to listen. If there is conflict, I want to hear what the other side says. . . . As long as I feel there is mutual respect, it does not hurt me to listen to someone with whom I am really in conflict, to hear what they are saying even if I disagree. If it's a conflict I really want to resolve, I try to find ways we can come to mutual points of agreement. One thing I always believe is if you talk long enough you can almost always reach a resolution. Just the process of talking has a de-fanging influence. I have great faith in human beings finding ways to relate if they have enough contact with each other.

Lucinda Watson, *How They Achieved: Stories of Personal Achievement and Business Success.* Copyright © 2001, pp. 208–212, John Wiley & Sons. Reprinted with permission.

**(1943–)
President of the Planned Parenthood Federation of America from 1978 until 1992. She is currently the founder and president of the Center for the Advancement of Women.**

Learn more about Faye Wattleton and other master students at the Master Student Hall of Fame.

7 Tests

Master Student Map

as you read, ask yourself

what if . . .

I could let go of stress over tests—
or anything else?

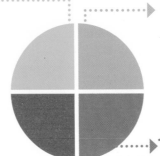

why this chapter matters . . .

Adopting a few simple techniques
can change your experience of
tests—and make a difference in how
you manage stress of any type.

what is included . . .

how

you can use this chapter . . .

- Predict test questions and use your
  study time more effectively.
- Harness the power of cooperative
  learning by studying with other people.
- Learn to look on an F as *feedback*
  rather than *failure*.
- Create value from performance
  reviews at work.

MASTER EMPLOYEE in *action*

When I first became a manager, I dreaded conducting the annual
performance reviews for my group. I expected my employees—
many of whom had been with the company
far longer than I had—to resent me evaluating
their performances. But for the most part, I
was happily surprised. Most people genuinely
wanted ideas about how they could improve
their performance. After all, if we can't accept
constructive criticism, none of us would be able to
hold onto our jobs for long.

—JEFF ROGERS, RESEARCH MANAGER

Photo courtesy of Jeff Rogers

Disarm tests

ON THE SURFACE, tests don't look dangerous. Maybe that's why we sometimes treat them as if they were land mines. Suppose a stranger walked up to you on the street and asked, "Does a finite abelian P-group have a basis?" Would you break out in a cold sweat? Would your muscles tense up? Would your breathing become shallow?

Probably not. Even if you had never heard of a finite abelian P-group, you probably would remain coolly detached. However, if you find the same question on a test and you have never heard of a finite abelian P-group, your hands might get clammy.

Grades (A to F) are what we use to give power to tests. However, there are lots of misconceptions about what grades are. Grades are not a measure of intelligence or creativity. They are not an indication of our ability to contribute to society. Grades are simply a measure of how well we do on tests.

Some people think that a test score measures what a student has accomplished in a course. This idea is false. A test score is a measure of what a student scored on a test. If you are anxious about a test and blank out, the grade cannot measure what you've learned. The reverse is also true: If you are good at taking tests and you are a lucky guesser, the score won't be an accurate reflection of what you know.

Grades are not a measure of self-worth. Yet we tend to give test scores the power to determine how we feel about ourselves. Common thoughts include "If I fail a test, I am a failure" or "If I do badly on a test, I am a bad person." The truth is that if you do badly on a test, you are a person who did badly on a test. That's all.

Carrying around misconceptions about tests and grades can put undue pressure on your performance. It's like balancing on a railroad track. Many people can walk along the rail and stay balanced for long periods. Yet the task seems entirely different if the rail is placed between two buildings, 52 stories up.

It is easier to do well on exams if you don't put too much pressure on yourself. Don't give the test some magical power over your own worth as a human being. Academic tests are not a matter of life and death. Scoring low on important tests—standardized tests, medical school exams, bar exams, CPA exams—usually means only a delay.

Whether the chance of doing poorly is real or exaggerated, worrying about it can become paralyzing. The way to deal with tests is to keep them in perspective. Keep the railroad track on the ground. ✳

journal entry 16

Discovery/Intention Statement

Transform your experience of tests

Mentally re-create a time when you had difficulty taking a test. Do anything that helps you re-experience this event. Briefly describe that experience in the following space. You could draw a picture of yourself in this situation, list some of the questions you had difficulty answering, or explain how you felt after finding out your score on the test.

I discovered that I . . .

_____

_____

_____

Now wipe your mental slate clean, and declare your intention to replace it with a new scenario. Describe how you want your experience of test taking to change. For example, you might write: "I intend to walk into every test I take feeling well rested and thoroughly prepared."

I intend to . . .

_____

_____

_____

Preview this chapter, looking for at least five strategies that can help you accomplish your goal. List those strategies in the following space, and note the page numbers where you can find out more about them.

Strategy   **Page number**

_____

_____

_____

_____

_____

_____

_____

What to do *before* the test

Do daily reviews. Daily reviews include short preclass and postclass reviews of lecture notes. You should also conduct brief daily reviews with textbooks: Before reading a new assignment, scan your notes and the sections you underlined or highlighted in the previous assignment. In addition, use the time you spend waiting for the bus or doing the laundry to conduct short reviews.

Concentrate daily reviews on two kinds of material. One is material you have just learned, either in class or in your reading. The other is material that involves simple memorization—equations, formulas, dates, and definitions.

Begin to review on the first day of class. Most instructors outline the whole course at that time. You can even start reviewing within seconds after learning. During a lull in class, go over the notes you just took. Immediately after class, review your notes again.

Do weekly reviews. Review each subject at least once a week, allowing about one hour per subject. Include reviews of assigned reading and lecture notes. Look over any mind map summaries or flash cards you have created. You should also practice working on sample problems.

Do major reviews. Major reviews are usually most helpful when conducted the week before finals or other critical exams. They help you integrate concepts and deepen your understanding of material presented throughout the term. These are longer review periods than a daily or weekly review—two to five hours at a stretch, with sufficient breaks. Remember that the effectiveness of your review begins to drop after an hour or so unless you give yourself a short rest.

After a certain point, short breaks every hour might not be enough to refresh you. That's when it's time to quit. Learn your limits by being conscious of the quality of your concentration.

During long sessions, study the most difficult subjects when you are the most alert: at the beginning of the session.

Schedule reviews. Schedule specific times in your calendar for reviews. Start reviewing key topics at least five days before you'll be tested on them. This allows plenty of time to find the answers to questions and close any gaps in your understanding.

© Gaetano Images Inc./Alamy

Create study checklists. You can use study checklists the way a pilot uses a preflight checklist. Pilots go through a standard routine before they take off. They physically mark off each item: test flaps, check magnetos, check fuel tanks, adjust instruments, check rudder. A written list helps them to be sure they don't miss anything. Once they are in the air, it's too late. Taking an exam is like flying a plane. Once the test begins, it's too late to memorize that one equation you forgot to include in your review.

Make a checklist for each subject. List reading assignments by chapters or page numbers. List dates of lecture notes. Write down various types of problems you will need to solve. Write down other skills to master. Include major ideas, definitions, theories, formulas, and equations. For math and science tests, choose some problems and do them over again as a way to review for the test.

Remember that a study checklist is not a review sheet; it is a to-do list. Checklists contain the briefest possible description of each item to study.

Instead of a checklist, you may want to use a test prep plan. This written plan goes beyond a study checklist to include the following:

■ The date and time of each test, along with the name of the course and instructor.

TESTS

7

- The type of items—such as essay or multiple choice—that are likely to appear on each test.
- Specific dates and times that you intend to study for each test (which you then enter on your calendar).
- Specific strategies that you intend to use while studying for each test.

Create mind map summary sheets. There are several ways to make a mind map as you study for tests. Start by creating a map totally from memory. You might be surprised by how much you already know. After you have gone as far as you can using recall alone, go over your notes and text, and fill in the rest of the map. Another option is to go through your notes and write down keywords as you pick them out. Then, without looking at your notes, create a mind map of everything you can recall about each keyword. Finally, go back to your notes and fill in material you left out.

Create flash cards. Flash cards can be used to make portable test questions. On one side of some 3×5 cards, write questions. On the other side, write the answers. It's that simple. Always carry a pack of flash cards with you, and review them whenever you have a minute to spare. Use flash cards for formulas, definitions, theories, keywords from your notes, axioms, dates, foreign language phrases, hypotheses, and sample problems. Create flash cards regularly as the term progresses. Buy an inexpensive card file to keep your flash cards arranged by subject.

Monitor your reviews. Each day that you prepare for a test, assess what you have learned and what you still want to learn. See how many items you've covered from your study checklist. Look at the tables of contents in your textbooks, and write an X next to the sections that you've summarized. This helps you gauge the thoroughness of your reviews and alerts you to areas that still need attention.

Take a practice test. Write up your own questions to make a practice test. Take this practice test several times before the actual exam. You might type this "test" so that it looks like the real thing. If possible, take your practice test in the same room where you will take the actual test.

In addition, meet with your instructor to go over your practice test. Ask whether your questions focus on appropriate topics and represent the kind of items you can expect to see. The instructor might decline to give you any of this information. More often, though, instructors will answer some or all of your questions about an upcoming test.

Get copies of old exams. Copies of previous exams for the class might be available from the instructor, the instructor's department, the library, or the counseling office. Old tests can help you plan a review strategy. One caution: If you rely on old tests exclusively, you might gloss over material the instructor has added since the last test. Also, check your school's policy about making past tests available to students. Some schools might not allow it. ✳

 See examples of mind map summary sheets and other review tools online.

How to cram . . . even though you shouldn't

Know the limitations of cramming, and be aware of its costs. Cramming won't work if you've neglected all of the reading assignments, or if you've skipped most of the lectures and daydreamed through the rest. The more courses you have to cram for, the less effective cramming will be. Also, cramming is not the same as learning: You won't remember what you cram.

If you *are* going to cram, however, then avoid telling yourself that you *should* have studied earlier, you *should* have read the assignments, or you *should* have been more conscientious. All those shoulds get you nowhere. Instead, write an Intention Statement about how you will change your study habits. Give yourself permission to be the fallible human being you are. Then make the best of the situation.

Make choices Pick out a *few* of the most important elements of the course and learn them backward, forward, and upside down. For example, devote most of your attention to the topic sentences, tables, and charts in a long reading assignment.

Make a plan After you've chosen what elements you want to study, determine how much time to spend on each one.

Recite and recite again The key to cramming is repetition. Go over your material again and again.

Ways to predict test questions

PREDICTING TEST QUESTIONS can do more than get you a better grade. It can also keep you focused on the purpose of a course and help you design your learning strategies. Making predictions can be fun, too—especially when they turn out to be accurate.

Ask about the nature of the test. Eliminate as much guesswork as possible. Ask your instructor to describe upcoming tests. Do this early in the term so you can be alert for possible test questions throughout the course. Some questions to ask are:

- What course material will the test cover—readings, lectures, lab sessions, or a combination?
- Will the test be cumulative, or will it cover just the most recent material you've studied?
- Will the test focus on facts and details or major themes and relationships?
- Will the test call on you to solve problems or apply concepts?
- Will you have choices about which questions to answer?
- What types of questions will be on the test—true/false, multiple choice, short answer, essay?

Note: In order to study appropriately for essay tests, find out how much detail the instructor wants in your answers. Ask how much time you'll be allowed for the test and about the length of essay answers (number of pages, blue books, or word limit). Having that information before you begin studying can help you gauge your depth for learning the material.

Put yourself in your instructor's shoes. If you were teaching the course, what kinds of questions would you put on an exam? Make up practice test questions and answer them. You can also brainstorm test questions with other students—this is a great activity for study groups.

Look for possible test questions in your notes and readings. Label a separate section in your notebook "Test questions." Add several questions to this section after every lecture and assignment. You can also create your own code or graphic signal—such as a *T!* in a circle—to flag possible test questions in your notes. Use the same symbol to flag review questions and problems in your textbooks that could appear on a test.

See the boxed feature "Words to Watch for in Essay Questions" on page 197. Use it as a guide to turn the keywords in your notes into test questions.

Look for clues to possible questions during class. During lectures, you can predict test questions by observing what an instructor says and how he says it. Instructors often give clues. They might repeat important points several times, write them on the board, or return to them in later classes.

Gestures can indicate critical points. For example, your instructor might pause, look at notes, or read passages word for word.

Notice whether your teacher has any strong points of view on certain issues. Questions on those issues are likely to appear on a test. Also pay attention to questions the instructor poses to students, and note questions that other students ask.

When material from reading assignments is covered extensively in class, it is likely to be on a test. For science courses and other courses involving problem solving, work on sample problems using different variables.

Save all quizzes, papers, lab sheets, and graded materials of any kind. Quiz questions have a way of reappearing, in slightly altered form, on final exams. If copies of previous exams and other graded materials are available, use them to predict test questions.

Apply your predictions. To get the most value from your predictions, use them to guide your review sessions.

Remember the obvious. Be on the lookout for these words: *This material will be on the test.* ✱

Cooperative learning: Working in teams

Yuri Arcurs/Shutterstock

STUDY GROUPS CAN lift your mood on days when you just don't feel like working. If you skip a solo study session, no one else will know. If you declare your intention to study with others who are depending on you, your intention gains strength.

Study groups are especially important if going to school has thrown you into a new culture. Joining a study group with people you already know can help ease the transition. To multiply the benefits of working with study groups, seek out people of other backgrounds, cultures, races, and ethnic groups. You can get a whole new perspective on the world, along with some valuable new friends. You can also experience what it's like to be part of a diverse team, which is an important asset in today's job market.

Form a study group

Choose a focus for your group. Many students assume that the purpose of a study group is to help its members prepare for a test. That's one valid purpose—but there are others. Through his research on cooperative learning, psychologist Joe Cuseo has identified several kinds of study groups.[1] For instance, members of *test review* groups compare answers and help one another discover sources of errors. *Note-taking* groups focus on comparing and editing notes, often meeting directly after the day's class. Members of *research* groups meet to help one another find, evaluate, and take notes on background materials for papers and presentations. *Reading* groups can be useful for courses in which test questions are based largely on textbooks. Meet with classmates to compare the passages you underlined or highlighted and the notes you made in the margins of your books.

Look for dedicated students. Find people you are comfortable with and who share your academic goals. Look for students who pay attention, participate in class, and actively take notes. Invite them to join your group.

Of course, you can recruit members in other ways. One way is to make an announcement during class. Another option is to post signs asking interested students to contact you. You can also pass around a sign-up sheet before class. These methods can reach many people, but they do take more time to achieve results. In addition, you have less control over who applies to join the group.

Limit groups to four people. Research on cooperative learning indicates that four people is an ideal group size.[2] Larger ones can be unwieldy.

Studying with friends is fine, but if your common interests are pizza and jokes, you might find it hard to focus.

In addition, remember that you'll gain the most benefit from study groups if you continue to take personal responsibility for your learning. Study group members can give you feedback, ask questions, and offer support. However, they cannot read, write papers, or take tests for you.

Hold a planning session. Ask two or three people to get together for a snack and talk about the group. You may define its goals, set up meeting times and locations, and clarify other logistics. You don't have to make an immediate commitment.

As you brainstorm about places to meet, aim for a quiet meeting room with plenty of space to spread out materials.

Do a trial run. Test the group first by planning a one-time session. If that session works, plan another. After a few successful sessions, you can schedule regular meetings.

Conduct your group

Ask your instructor for guidelines on study group activity. Many instructors welcome and encourage study groups. However, they have different

TESTS

7

ideas about what kinds of collaboration are acceptable. Some activities—such as sharing test items or writing papers from a shared outline—are considered cheating and can have serious consequences. Let your instructor know that you're forming a group, and ask for clear guidelines.

Set an agenda for each meeting. At the beginning of each meeting, reach an agreement on what you intend to do. Set a time limit for each agenda item, and determine a quitting time. End each meeting with assignments for all members to complete before the next meeting.

Assign roles. To make the most of your time, ask one member to lead each group meeting. The leader's role is to keep the discussion focused on the agenda and ask for contributions from all members. Assign another person to act as recorder. This person will take notes on the meeting, recording possible test questions, answers, and main points from group discussions. Rotate both of these roles so that every group member takes a turn.

Cycle through learning styles. As you assign roles, think about the learning styles present in your group. Some people excel at raising questions and creating lots of ideas. Others prefer to gather information and think critically. Some like to answer questions and make decisions, while others excel at taking action. Each of these distinct modes of learning are explained in "Learning Styles: Discovering How You Learn" on page 32. To create an effective group, match people with their preferred activities. You should also change roles within the group periodically. This gives group members a chance to explore new learning styles.

Teach each other. Teaching is a great way to learn something. Turn the material you're studying into a list of topics and assign a specific topic to each person, who will then teach it to the group. When you're done presenting your topic, ask for questions or comments. Prompt each other to explain ideas more clearly, find gaps in understanding, consider other points of view, and apply concepts to settings outside the classroom.

Test one another. During your meeting, take a practice test created from questions contributed by group members. When you're finished, compare answers. You can also turn testing into a game by pretending you're on a television game show. Use sample test questions to quiz one another.

Compare notes. Make sure that all the group's members heard the same thing in class and that you all recorded the important information. Ask others to help explain material in your notes that is confusing to you.

Create wall-size mind maps or concept maps to summarize a textbook or series of lectures. Work on large sheets of butcher paper, or tape together pieces of construction paper. When creating a mind map, assign one branch to each member of the study group. Use a different colored pen or marker for each branch of the mind map. (For more information on concept maps and mind maps, see Chapter 6: "Notes.")

Monitor effectiveness. On your meeting agenda, include an occasional discussion about your group's effectiveness. Are you meeting consistently? Is the group helping members succeed in class?

Use this time to address any issues that are affecting the group as a whole. If certain members are routinely unprepared for study sessions, brainstorm ways to get them involved. If one person tends to dominate meetings, reel her in by reminding her that everyone's voice needs to be heard.

To resolve conflict among group members, keep the conversation constructive. Focus on solutions. Move from vague complaints ("You're never prepared") to specific requests ("Will you commit to bringing 10 sample test questions next time?"). Asking a "problem" member to lead the next meeting might make an immediate difference. ✳

journal entry 17

Intention Statement

Start a study group

In the following space, outline a plan to form a study group. Explain the steps you will take to get the group organized and set a first meeting date. Also describe the reward you anticipate for acting on this intention.

I intend to . . .

_____

_____

_____

_____

_____

_____

_____

_____

© image100/Corbis

What to do during the test

PREPARE YOURSELF FOR the test by arriving early. Being early often leaves time to do a relaxation exercise. While you're waiting for the test to begin and talking with classmates, avoid asking the question, "How much did you study for the test?" This question might fuel anxious thoughts that you didn't study enough.

As you begin

Ask the teacher or test administrator if you can use scratch paper during the test. (If you use a separate sheet of paper without permission, you might appear to be cheating.) If you *do* get permission, use this paper to jot down memory aids, formulas, equations, definitions, facts, or other material you know you'll need and might forget. An alternative is to make quick notes in the margins of the test sheet.

Pay attention to verbal directions given as a test is distributed. Then scan the whole test immediately. Evaluate the importance of each section. Notice how many points each part of the test is worth; then estimate how much time you'll need for each section, using its point value as your guide. For example, don't budget 20 percent of your time for a section that is worth only 10 percent of the points.

Read the directions slowly. Then reread them. It can be agonizing to discover that you lost points on a test merely because you failed to follow the directions. When the directions are confusing, ask to have them clarified.

Now you are ready to begin the test. If necessary, allow yourself a minute or two of "panic" time. Notice any tension you feel, and apply one of the techniques explained in the article "Let Go of Test Anxiety" later in this chapter.

Answer the easiest, shortest questions first. This gives you the experience of success. It also stimulates associations and prepares you for more difficult questions. Pace yourself, and watch the time. If you can't think of an answer, move on. Follow your time plan.

Multiple-choice questions

- *Answer each question in your head first.* Do this step before you look at the possible answers. If you come up with an answer that you're confident is right, look for that answer in the list of choices.

- *Read all possible answers before selecting one.* Sometimes two answers will be similar and only one will be correct.

- *Test each possible answer.* Remember that multiple-choice questions consist of two parts: the stem (an incomplete statement or question at the beginning) and a list of possible answers. Each answer, when combined with the stem, makes a complete statement or question-and-answer pair that is either true or false. When you combine the stem with each possible answer, you are turning each multiple-choice question into a small series of true/false questions. Choose the answer that makes a true statement.

- *Eliminate incorrect answers.* Cross off the answers that are clearly not correct. The answer you cannot eliminate is probably the best choice.

True/false questions

- *Read the entire question.* Separate the statement into its grammatical parts—individual clauses and phrases—and then test each part. If any part is false, the entire statement is false.

- *Look for qualifiers.* Qualifiers include words such as *all, most, sometimes,* or *rarely.* Absolute qualifiers such as *always* or *never* generally indicate a false statement.

7

TESTS

- *Find the devil in the details.* Double-check each number, fact, and date in a true/false statement. Look for numbers that have been transposed or facts that have been slightly altered. These are signals of a false statement.

- *Watch for negatives.* Look for words such as *not* and *cannot.* Read the sentence without these words and see if you come up with a true or false statement. Then reinsert the negative words and see if the statement makes more sense. Watch especially for sentences with two negative words. As in math operations, two negatives cancel each other out: *We cannot say that Chekhov never succeeded at short story writing* means the same as *Chekhov succeeded at short story writing.*

Computer-graded tests

- Make sure that the answer you mark corresponds to the question you are answering.

- Check the test booklet against the answer sheet whenever you switch sections and whenever you come to the top of a column.

- Watch for stray marks on the answer sheet; they can look like answers.

- If you change an answer, be sure to erase the wrong answer thoroughly, removing all pencil marks completely.

Open-book tests

- Carefully organize your notes, readings, and any other materials you plan to consult when writing answers.

- Write down any formulas you will need on a separate sheet of paper.

- Bookmark the table of contents and index in each of your textbooks. Place sticky notes and stick-on tabs or paper clips on other important pages of books (pages with tables, for instance).

- Create an informal table of contents or index for the notes you took in class.

- Predict which material will be covered on the test, and highlight relevant sections in your readings and notes.

Short-answer/fill-in-the-blank tests

- Concentrate on keywords and facts. Be brief.

- Remember that overlearning material can really pay off. When you know a subject backward and forward, you can answer this type of question almost as fast as you can write.

Matching tests

- Begin by reading through each column, starting with the one with fewer items. Check the number of items in each column to see if they're equal. If they're not, look for an item in one column that you can match with two or more items in the other column.

- Look for any items with similar wording, and make special note of the differences between these items.

- Match words that are similar grammatically. For example, match verbs with verbs and nouns with nouns.

- When matching individual words with phrases, first read a phrase. Then look for the word that logically completes the phrase.

- Cross out items in each column when you are through with them.

What to do when you get stuck on a test question

- *Read it again.* Eliminate the simplest sources of confusion, such as misreading the question.

- *Skip the question for now.* This advice is simple—and it works. Let your subconscious mind work on the answer while you respond to other questions.

- *Look for answers in other test questions.* A term, name, date, or other fact that escapes you might appear in another question on the test itself.

- *Treat intuitions with care.* In quick-answer questions (multiple choice, true/false), go with your first instinct as to which answer is correct. If you think your first answer is wrong because you misread the question, do change your answer.

- *Rewrite the question.* See if you can put a confusing question into your own words. Doing so might release the answer.

- *Free-write.* On scratch paper or in the margins of your test booklet, record any response to the test question that pops into your head. Instead of just sitting there, stumped, you're doing something—a fact that can reduce anxiety. Writing might also trigger a mental association that answers the question.

- *Write a close answer.* Answer the question as best as you can, even if you don't think your answer is fully correct. This technique might help you get partial credit for short-answer questions, essay questions, and problems on math or science tests.

Essay questions

Managing your time is crucial in answering essay questions. Note how many questions you have to answer, and monitor your progress during the test period. Writing shorter answers and completing all of the questions on an essay test will probably yield a better score than leaving some questions blank.

Find out what an essay question is asking—precisely. If a question asks you to *compare* the ideas of Sigmund Freud and Karl Marx, no matter how eloquently you *explain* them, you are on a one-way trip to No Credit City.

Before you write, make a quick outline. An outline can help speed up the writing of your detailed answer. You're then less likely to leave out important facts. Even if you don't have time to finish your answer, your outline could win you some points. To use test time efficiently, keep your outline brief. Focus on keywords to use in your answer.

Introduce your answer by getting to the point. General statements such as "There are many interesting facets to this difficult question" can cause acute irritation to teachers grading dozens of tests.

One way to get to the point is to begin your answer with part of the question. Suppose the question is, "Discuss how increasing the city police budget might or might not contribute to a decrease in street crime." Your first sentence might be this: "An increase in police expenditures will not have a significant effect on street crime for the following reasons." Your position is clear. You are on your way to an answer.

Next, expand your answer with supporting ideas and facts. Start out with the most solid points. Be brief and avoid filler sentences.

Write legibly. Grading essay questions is in large part a subjective process. Sloppy, difficult-to-read handwriting might actually lower your grade.

Write on one side of the paper only. If you write on both sides of the paper, writing may show through and obscure the words on the other side. If necessary, use the blank side to add points you missed. Leave a generous left-hand margin and plenty of space between your answers, in case you want to add points that you missed later on.

Finally, if you have time, review your answers for grammar and spelling errors, clarity, and legibility. ✳

Words to watch for in essay questions

The following words are commonly found in essay test questions. They give you precise directions about what to include in your answer. Get to know these words well. When you see them on a test, underline them. Also look for them in your notes. Locating such keywords can help you predict test questions.

Analyze. Break into separate parts and discuss, examine, or interpret each part. Then give your opinion.

Compare. Examine two or more items. Identify similarities and differences.

Contrast. Show differences. Set in opposition.

Criticize. Make judgments. Evaluate comparative worth. Criticism often involves analysis.

Define. Explain the exact meaning—usually, a meaning specific to the course or subject. Definitions are usually short.

Describe. Give a detailed account. Make a picture with words. List characteristics, qualities, and parts.

Discuss. Consider and debate or argue the pros and cons of an issue. Write about any conflict. Compare and contrast.

Explain. Make an idea clear. Show logically how a concept is developed. Give the reasons for an event.

Prove. Support with facts (especially facts presented in class or in the text).

Relate. Show the connections between ideas or events. Provide a larger context for seeing the big picture.

State. Explain precisely.

Summarize. Give a brief, condensed account. Include conclusions. Avoid unnecessary details.

Trace. Show the order of events or the progress of a subject or event.

Notice how these words differ. For example, *compare* asks you to do something different than *contrast*. Likewise, *criticize* and *explain* call for different responses. If any of these terms are still unclear to you, look them up in an unabridged dictionary.

The test isn't over until . . .

MANY STUDENTS BELIEVE that a test is over as soon as they turn it in. Consider another point of view: You're not done with a test until you know the answer to any question that you missed—and why you missed it.

This point of view offers major benefits. Tests in many courses are cumulative. In other words, the content included on the first test is assumed to be working knowledge for future tests. When you understand the reason for lost points you learn something—and you greatly increase your odds of achieving better scores later in the course.

To get the most value from any test, take control of what you do at two critical points: immediately following the test and when the test is returned to you.

Immediately following the test. After finishing a test, your first thought might be to nap, snack, or celebrate with friends. Restrain those impulses for a short while so that you can reflect on the test. The time you invest now carries the potential to raise your grades in the future.

To begin with, sit down in a quiet place. Take a few minutes to write some Discovery Statements related to your experience. Describe how you felt about taking the test, how effective your review strategies were, and whether you accurately predicted the questions that appeared.

Follow up with an Intention Statement or two. State what you will do differently to prepare for the next test.

When the test is returned. First, make sure that the point totals add up correctly, and double-check for any other errors in grading. Even the best teachers make an occasional mistake.

Next, ask these questions:

On what material did the teacher base test questions—readings, lectures, discussions, or other class activities?

What types of questions appeared in the test—objective (such as matching items, true/false questions, or multiple choice), short answer, or essay?

What types of questions did you miss?

What can you learn from the instructor's comments that will help you prepare for the next test?

How will you prepare differently for your next test?

Also see if you can correct any answers that lost points. Consult the following chart for help. ✳

Source of test error	Possible solutions
Study errors—studying material that was not included on the test, or spending too little time on material that *did* appear on the test	• Ask your teacher about specific topics that will be included on a test. • Practice predicting test questions. • Form a study group with class members to create mock tests.
Careless errors, such as skipping or misreading directions	• Read directions more carefully—especially when tests are divided into several sections. • Set aside time during the next test to proofread your answers.
Concept errors—mistakes made when you do not understand the underlying principles needed to answer a question or solve a problem	• Look for patterns in the questions you missed. • Make sure that you complete all assigned readings, attend all lectures, and show up for laboratory sessions. • Ask your teacher for help with specific questions.
Application errors—mistakes made when you understand underlying principles but fail to apply them correctly	• Rewrite your answers correctly. • Spend more time solving sample problems. • Predict application questions that will appear in future tests, and practice answering them.
Test mechanics errors—missing more questions in certain parts of the test than others, changing correct answers to incorrect ones at the last minute, leaving items blank, miscopying answers from scratch paper to the answer sheet	• Set time limits for taking each section of a test. • Proofread your test answers carefully. • Look for patterns in the kind of answers you change at the last minute. • Change answers only if you can state a clear and compelling reason to do so.

TESTS

7

Let go of test anxiety

If you freeze during tests and flub questions when you know the answers, you might be dealing with test anxiety.

© Masterfile Royalty Free

A LITTLE TENSION before a test is fine. That tingly, butterflies-in-the-stomach feeling you get from extra adrenaline can sharpen your awareness and keep you alert. You can enjoy the benefits of a little tension while you stay confident and relaxed.

Sometimes, however, tension is persistent and extreme. If it interferes with your daily life and consistently prevents you from doing your best in school, you might be suffering from test anxiety.

Symptoms of anxiety include the following:[3]

- Inability to concentrate
- Insomnia
- Sweating
- Shortness of breath
- Fatigue
- Irritability
- Stomachache
- Diarrhea
- Headache

Anxiety has mental, physical, and emotional elements. The mental element includes your thoughts, including predictions of failure. The physical component includes physical sensations such as shallow breathing and muscle tension. The emotional element occurs when thoughts and physical sensations combine. The following techniques can help you deal with these elements of stress in *any* situation, from test anxiety to stage fright.

Dealing with thoughts

Yell "Stop!" When you notice that your mind is consumed with worries and fears—that your thoughts are spinning out of control—mentally yell "Stop!" If you're in a situation that allows it, yell it out loud. This action can allow you to redirect your thoughts. Once you've broken the cycle of worry or panic, you can use any of the following techniques.

Dispute your thoughts. Certain thoughts tend to increase test anxiety. They often boil down to this statement: *Getting a low grade on a test is a disaster*. Do the math, however: A four-year degree often involves taking about 32 courses (eight courses per year over four years for a full-time student). This means that your final grade on any one course amounts to about only 3 percent of your total grade point average.

Also consider that your final grade in any one course is usually based on more than one test. This means that

F is for feedback, not failure

When some students get an F on an assignment, they interpret that letter as a message: "You are a failure." That interpretation is not accurate. Getting an F means only that you failed a test—not that you failed your life.

From now on, imagine that the letter F when used as a grade represents another word: *feedback.* An F is an indication that you didn't understand the material well enough. It's a message to do something differently before the next test or assignment.

If you interpret F as *failure,* you don't get to change anything. But if you interpret F as *feedback,* you can change your thinking and behavior in ways that promote your success.

7

TESTS

a single test score is not going to make or break your college career.

This argument is not meant to convince you to stop preparing for tests. It *is* an argument to keep each test in perspective—and to dispute thoughts that only serve to create anxiety.

Praise yourself. Talk to yourself in a positive way. Many of us take the first opportunity to belittle ourselves: "Way to go, dummy! You don't even know the answer to the first question on the test." We wouldn't dream of treating a friend this way, yet we do it to ourselves. An alternative is to give yourself some encouragement. Treat yourself as if you were your own best friend. Consider telling yourself, "I am prepared. I can do a great job on this test."

Consider the worst. Rather than trying to put a stop to your worrying, consider the very worst thing that could happen. Take your fear to the limit of absurdity.

Imagine the catastrophic problems that might occur if you were to fail the test. You might say to yourself, "Well, if I fail this test, I might fail the course, lose my financial aid, and get kicked out of school. Then I won't be able to get a job, so the bank will repossess my car, and I'll start drinking." Keep going until you see the absurdity of your predictions. After you stop chuckling, you can backtrack to discover a reasonable level of concern. Your worry about failing the entire course if you fail the test might be justified. At that point, ask yourself, "Can I live with that?" Unless you are taking a test in parachute packing and the final question involves jumping out of a plane, the answer will almost always be yes. (If the answer is no, use another anxiety-relieving technique. In fact, use several other techniques.)

Dealing with physical sensations

Breathe. You can calm physical sensations within your body by focusing your attention on your breathing. Concentrate on the air going in and out of your lungs. Experience it as it passes through your nose and mouth. Do this exercise for two to five minutes. If you notice that you are taking short, shallow breaths, begin to take longer and deeper breaths. Imagine your lungs to be a pair of bagpipes. Expand your chest to bring in as much air as possible. Then listen to the plaintive chords as you slowly release the air.

Describe sensations. In your mind, describe your anxiety to yourself in detail; don't resist it. Think about all the ways in which your anxiety manifests itself. When you completely experience a physical sensation, it will often disappear. People suffering from chronic pain have also used this technique successfully.[4]

Scan your body. Simple awareness is an effective response to unpleasant physical sensations. Discover this for yourself by bringing awareness to each area of your body.

To begin, sit comfortably and close your eyes. Focus your attention on the muscles in your feet, and notice if they are relaxed. Tell the muscles in your feet that they can relax.

Move up to your ankles, and repeat the procedure. Next, go to your calves and thighs and buttocks, telling each group of muscles to relax.

Do the same for your lower back, diaphragm, chest, upper arms, lower arms, fingers, upper back, shoulders, neck, jaw, face, and scalp.

Use guided imagery. Relax completely, and take a quick fantasy trip. Close your eyes, free your body of tension, and imagine yourself in a beautiful, peaceful, natural setting. Create as much of the scene as you can. Be specific. Use all of your senses.

For example, you might imagine yourself at a beach. Hear the surf rolling in and the seagulls calling to each other. Feel the sun on your face and the hot sand between your toes. Smell the sea breeze. Taste the salty mist from the surf. Notice the ships on the horizon and the rolling sand dunes. Use all of your senses to create a vivid imaginary trip.

Find a place that works for you, and practice getting there. When you become proficient, you can return to it quickly for trips that might last only a few seconds.

With practice, you can use this technique even while you are taking a test.

Exercise aerobically. Performing aerobic exercise is one technique that won't work in the classroom or while you're taking a test. Yet it is an excellent way to reduce body tension. Exercise regularly during the days you review for a test. See what effect it has on your ability to focus and relax during the test.

Do some kind of exercise that will get your heart beating at twice your normal rate and keep it beating at that rate for 15 or 20 minutes. Aerobic exercise includes rapid walking, jogging, swimming, bicycling, playing basketball, and anything else that elevates your heart rate and keeps it elevated.

Find alternatives to chemicals. When faced with stress, some people turn to relief in the form of a pill, a drink, or a drug in some other form. Chemicals such as caffeine and alcohol *can* change the way you feel. They also come with costs that go beyond money. For example, drinking alcohol can relax you *and* interfere with your attention and memory. Caffeine or energy drinks might make you feel more confident in the short term. Watch what happens, though, when you start to come down from a caffeine-induced high. You might feel even more irritable than you did *before* drinking that double espresso.

All moral lectures aside, chemicals that you take without a prescription are ineffective ways to manage anxiety. Use other techniques instead.

Dealing with emotions

Accept emotions—whatever they are. Consider our typical response to problems. If a car has a flat tire, that's a problem. The solution is to repair or replace the tire. If a bathroom faucet drips, that's a problem. The solution is to repair or replace part of the faucet.

This problem–solution approach often works well when applied to events outside us. It does not work so well, however, when applied to events *inside* us. When we define anger, sadness, fear, or any emotion as a problem, we tend to search for a solution. However, emotions respond differently than flat tires and drippy faucets.

Typical attempts to "solve" unpleasant emotions include eating, drinking, watching TV, or surfing the Internet. These are actually attempts to resist the emotions and try to make them go away. For a short time, this strategy might work. Over the long term, however, our efforts to repair or replace emotions often have the opposite effect: The emotions persist or even get stronger. Our solutions actually become part of the problem.

An alternative to problem solving is *acceptance*. We can stop seeing emotions as problems. This attitude frees us from having to search for solutions (which often fail anyway).

Acceptance means just letting our emotions be. It means releasing any resistance to emotions. This approach is a wise one, since what we *resist* usually *persists*. Our emotions are just bundles of thoughts and physical sensations. Even the most unpleasant ones fade sooner or later.

The next time you are feeling anxious before a test, simply let that feeling arise and then pass away.

Practice detachment. To *detach* means to step back from something and see it as separate from ourselves. When we detach from an emotion, we no longer identify with it. We no longer say, "*I* am afraid" or "*I* am sad." We say something like "There's fear again" or "I feel sadness right now." Using language such as this offers us a way to step back from our internal experiences and keep them in perspective.

Before a test, you might find it especially useful to detach from your thoughts. Borrow some ideas from Acceptance and Commitment Therapy (ACT), which is used by a growing number of therapists.[5] Take an anxiety-producing thought—such as *I always screw up on tests*—and do any of the following:

- Repeat the thought over and over again out loud until it becomes just a meaningless series of sounds.
- Repeat the thought while using the voice of a cartoon character such as Mickey Mouse or Homer Simpson.
- Rephrase the thought so that you can sing it to the tune of a nursery rhyme or the song "Happy Birthday."
- Preface the thought with "I'm having the thought that . . ." (For example, *I'm having the thought that I always screw up on tests.*)
- Talk back to your mind by saying, "That's an interesting thought, mind; thanks a lot for sharing." Or simply say, "Thanks, mind."

Make contact with the present moment. If you feel anxious, see if you can focus your attention on a specific sight, sound, or other sensation that's happening in the present moment. Examine the details of a painting. Study the branches on a tree. Observe the face of your watch right down to the tiny scratches in the glass. During an exam, take a few seconds to listen to the sounds of squeaking chairs, the scratching of pencils, the muted coughs. Touch the surface of your desk and notice the texture. Focus all of your attention on one point—anything other than the flow of thoughts through your head. Focusing in this manner is one way to use the Power Process: "Be Here Now."

Get help. If you use any of the previous techniques for a couple of weeks and they fail to work, then turn to other people. Sometimes help with a specific situation—such as a lack of money—can relieve a source of stress that affects your test performance. Turn to the appropriate campus resource, such as the financial aid office.

If you become withdrawn, have thoughts about death or suicide, feel depressed for more than a few days, or have prolonged feelings of hopelessness, then see your doctor or a counselor at your student health center. No matter what the source of anxiety, help is always available. ✳

critical thinking exercise
20 things I like to do

One way to relieve tension is to mentally yell "Stop!" and substitute a pleasant daydream for the stressful thoughts and emotions you are experiencing.

To create a supply of pleasant images to recall during times of stress, conduct an 8-minute brainstorm about things you like to do. Your goal is to generate at least 20 ideas. Time yourself, and write as fast as you can in the following space.

When you have completed your list, study it. Pick out two activities that seem especially pleasant, and elaborate on them by creating a mind map. Write down all of the memories you have about that activity.

You can use these images to calm yourself in stressful situations.

Have some FUN!

Contrary to popular belief, finals week does not have to be a drag.

In fact, if you have used the techniques in this chapter, exam week can be fun. You will have done most of your studying long before finals arrive.

When you are well prepared for tests, you can even use fun as a technique to enhance your performance.

The day before a final, go for a run or play a game of basketball. Take in a movie or a concert. A relaxed brain is a more effective brain. If you have studied for a test, your mind will continue to prepare itself even while you're at the movies.

Get plenty of rest, too. There's no need to cram until 3 a.m. when you have reviewed material throughout the term.

On the first day of finals, you can wake up refreshed, have a good breakfast, and walk into the exam room with a smile on your face. You can also leave with a smile on your face, knowing that you are going to have a fun week. It's your reward for studying regularly throughout the term.

Discovery/Intention Statement

Notice your excuses and let them go

Do a timed, four-minute brainstorm of all the reasons, rationalizations, justifications, and excuses you have used to avoid studying. Be creative. List your thoughts in the following space and continue them on a separate sheet if needed:

_____

_____

_____

_____

_____

_____

_____

_____

Now write a Discovery Statement about the list you just created.

I discovered that I . . .

_____

_____

_____

_____

_____

Next, review your list, pick the excuse that you use the most, and circle it. In the following space, write an Intention Statement about what you will do to begin eliminating your favorite excuse. Make this Intention Statement one that you can keep, with a timeline and a reward.

I intend to . . .

_____

_____

_____

_____

_____

Discovery Statement

Explore your feelings about tests

Complete the following sentences.

As exam time gets closer, one thing I notice that I do is . . .

_____

_____

When it comes to taking tests, I have trouble . . .

_____

_____

The night before a test, I usually feel . . .

_____

_____

The morning of a test, I usually feel . . .

_____

_____

During a test, I usually feel . . .

_____

_____

After a test, I usually feel . . .

_____

_____

When I learn a test score, I usually feel . . .

_____

_____

 An online version of this exercise is available.

7

TESTS

Getting ready for math tests

© Bloomimage/Corbis

MANY STUDENTS WHO could succeed in math shy away from the subject. Some had negative experiences in past courses. Others believe that math is only for gifted students.

At some level, however, math is open to all students. There's more to this subject than memorizing formulas and manipulating numbers. Imagination, creativity, and problem-solving skills are important, too.

Consider a three-part program for math success. Begin with strategies for overcoming math anxiety. Next, boost your study skills. Finally, let your knowledge shine during tests.

Overcome math anxiety

Many schools offer courses in overcoming math anxiety. Ask your advisor about resources on your campus. You can also experiment with the following suggestions.

Connect math to life. Think of the benefits of mastering math courses. You'll have more options for choosing a major and a career. Math skills can also put you at ease in everyday situations—for example, calculating the tip for a waiter, balancing your checkbook, or working with a spreadsheet on a computer. If you follow baseball statistics, cook, do construction work, or snap pictures with a camera, you'll use math. In addition, speaking the language of math can help you feel at home in a world driven by technology.

Pause occasionally to get an overview of the branch of math that you're studying. What's it all about? What basic problems is it designed to solve? How do people apply this knowledge in daily life? For example, many architects, engineers, and space scientists use calculus daily.

Take a first step. Math is cumulative. Concepts build upon each other in a certain order. If you struggled with algebra, you may have trouble with trigonometry or calculus.

To ensure that you have an adequate base of knowledge, tell the truth about your current level of knowledge and skill. Before you register for a math course, locate assigned texts for the prerequisite courses. If the material in those books seems new or difficult for

you, see the instructor. Ask for suggestions on ways to prepare for the course.

Remember that it's OK to continue your study of math from your current level of ability, whatever that level might be.

Notice your pictures about math. Sometimes what keeps people from succeeding at math is their mental picture of mathematicians. They see a man dressed in a baggy plaid shirt and brown wingtip shoes. He's got a calculator on his belt and six pencils jammed in his shirt pocket.

These pictures are far from realistic. Succeeding in math won't turn you into a nerd. Actually, you'll be able to enjoy school more, and your friends will still like you.

Mental pictures about math can be funny, but they can have serious effects. If math is seen as a field for white males, then women and people of color are likely to get excluded. Promoting math success for all students helps to overcome racism and sexism.

Change your conversation about math. When students fear math, they often say negative things to themselves about their abilities in this subject. Many times this self-talk includes statements such as *I'll never be fast enough at solving math problems* or *I'm good with words, so I can't be good with numbers.*

Get such statements out in the open, and apply some emergency critical thinking. You'll find two self-defeating assumptions lurking there: *Everybody else is better at math and science than I am* and *Since I don't understand a math concept right now, I'll never understand it.* Both of these statements are illogical.

Replace negative beliefs with logical, realistic statements that affirm your ability to succeed in math: *Any confusion I feel now can be resolved. I learn math without comparing myself to others.* And *I ask whatever questions are needed to aid my understanding.*

Choose your response to stress. Math anxiety is seldom just "in your head." It can also register as sweaty palms, shallow breathing, tightness in the chest, or a mild headache. Instead of trying to ignore these sensations, just notice them without judgment. Over time, simple awareness decreases their power.

In addition, use stress management techniques. "Let Go of Test Anxiety" on page 199 offers a bundle of them.

No matter what you do, remember to breathe. You can relax in any moment just by making your breath slower and deeper. Practice doing this while you study math. It will come in handy at test time.

Boost study skills for math

Choose teachers with care. Whenever possible, find a math teacher whose approach to math matches your learning style. Talk with several teachers until you find one you enjoy.

Another option is to ask around. Maybe your academic advisor can recommend math teachers. You can also ask classmates to name their favorite math teachers—and to explain the reasons for their choices.

In some cases, only one teacher will be offering the math course you need. The suggestions that follow can be used to learn from a teacher regardless of her teaching style.

Take math courses back to back. Approach math in the same way that you learn a foreign language. If you take a year off in between Spanish I and Spanish II, you won't gain much fluency. To master a language, you take courses back to back. It works the same way with math, which is a language in itself.

Form a study group. During the first week of each math course, organize a study group. Ask each member to bring five problems to group meetings, along with solutions. You should also exchange contact information so that you can stay in touch via e-mail, phone, and text messaging.

Avoid short courses. Courses that you take during summer school or another shortened term are condensed. You might find yourself doing far more reading and homework each week than you do in longer courses. If you enjoy math, the extra intensity can provide a stimulus to learn. However, if math is not your favorite subject, give yourself extra time. Enroll in courses spread out over more calendar days.

Participate in class. Success in math depends on your active involvement. Attend class regularly. Complete homework assignments *when they're due*—not just before the test. If you're confused, get help right away from an instructor, tutor, or study group. Instructors' office hours, free on-campus tutoring, and classmates are just a few of the resources available to you. In addition, support your class participation with time for homework. Make daily contact with math.

Prepare for several types of tests. Math tests often involve lists of problems to solve. Ask your instructor about what types of tests to expect. Then prepare for the tests using strategies from this chapter.

Ask questions fearlessly. It's a cliché, but it's true: In math, there are no dumb questions. Ask whatever questions will aid your understanding. Keep a running list of them, and bring the list to class.

Make your text your top priority. Math courses are often text driven. Class activities closely follow the book. This fact underscores the importance of completing your reading assignments. Master one

Succeeding in science courses

Many of the strategies that help you prepare for math tests can also help you succeed in science courses. For example, forming small study groups can be a fun way to learn these subjects. Following are some additional ideas.

Relate science to your career interests and daily life   People in many professions—from dentists to gardeners—rely on science to do their job. Even if you don't choose a science-driven career, you will live in a world that's driven by technology. Understanding how scientists observe, collect data, and arrive at conclusions can help you feel more at home in this world.

Prepare for variety   Remember that the word *science* refers to a vast range of subjects—astronomy, biology, chemistry, physics, physiology, geology, ecology, geography, and more. Most of these subjects include math as one of their tools. Beyond that, however, are many differences.

You can take advantage of this variety. Choose science courses that match your personal interests and comfort level for technical subjects.

Prepare for lab sessions   Laboratory work is crucial to many science classes. To get the most out of these sessions, be prepared. Complete required reading before you enter the lab. Be sure you also gather the materials you'll need ahead of time.

 Find more strategies for succeeding in science online.

1: Prepare

- Read each problem two or three times, slowly and out loud whenever possible.
- Consider creating a chart with three columns labeled *What I already know, What I want to find out,* and *What connects the two.* The third column is the place to record a formula that can help you solve the problem.
- Determine which arithmetic operations (addition, subtraction, multiplication, division) or formulas you will use to solve the problem.
- See if you can estimate the answer before you compute it.

2: Compute

- Reduce the number of unknowns as much as you can. Consider creating a separate equation to solve each unknown.
- When solving equations, carry out the algebra as far as you can before plugging in the actual numbers.
- Cancel and combine. For example, if the same term appears in both dividend and divisor, they will cancel each other out.
- Remember that it's OK to make several attempts at solving the problem before you find an answer.

3: Check

- Plug your answer back into the original equation or problem and see if it works out correctly.
- Ask yourself if your answer seems likely when compared with your estimate. For example, if you're asked to apply a discount to an item, that item should cost less in your solution.
- Perform opposite operations. If a problem involves multiplication, check your work by division; add, then subtract; factor, then multiply; find the square root, then the square; differentiate, then integrate.
- Keep units of measurement clear. Say that you're calculating the velocity of an object. If you're measuring distance in meters and time in seconds, the final velocity should be in meters per second.

concept before going on to the next, and stay current with your reading. Be willing to read slowly and reread sections as needed.

Read actively. To get the most out of your math texts, read with paper and pencil in hand. Work out examples. Copy diagrams, formulas, and equations. Use chapter summaries and introductory outlines to organize your learning.

From time to time, stop, close your book, and mentally reconstruct the steps in solving a problem. Before you memorize a formula, understand the basic concepts behind it.

Practice solving problems. To get ready for math tests, work *lots* of problems. Find out if practice problems or previous tests are on file in the library, in the math department, or with your math teacher.

Isolate the types of problems that you find the most difficult. Practice them more often. Be sure to get help with these kinds of problems *before* exhaustion or frustration sets in.

To prepare for tests, practice working problems fast. Time yourself. This activity is a great one for math study groups.

Approach problem solving with a three-step process, as shown in the chart on this page. During each step, apply an appropriate strategy.

Use tests to show what you know

Practice test taking. Part of preparing for any math test is rehearsal. Instead of passively reading through your text or scanning class notes, do a practice test:

- Print out a set of practice problems, and set a timer for the same length of time as your testing period.
- Whenever possible, work practice problems in the same room where you will take the actual test.
- Use only the kinds of supporting materials—such as scratch paper or lists of formulas—that will be allowed during the test.
- As you work problems, use deep breathing or another technique to enter a more relaxed state.

Ask appropriate questions. During the test, if you don't understand a test item, ask for clarification. The worst that can happen is that an instructor or proctor will politely decline to answer your question.

Write legibly. Put yourself in the instructor's place. Imagine the prospect of grading stacks of illegible answer sheets. Make your answers easy to read. If you show your work, underline key sections and circle your answer.

Do your best. There are no secrets involved in getting ready for math tests. Master some stress management techniques, do your homework, get answers to your questions, and work sample problems. If you've done those things, you're ready for the test and deserve to do well. If you haven't done all those things, just do the best you can.

Remember that your personal best can vary from test to test, and even from day to day. Even if you don't answer all test questions correctly, you can demonstrate what you *do* know right now.

During the test, notice when solutions come easily. Savor the times when you feel relaxed and confident. If you ever feel math anxiety in the future, these are the times to remember.[6] ✳

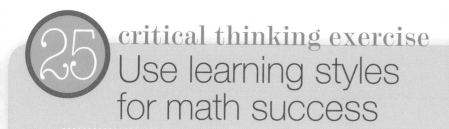

25 critical thinking exercise
Use learning styles for math success

Review the articles about learning styles in Chapter 1: "First Steps." Look for strategies that could promote your success in math. Modify any of the suggested strategies so that they work for you.

See if you can invent techniques that work especially well for math courses. If you're a visual learner, for example, you might color code your notes by writing key terms and formulas in red ink. If you like to learn by speaking and listening, then consider reading key passages in your textbooks out loud. Alternatively, if you're a kinesthetic learner, use "manipulatives"—such as magnetic boards with letters and numbers—when you study math.

Whatever you choose, commit to using at least one new strategy. In the following space, describe what you will do.

© Lawrence Manning/Corbis

Make performance reviews work for you

PERFORMANCE REVIEWS usually take place in a meeting with your direct supervisor at work. These meetings follow various formats, and many organizations have their own systems for rating performance. Yet the basic idea in any case is for you to walk away with answers to three questions: *What am I doing well? What could I do better?* and *How can I develop the skills to do better?* When handled with skill, performance reviews are tools for taking charge of your career.

Set goals early. Your organization may schedule performance reviews only once or twice per year. However, effective performance review is a continuous process. For optimum results, begin this process on your first day at work. When you start a new job, meet with your direct supervisor to define exactly what "effective performance" means for you.

Set work-related goals that you can achieve (see Chapter 3: "Time"). State them in specific, measurable terms, as explained later in this article. Whenever possible, include a specific date to meet each goal. Put your goals in writing and share them with your supervisor.

Prepare for the review. As the date of your performance review approaches, anticipate the kinds of questions your supervisor will ask. For example:

- What was your biggest accomplishment since your last performance review?

- In light of your stated goals, how did you feel about your performance?

- What prevented you from performing well or meeting any of your goals?

- What can you do to overcome those obstacles?

- What can coworkers and managers do to help you overcome those obstacles?

Keep the tone positive. When you meet with your supervisor, refer to your list of goals and note which ones you met. Take time to celebrate your accomplishments and set new goals.

If you missed a goal, talk about how that happened. Instead of focusing on failure or placing blame, take a problem-solving approach. If you made a mistake, talk about what you learned from the experience and what you intend to do differently in the future. Revise the goal and create a new plan for achieving it.

Effective performance reviews include time for you to *give* feedback as well as receive it. Discuss what you like about your job and what you would like to change. If meeting your goals calls for extra resources or changes in your job description, then ask for them.

Instead of complaining about working conditions, make suggestions. "My office is way too noisy for me to be productive" is a complaint. "Let's set up a quiet room in our building where people can go to do work that requires long periods of concentration" is a suggestion. Suggestions are easier to hear than complaints and naturally lend themselves to follow-up action.

Create a focused plan for personal development. Performance reviews often end with a development plan that includes specific ways to improve performance. Standard advice from many self-development "experts" is to focus this plan on identifying your greatest personal weakness and changing that right away.

Think critically about this advice for three reasons. First, tackling your biggest weakness first can feel threatening and lead to procrastination. Second, this weakness may be hard to change before your next performance review. And third, eliminating this weakness might affect your life outside work but have little or no impact on your career.

Another option is to focus your development plan on your strengths. Think about any of your recent accomplishments at work. Describe them in writing, including specific details about what you did and the results of your actions.

Next, set a goal to build on one of these accomplishments. Say that you made a suggestion to change the work flow in your department, and this change allowed your team to finish a project well before the scheduled due date. Consider setting a goal to make this a permanent change in your department's procedures. You could also set a goal to find other time-saving procedures.

Of course, you can always set a goal that targets one of your weaknesses. Just stay positive. Instead of focusing on a current behavior that you want to *stop*, for example, describe a new behavior that you want to *start*. Change "I will stop taking unclear notes at meetings" to "I will review my meeting notes to clarify the major agreements we made and next actions to take."

In any case, focus your development plan on goals that you can actually achieve in the near future, leading to clear benefits at work. Translate your goal into concrete behaviors. Ask yourself: What exactly will I *do* differently based on my goal? And how will I *monitor* this behavior?

If you did the Time Monitor/Time Plan exercise in Chapter 3: "Time," you already have some experience with monitoring your behavior. You can monitor your progress toward any goal, no matter how ambitious. To monitor listening skills, for example, you could count the number of times each day that you interrupt other people.

Remember that the point of monitoring your behavior is not to become a cold-blooded measurement machine. Rather, the idea is to make a change that really makes a difference over the long term. The behaviors that we measure are the ones most likely to change.

As you monitor your behavior, suspend all self-judgment. Just record the facts. If you deviate from your plan, just look for the next opportunity to practice your new behavior.

Act on your plan every day. For your development plan, choose a behavior that you can do every day at work. Also describe how you will record the measurements that you make while monitoring your behavior. For instance, you could tally the number of your work breaks on a 3×5 card.

Do a daily debriefing on your way home from work. This can take only a minute or two. Estimate how often you're succeeding at changing your behavior. Make any adjustments to your plan that seem necessary. Then set a clear intention about when and where you will practice a new behavior at work tomorrow. By creating a continuous cycle of planning and monitoring, you set yourself up for long-term success at work.

Based on this feedback about performance in your current job, you can define the next job you want. Every performance review can be one more step to the career of your dreams. ✳

journal entry 20

Intention Statement

Set a goal for personal development

Reflect for a few minutes on your recent performance at your current job, or your overall performance at a previous job. In a single sentence, describe one success that you experienced—any goal that you were proud to meet or any task that you did especially well:

_____

_____

_____

Now reflect on this experience by completing the following sentences:

In creating this success, the attitude or behavior that helped me most was . . .

_____

_____

To experience this kind of success on a more consistent basis, I intend to . . .

_____

_____

Celebrate mistakes

PKruger/Shutterstock

A CREATIVE ENVIRONMENT is one in which failure is not fatal. Businesses striving to be on the cutting edge of competition desperately seek innovative changes. They know that innovation requires risk taking, despite the chance of failure.

This is not idle talk. There are people who actually celebrate mistakes:[7]

- The Coca-Cola company launched a number of beverages that bombed—including Choglit, OK Soda, Surge, and New Coke. But at the company's annual meeting in 2006, chair and chief executive officer E. Neville Isdell told investors to accept failures as a way to regenerate the company.

- Scott Anthony, director of a consulting firm named Innosight, coaches companies to fumble to success by failing early and cheaply as they develop new products.

- Thomas D. Kuczmarski, a Chicago-based consultant, suggests that companies hold "failure parties" to reward mistakes that lead to better products.

This is *not* an argument in favor of making mistakes. Rather, the goal is to learn from mistakes that happen as we aim for success. In fact, there are several reasons that we can even celebrate mistakes.

Celebration allows us to notice the mistake. Covering up mistakes or blaming others for them takes a lot of energy. That energy could be channeled into correcting errors instead. Celebrating mistakes gets them out into the open.

Mistakes are valuable feedback. There's an old story about the manager of a major corporation who made a mistake that cost his company $100,000. The manager predicted that he would be fired. Instead, his boss said, "Fire you? I can't afford to do that. I just spent $100,000 training you." This story may be fictional, but it makes a point: Mistakes are part of the learning process. In fact, mistakes are often more interesting and more instructive than are successes.

Mistakes demonstrate that we're taking risks. People who play it safe make few mistakes. Making mistakes can be evidence that we're stretching to the limit of our abilities—growing, risking, and learning. Fear of making mistakes can paralyze us into inaction. Celebrating mistakes helps us move into gear and get things done.

Celebrating mistakes includes everyone. Celebrating mistakes reminds us that the exclusive club named the Perfect Performance Society has no members. All of us make mistakes. When we notice them, we can work together to find a solution. ✳

Notable failures

As you experiment with new techniques, you may try a few that fail at crucial moments—such as during a test. Just remember that many people before you have failed miserably before succeeding brilliantly. Consider a few examples:

In his first professional race, cyclist *Lance Armstrong* finished last.

The first time *Jerry Seinfeld* walked onstage at a comedy club as a professional comic, he looked out at the audience and froze.

In high school, actor and comic *Robin Williams* was voted "Least Likely to Succeed."

Walt Disney was fired by a newspaper editor because "he lacked imagination and had no good ideas."

R. H. Macy failed seven times before his store in New York City caught on.

Decca Records turned down a recording contract with *The Beatles* with an unprophetic evaluation: "We don't like their sound. Groups of guitars are on their way out."

In 1954, Jimmy Denny, manager of the Grand Ole Opry, fired *Elvis Presley* after one performance.

Babe Ruth is famous for his past home run record, but for decades he also held the record for strikeouts. *Mark McGwire* broke that record.

Adapted from "But They Did Not Give Up," www.des.emory.edu/mfp/OnFailingG.html (accessed November 11, 2009).

DETACH

This Power Process helps you release the powerful, natural student within you. It is especially useful whenever negative emotions are getting in your way.

Attachments are addictions. When we are attached to something, we think we cannot live without it, just as a drug addict feels he cannot live without drugs. We believe our well-being depends on maintaining our attachments.

We can be attached to just about anything: beliefs, emotions, people, roles, objects. The list is endless.

One person, for example, might be so attached to his car that he takes an accident as a personal attack. Pity the poor unfortunate who backs into this person's car. He might as well have backed into the owner himself.

Another person might be attached to her job. Her identity and sense of well-being depend on it. She could become deeply depressed, almost to the point of suicide, if she ever gets fired.

When we are attached and things don't go our way, we can feel angry, sad, afraid, or confused.

Suppose you are attached to getting an A on your physics test. You feel as though your success in life depends on getting that A. As the clock ticks away, you work harder on the test, getting more stuck. That voice in your head gets louder: "I must get an A. I MUST get an A. I MUST GET AN A!"

Now is a time to detach. Practice observer consciousness. See if you can just *observe* what's going on, letting go of all your judgments. When you just observe, you reach a quiet state above and beyond your usual thoughts. This is a place where you can be aware of being aware. It's a tranquil spot, apart from your emotions. From here, you can observe yourself objectively, as if you were someone else. Pay attention to your thoughts and physical sensations. If you are confused and feeling stuck, tell yourself, "Here I am, confused and stuck." If your palms are sweaty and your stomach is one big knot, admit it. Put your current circumstances into a broader perspective. View your personal issues within the larger context of your community, nation, or even planet.

Practice breathing. Calm your mind and body with relaxation techniques.

Practice detaching before the big test. The key is to let go of automatic emotional reactions when you don't get what you want.

Caution: Giving up an *attachment* to being an A student does not mean giving up *being* an A student. Giving up an attachment to a job doesn't mean giving up the job. When you detach, you get to keep your values and goals. However, you know that you will be OK even if you fail to achieve a goal. You are more than your goals. You are more than your thoughts and feelings. You are more than your current circumstances. These things come and go. Meanwhile, the part of you that can just *observe* everything that happens and learn from it is always there and always safe, no matter what happens.

Behind your attachments is a master student. Release that mastery. Detach.

 Learn more about using this Power Process online.

Katsuo Yamagishi/SPORT/Jupiter Images

Career Application

Red Chopsticks/Getty

D uring his senior year of high school, Chang Lee read about the favorable job market for medical assistants. He set a goal to enroll in a local community college and earn his A.A. degree in medical assisting. This was a logical choice for Chang. His mother worked as a psychiatric nurse, and he'd always been interested in health care. He figured that his degree would equip him with marketable skills and a way to contribute to society.

Chang's choice paid off. He excelled in his classes. With his career goal in mind, he often asked himself: *How could I use this information to become a better medical assistant?*

During his second year of college, Chang landed an internship with a large medical clinic near campus. The clinic offered him a job after he graduated, and he accepted.

Chang enjoyed the day-to-day tasks of medical assisting. He helped doctors run medical tests and perform physical exams. In addition, he ordered lab work and updated medical records.

After three months on the job, Chang was on a first-name basis with many of the clinic's regular patients. No matter how busy the clinic's schedule, Chang made time for people. When

they finished describing their symptoms, he frequently asked, "Is there anything else that's on your mind?" Then he listened without interrupting. Chang's ability to put people at ease made him popular with patients, who often asked specifically to see him.

The only part of his job that Chang dreaded was performance reviews, which took place twice during each year of employment. Even though he was respected by coworkers, Chang felt nervous whenever the topic of evaluating work performance came up. "It just reminds me too much of final exams during school," he said. "I like my job and I try to do it well every day. Having a performance review just raises my anxiety level and doesn't really benefit me."

Reflecting on this scenario

Briefly describe three strategies from this chapter that Chang could use to change his experience of performance reviews. Be specific about how he could use each strategy.

Quiz

Name _____   Date ____/____/____

1. According to the text, test scores measure your intelligence. True or false? Explain your answer.

2. When answering multiple-choice questions, it is generally effective to read all of the possible answers before answering the question in your head. True or false? Explain your answer.

3. The presence of absolute qualifiers, such as *always* or *never,* generally indicates a false statement. True or false? Explain your answer.

4. Briefly explain the difference between a daily review and a major review.

5. Define the term *study checklist,* and give three examples of what to include on such checklists.

6. Describe how using the Power Process: "Detach" differs from giving up.

7. Study groups can focus on which of the following?
    (a) Comparing and editing class notes.
    (b) Doing research to prepare for papers and presentations.
    (c) Finding and understanding key passages in assigned readings.
    (d) Creating and taking practice tests.
    (e) All of the above.

8. Give an example of "changing your conversation" about learning math.

9. Describe three techniques for dealing with the thoughts connected to test anxiety.

10. Describe three techniques for dealing with the physical sensations or emotions connected to test anxiety.

Focus on Transferable Skills

Now that you've had some concrete experience with the strategies presented in this chapter, take a minute to reflect on your responses to the "Tests" section of the Discovery Wheel in Chapter 1: "First Steps." Think about your current skills in this area and plan to expand on them.

You might want to prepare for this exercise by reviewing the articles "Jumpstart Your Education with Transferable Skills" on page 58 and "101 Transferable Skills" on page 60.

PREPARING FOR TESTS

When studying for a test, the first thing I usually do is to . . .

In addition, I . . .

TAKING TESTS

One strategy that helps me with objective tests (true/false and multiple choice) is . . .

One strategy that helps me with short-answer and essay tests is . . .

MANAGING MY RESPONSE TO TESTS AND PERFORMANCE REVIEWS

On the day of a test, my level of confidence is generally . . .

For a performance review at work, my level of confidence is generally . . .

NEXT ACTION

The skill related to tests and performance reviews that I would most like to develop is . . .

To develop this skill, the most important thing I can do next is to . . .

Master Student PROFILE

Al Gore

. . . is optimistic

© Joseph Sohm/Visions
of America/Corbis

One hundred and nineteen years ago, a wealthy inventor read his own obituary, mistakenly published years before his death. Wrongly believing the inventor had just died, a newspaper printed a harsh judgment of his life's work, unfairly labeling him "The Merchant of Death" because of his invention—dynamite. Shaken by this condemnation, the inventor made a fateful choice to serve the cause of peace.

Seven years later, Alfred Nobel created this prize and the others that bear his name.

Seven years ago tomorrow, I read my own political obituary in a judgment that seemed to me harsh and mistaken—if not premature. But that unwelcome verdict also brought a precious if painful gift: an opportunity to search for fresh new ways to serve my purpose.

Unexpectedly, that quest has brought me here. Even though I fear my words cannot match this moment, I pray what I am feeling in my heart will be communicated clearly enough that those who hear me will say, "We must act." . . .

In the last few months, it has been harder and harder to misinterpret the signs that our world is spinning out of kilter. Major cities in North and South America, Asia and Australia are nearly out of water due to massive droughts and melting glaciers. Desperate farmers are losing their livelihoods. Peoples in the frozen Arctic and on low-lying Pacific islands are planning evacuations of places they have long called home. Unprecedented wildfires have forced a half million people from their homes in one country and caused a national emergency that almost brought down the government in another. Climate refugees have migrated into areas already inhabited by people with different cultures, religions, and traditions, increasing the potential for

conflict. Stronger storms in the Pacific and Atlantic have threatened whole cities. Millions have been displaced by massive flooding in South Asia, Mexico, and 18 countries in Africa. As temperature extremes have increased, tens of thousands have lost their lives. We are recklessly burning and clearing our forests and driving more and more species into extinction.

There is an African proverb that says, "If you want to go quickly, go alone. If you want to go far, go together." We need to go far, quickly. . . .

Fifteen years ago, I made that case at the "Earth Summit" in Rio de Janeiro. Ten years ago, I presented it in Kyoto. This week, I will urge the delegates in Bali to adopt a bold mandate for a treaty that establishes a universal global cap on emissions and uses the market in emissions trading to efficiently allocate resources to the most effective opportunities for speedy reductions.

This treaty should be ratified and brought into effect everywhere in the world by the beginning of 2010—two years sooner than presently contemplated. The pace of our response must be accelerated to match the accelerating pace of the crisis itself. . . .

The future is knocking at our door right now. Make no mistake, the next generation will ask us one of two questions. Either they will ask: "What were you thinking; why didn't you act?" Or they will ask instead: "How did you find the moral courage to rise and successfully resolve a crisis that so many said was impossible to solve?"

© The Nobel Foundation 2007. Reprinted with permission.

(1948–) Former vice president of the United States, Gore refocused his career on climate change, won a Nobel Peace Prize, and—in the film *An Inconvenient Truth*—invented a new type of documentary.

Learn more about Al Gore and other master students at the Master Student Hall of Fame.

8 Thinking

Master Student Map

as you read, ask yourself

what if . . .

I could solve problems more creatively and make decisions in every area of life with more confidence?

why this chapter matters . . .

The ability to think helps you succeed in school and promotes many skills that transfer to the workplace—including reading, writing, speaking, and listening

how

you can use this chapter . . .

- Learn to create and refine ideas.
- Choose attitudes that promote your success.
- Avoid common mistakes in thinking.
- Enhance your success in problem solving.
- Put your thinking skills to practical use in making decisions.

what is included . . .

MASTER EMPLOYEE in *action*

I am lucky to work for a company that actively encourages creativity. Although we are expected to fulfill all the responsibilities of our position, there is also time set aside during which we can pursue more free-thinking activities. I stay motivated by remembering that there is an outlet for my creativity and always come back to the more mundane tasks with a renewed energy.

—KATE CHIU, ASSOCIATE DIRECTOR OF COMMUNICATIONS

Photo courtesy of Kate Chiu

Critical thinking:
A survival skill

SOCIETY DEPENDS ON persuasion. Advertisers want us to spend money on their products. Political candidates want us to "buy" their stands on the issues. Teachers want us to agree that their classes are vital to our success. Parents want us to accept their values. Authors want us to read their books. Broadcasters want us to spend our time in front of the radio or television, consuming their programs and not those of the competition. The business of persuasion has an impact on all of us.

A typical American sees thousands of television commercials each year—and TV is just one medium of communication. Add to that the writers and speakers who enter our lives through radio shows, magazines, books, billboards, brochures, Internet sites, and fund-raising appeals—all with a product, service, cause, or opinion for us to embrace.

This flood of appeals leaves us with hundreds of choices about what to buy, where to go, and who to be. It's easy to lose our heads in the crosscurrent of competing ideas—unless we develop skills in critical thinking. When we think critically, we can make choices with open eyes.

Uses of critical thinking. *Critical thinking informs reading, writing, speaking, and listening.* These elements are the basis of communication—a process that occupies most of our waking hours.

Critical thinking promotes social change. The institutions in any society—courts, governments, schools, businesses, nonprofit groups—are the products of cultural customs and trends. All social movements—from the American Revolution to the Civil Rights movement—came about through the work of engaged individuals who actively participated in their communities and questioned what was going on around them. As critical thinkers, we strive to understand and influence the institutions in our society.

Critical thinking uncovers bias and prejudice. Working through our preconceived notions is a first step toward communicating with people of other races, ethnic backgrounds, and cultures.

Critical thinking reveals long-term consequences. Crises occur when our thinking fails to keep pace with reality. An example is the world's ecological crisis, which arose when people polluted the earth, air, and water without considering the long-term consequences.

Discovery/Intention Statement

Choose to create value from this chapter

Think back to a time when you felt unable to choose among several different solutions to a problem or several stands on a key issue in your life. In the following space, describe this experience.

I discovered that . . .

_____

_____

_____

Now scan this chapter to find useful suggestions for decision making, problem solving, and critical thinking. Note in the following space at least four techniques that look especially promising to you.

Strategy	Page number
_____	_____
_____	_____
_____	_____
_____	_____
_____	_____
_____	_____

Finally, declare your intention to explore these techniques in detail and apply them to a situation coming up during this term.

I intend to use critical thinking strategies to . . .

_____

_____

_____

_____

_____

_____

THINKING

8

Imagine how different our world would be if our leaders had thought like the first female chief of the Cherokees. Asked about the best advice her elders had given her, she replied, "Look forward. Turn what has been done into a better path. If you are a leader, think about the impact of your decision on seven generations into the future."

Critical thinking reveals nonsense. Novelist Ernest Hemingway once said that anyone who wants to be a great writer must have a built-in, shockproof "crap" detector.[1] That inelegant comment points to a basic truth: As critical thinkers, we are constantly on the lookout for thinking that's inaccurate, sloppy, or misleading.

Critical thinking is a skill that will never go out of style. At various times in human history, nonsense has been taken for the truth. For example, people have believed the following:

- Use of blood-sucking leeches is the only recommended treatment for disease.
- Illness results from an imbalance in the four vital fluids: blood, phlegm, water, and bile.
- Caucasians are inherently more intelligent than people of other races.
- Racial intermarriage will lead to genetically inferior children.
- Racial integration of the armed forces will lead to destruction of soldiers' morale.
- Women are incapable of voting intelligently.
- We will never invent anything smaller than a transistor. (That was before the computer chip.)
- Computer technology will usher in the age of the paperless office.

The critical thinkers of history arose to challenge short-sighted ideas such as those in the previous list. These courageous men and women pointed out that, metaphorically speaking, the emperor had no clothes.

Even in mathematics and the hard sciences, the greatest advances take place when people reexamine age-old beliefs. Scientists continually uncover things that contradict everyday certainties. For example, physics presents us with a world where solid objects are made of atoms spinning around in empty space, where matter and energy are two forms of the same substance. At a moment's notice, the world can deviate from the "laws of nature." That is because those "laws" exist in our heads, not in the world.

Critical thinking is a path to freedom from half-truths and deception. You have the right to question everything that you see, hear, and read. Acquiring this ability is a major goal of a liberal education.

Critical thinking as thorough thinking. For some people, the term *critical thinking* has negative connotations. If you prefer, use *thorough thinking* instead. Both terms point to the same activities: sorting out conflicting claims, weighing the evidence, letting go of personal biases, and arriving at reasonable conclusions. These activities add up to an ongoing conversation—a constant process, not a final product.

We live in a culture that values quick answers and certainty. These concepts are often at odds with effective thinking. Thorough thinking is the ability to examine and reexamine ideas that might seem obvious. This kind of thinking takes time and the willingness to say three subversive words: *I don't know.*

Thorough thinking is also the willingness to change our opinions as we continue to examine a problem. This calls for courage and detachment. Just ask anyone who has given up a cherished point of view in light of new evidence.

Thorough thinking is the basis for much of what you do in school—reading, writing, speaking, listening, note taking, test taking, problem solving, and other forms of decision making. Skilled students have strategies for accomplishing all of these tasks. They distinguish between opinion and fact. They ask probing questions and make detailed observations. They uncover assumptions and define their terms. They make assertions carefully, basing them on sound logic and solid evidence. Almost everything that we call *knowledge* is a result of these activities. This means that critical thinking and learning are intimately linked.

One kind of thorough thinking—planning—has the power to lift the quality of our lives almost immediately. When you plan, you are the equal of the greatest sculptor, painter, or playwright. More than creating a work of art, you are designing your life. *From Master Student to Master Employee* invites you to participate in this form of thinking by choosing your major, planning your career, and setting long-term goals.

It's been said that human beings are rational creatures. Yet no one is born a thorough thinker. Critical thinking is a learned skill. Use the suggestions in this chapter to claim the thinking powers that are your birthright. The critical thinker is one aspect of the master student who lives inside you. ✳

Becoming a critical thinker

Critical thinking is a path to intellectual adventure. Although there are dozens of possible approaches, the process boils down to asking and answering questions.

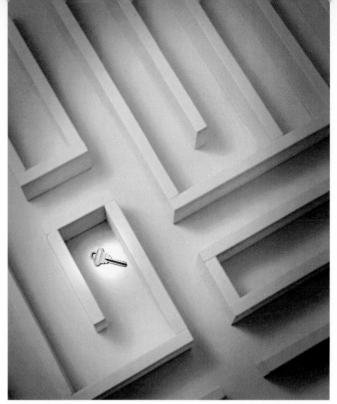
© Steve Cole/Getty

ACCORDING TO "Learning Styles: Discovering How You Learn" (p. 32) there are four modes of learning based on four questions: *Why? What? How?* and *What if?* These questions are also powerful guides to critical thinking. Following are a variety of tools for answering those questions. For more handy implements, see *Becoming a Critical Thinker* by Vincent Ryan Ruggiero.

1 **Why am I considering this issue?** Critical thinking and personal passion go together. Begin critical thinking with a question that matters to you. Seek a rationale for your learning. Understand why it is important for you to think about a specific topic. You might want to arrive at a new conclusion, make a prediction, or solve a problem. By finding a personal connection with an issue, your interest in acquiring and retaining new information increases.

2 **What are various points of view on this issue?** Imagine Karl Marx, Cesar Chavez, and Warren Buffett assembled in one room to choose the most desirable economic system. Picture Mahatma Gandhi, Nelson Mandela, and General George Patton lecturing at a United Nations conference on conflict resolution. Visualize Al Gore, Bill Gates, and Ban Ki-moon in a discussion about distributing the world's resources equitably. When seeking out alternative points of view, let such scenarios unfold in your mind.

Dozens of viewpoints exist on every important issue—reducing crime, ending world hunger, preventing war, educating our children, and countless other concerns. In fact, few problems have any single, permanent solution. Each generation produces its own answers to critical questions, based on current conditions. Our search for answers is a conversation that spans centuries. On each question, many voices are waiting to be heard.

You can take advantage of this diversity by seeking out alternative views with an open mind. When talking to another person, be willing to walk away with a new point of view—even if it's the one you brought to the table, but now supported with new evidence.

Examining different points of view is an exercise in analysis, which you can do with the suggestions that follow.

Define terms. Imagine a situation in which two people are arguing about whether an employer should limit health care benefits to members of a family. To one person, the word *family* means a mother, father, and children; to the other person, the word *family* applies to any individuals who live together in a long-term, supportive relationship. Chances are, the debate will go nowhere until these two people realize that they're defining the same word in different ways.

Conflicts of opinion can often be resolved—or at least clarified—when we define our key terms up front. This is especially true with abstract, emotion-laden terms such as *freedom, peace, progress,* or *justice.* Blood has been shed over the meaning of those words. Define them with care.

Look for assertions. Speakers and writers present their key terms in a larger context called an *assertion.* An assertion is a complete sentence that directly answers a key question. For example, consider this sentence from the article "The Master Student" in Chapter 1: "Mastery means attaining a level of skill that goes beyond technique." This sentence is an assertion that answers an important question: How do we recognize mastery?

8

THINKING

Look for at least three viewpoints. When asking questions, let go of the temptation to settle for just a single answer. Once you have come up with an answer, say to yourself, "Yes, that is one answer. Now what's another?" Using this approach can sustain honest inquiry, fuel creativity, and lead to conceptual breakthroughs. Be prepared: The world is complicated, and critical thinking is a complex business. Some of your answers might contradict others. Resist the temptation to have all of your ideas fit together in a neat, orderly bundle.

Practice tolerance. One path to critical thinking is tolerance for a wide range of opinions. Taking a position on important issues is natural. When we stop having an opinion on things, we've probably stopped breathing.

Problems occur when we become so attached to our current viewpoints that we refuse to consider alternatives. Many ideas that are widely accepted in Western cultures—for example, civil liberties for people of color and the rights of women to vote—once were considered dangerous. Viewpoints that seem outlandish today might become widely accepted a century, a decade, or even a year from now. Remembering this idea can help us practice tolerance for differing beliefs and, in doing so, make room for new ideas that might alter our lives.

3 How well is each point of view supported? Uncritical thinkers shield themselves from new information and ideas. As an alternative, you can follow the example of scientists, who constantly search for evidence that contradicts their theories. The following suggestions can help you do so.

Look for logic and evidence. The aim of using logic is to make statements that are clear, consistent, and coherent. As you examine a speaker's or writer's assertions, you might find errors in logic—assertions that contradict each other or assumptions that are unfounded.

Also assess the evidence used to support points of view. Evidence comes in several forms, including facts, expert testimony, and examples. To think critically about evidence, ask questions such as the following:

■ Are all or most of the relevant facts presented?

■ Are the facts consistent with one another?

■ Are facts presented accurately—or in a misleading way?

■ Are enough examples included to make a solid case for the viewpoint?

■ Do the examples truly support the viewpoint?

■ Are the examples typical? That is, could the author or speaker support the assertion with other examples that are similar?

■ Is the expert credible—in other words, is the expert truly knowledgeable about the topic?

Consider the source. Carefully consider that article on the problems of manufacturing cars powered by natural gas. It might have been written by an executive from an oil company. Check out the expert who disputes the connection between smoking and lung cancer. That "expert" might be the president of a tobacco company.

This is not to say that we should dismiss the ideas of people who have a vested interest in a topic or keep them from stating their opinions. Rather, we should take their self-interest into account as we consider their ideas.

Understand before criticizing. Polished debaters are good at summing up their opponents' viewpoints—in fact, they are often better than the people who support those viewpoints themselves. Likewise, critical thinkers take the time to understand a statement of opinion before agreeing or disagreeing with it.

Effective understanding calls for listening without judgment. Enter another person's world by expressing her viewpoint in your own words. If you're conversing with that person, keep revising your summary until she agrees that you've stated her position accurately. If you're reading an article, write a short summary of it. Then scan the article again, checking to see if your synopsis is on target.

Watch for hot spots. Many people have mental "hot spots"—topics that provoke strong opinions and feelings. Examples are abortion, homosexuality, gun control, and the death penalty.

To become more skilled at examining various points of view, notice your own particular hot spots. Make a clear intention to accept your feelings about these topics and to continue using critical thinking techniques in relation to them.

One way to cool down our hot spots is to remember that we can change—or even give up—our current opinions without giving up ourselves. That's a key message behind the Power Processes: "Ideas Are Tools" and "Detach." These articles remind us that human beings are much more than the sum of their current opinions.

Be willing to be uncertain. Some of the most profound thinkers have practiced the art of thinking by using a magic sentence: "I'm not sure yet."

THINKING

8

Those are words that many people do not like to hear. Our society rewards quick answers and quotable sound bites. We're under considerable pressure to utter the truth in 10 seconds or less.

In such a society, it is courageous and unusual to take the time to pause, to look, to examine, to be thoughtful, to consider many points of view—and to be unsure. A society that adopts half-truths in a blind rush for certainty is likely to falter. A willingness to embrace uncertainty can move us forward.

4 What if I could combine various points of view or create a new one? The search for truth is like painting a barn door by tossing an open can of paint at it. Few people who throw paint at the door miss it entirely. Yet no one can cover the whole door in a single toss.

People who express a viewpoint are seeking the truth. No reasonable person claims to understand the whole truth about anything. Instead, each viewpoint can be seen as one approach among many possible alternatives. If you don't think that any one opinion is complete, combine different perspectives on the issue. Experiment with the following strategies.

Create a critical thinking "spreadsheet." When you consult authorities with different stands on an issue, you might feel confused about how to sort, evaluate, and combine their points of view. To overcome confusion, create a critical thinking "spreadsheet." List the authorities (and yourself) across the top of a page and key questions down the left side. Then indicate each authority's answer to each question, along with your own answers.

For example, the following spreadsheet clarifies different points of view on the issue of whether to outlaw boxing.

You could state your own viewpoint by combining your answers to the questions in the previous spreadsheet: "I favor legalized boxing. Although boxing poses dangers, so do other sports. And like other sports, the risk of injury can be reduced when boxers get proper training."

Write about it. Thoughts can move at blinding speed. Writing slows down that process. Gaps in logic that slip by us in thought or speech are often exposed when we commit the same ideas to paper. Writing down our thoughts allows us to compare, contrast, and combine points of view more clearly—and therefore to think more thoroughly.

Accept your changing perspectives. Researcher William Perry found that students in higher education move through stages of intellectual development.[2] In earlier stages, students tend to think there is only one correct viewpoint on each issue, and they look to their instructors to reveal that truth. Later, students acknowledge a variety of opinions on issues and construct their own viewpoints.

Monitor changes in your thinking processes as you combine viewpoints. Distinguish between opinions that you accept from authorities and opinions that are based on your own use of logic and your search for evidence. Also look for opinions that result from objective procedures (such as using the *Why? What? How?* and *What if?* questions in this article) and personal sources (using intuition or "gut feelings").

Remember that the process of becoming a critical thinker will take you through a variety of stages. Give yourself time, and celebrate your growing mastery. ✳

 Find more strategies for becoming a critical thinker online.

	Medical doctor	Former boxer	Sports journalist	Me
Is boxing a sport?	No	Yes	Yes	Yes
Is boxing dangerous?	Yes	Yes	Yes	Yes
Is boxing more dangerous than other sports?	Yes	No	Yes	No
Can the risk of injury be overcome by proper training?	No	No	No	Yes

THINKING

8

Attitudes, affirmations, and visualizations

"I HAVE A BAD ATTITUDE." Some of us say this as if we were talking about having the flu. An attitude is certainly as strong as the flu, but it isn't something we have to succumb to or accept.

Attitudes are powerful. They mold behavior. If your attitude is that you're not interesting at a party, then your behavior will probably match your attitude. If your attitude is that you are fun at a party, then your behavior is more likely to be playful.

Visible measures of success—such as top grades and résumés filled with accomplishments—start with invisible assets called attitudes. Some attitudes will help you benefit from all the money and time you invest in higher education. Other attitudes will render your investment worthless.

You can change your attitudes through regular practice with affirmations and visualizations.

Affirm it. An affirmation is a statement describing what you want. The most effective affirmations are personal, positive, and written in the present tense.

To use affirmations, first determine what you want; then describe yourself as if you already have it. To get what you want from your education, you could write, "I, Malika Jones, am a master student. I take full responsibility for my education. I learn with joy, and I use my experiences in each course to create the life that I want."

If you decide that you want a wonderful job, you might write, "I, Peter Webster, have a wonderful job. I respect and love my colleagues, and they feel the same way about me. I look forward to going to work each day."

Effective affirmations include detail. Use brand names, people's names, and your own name. Involve all of your senses—sight, sound, smell, taste, and touch. Take a positive approach. Instead of saying, "I am not fat," say, "I am slender."

Once you have written an affirmation, repeat it. Practice saying it out loud several times a day. Do this at a regular time, such as just before you go to sleep or just after you wake up. Sit in a chair in a relaxed position. Take a few deep and relaxing breaths, and then repeat your affirmation with emotion. It's also effective to look in a mirror while saying the affirmation. Keep looking and repeating until you are saying your affirmation with conviction.

Attitude replacements

You can use affirmations to replace a negative attitude with a positive one. There are no limitations, other than your imagination and your willingness to practice. Here are some sample affirmations. Modify them to suit your individual hopes and dreams, and then practice them.

- I, _____, have abundant energy and vitality throughout the day.
- I, _____, exercise regularly.
- I, _____, work effectively with many different kinds of people.
- I, _____, eat wisely.
- I, _____, plan my days and use time wisely.
- I, _____, have a powerful memory.

- I, _____, take tests calmly and confidently.
- I, _____, fall asleep quickly and sleep soundly.
- I, _____, have relationships that are mutually satisfying.
- I, _____, contribute to other people through my job.
- I, _____, know ways to play and have fun.
- I, _____, focus my attention easily.
- I, _____, like myself.
- I, _____, have an income that far exceeds my expenses.
- I, _____, live my life in positive ways for the highest good of all people.

Visualize it. You can improve your golf swing, tennis serve, or batting average while lying in bed. You can become a better driver, speaker, or cook while sitting silently in a chair. While you're in line at the grocery store, you can improve your ability to type or to take tests. This is all possible through visualization—the technique of seeing yourself being successful.

Here's one way to begin. Choose what you want to improve. Then describe in writing what it would look like, sound like, and feel like to have that improvement in your life. If you are learning to play the piano, write down briefly what you would see, hear, and feel if you were playing skillfully. If you want to improve your relationships with your children, write down what you would see, hear, and feel if you were communicating with them successfully.

Practice at least once a day. Once you have a sketch of what it would be like to be successful, practice it in your imagination. Whenever you shoot the basketball, it swishes through the net. Every time you invite someone out on a date, the person says yes. Each test the teacher hands back to you is graded an A. Practice at least once a day. Then wait for the results to unfold in your life.

You can also use visualizations to replay errors. When you make a mistake, replay it in your imagination. After a bad golf shot, stop and imagine yourself making that same shot again, this time successfully. If you just had a discussion with your roommate that turned into a fight, replay it successfully.

Visualizations and affirmations can restructure your attitudes and behaviors. Be clear about what you want—and then practice it. ✳

Attitudes of a critical thinker

The American Philosophical Association invited a panel of 46 scholars from the United States and Canada to come up with answers to the following two questions: "What is college-level critical thinking?" and "What leads us to conclude that a person is an effective critical thinker?"[3] After two years of work, this panel concluded that critical thinkers share the attitudes summarized in the following chart.

Attitude	Sample statement
Truth seeking	"Let's follow this idea and see where it leads, even if we feel uncomfortable with what we find out."
Open minded	"I have a point of view on this subject, and I'm anxious to hear yours as well."
Analytical	"Taking a stand on the issue commits me to take some new action."
Systematic	"The speaker made several interesting points, and I'd like to hear some more evidence to support each one."
Self-confident	"After reading the book for the first time, I was confused. I'll be able to understand it after studying the book some more."
Inquisitive	"When I first saw that painting, I wanted to know what was going on in the artist's life when she painted it."
Mature	"I'll wait until I gather some more facts before reaching a conclusion on this issue."

8

THINKING

critical thinking exercise

26 Reprogram your attitude

Affirmations and visualizations can be used to successfully reprogram your attitudes and behaviors. Use this exercise to change your approach to any situation in your life.

Step 1

Pick something in your life that you would like to change. It can be related to anything—relationships, work, money, or personal skills. In the following space, write a brief description of what you choose to change.

_____

_____

_____

_____

_____

_____

_____

_____

_____

Step 2

Add more details about the change you described in Step 1. Write down how you would like the change to come about. Be outlandish. Imagine that you are about to ask your fairy godmother for a wish that you know she will grant. Be detailed in your description of your wish.

_____

_____

_____

_____

_____

_____

_____

_____

_____

Step 3

Here comes the fairy godmother. Use affirmations and visualizations to start yourself on the path to creating exactly what you wrote about in Step 2. In the following space, write at least two affirmations that describe your dream wish. Also, briefly outline a visualization that you can use to picture your wish. Be specific, detailed, and positive.

_____

_____

_____

_____

_____

_____

_____

_____

_____

Step 4

Put your new attitudes to work. Set up a schedule to practice them. Let the first time you practice be right now. Then set up at least five other times and places where you intend to practice your affirmations and visualizations.

I intend to relax and practice my affirmations and visualizations for at least 5 minutes on the following dates and at the time(s) and location(s) given.

	Date	Time	Location
1.			
2.			
3.			
4.			
5.			

 Complete this exercise online.

THINKING

8

Ways to create ideas

CREATIVE THINKING can give you an edge in the job market. In the face of global competition, employers are looking for people who can create new products, develop new services, and think in fresh ways about what customers and clients want.

Anyone can think creatively. Use the following techniques to generate ideas about anything—whether you're studying math problems, remodeling a house, or writing a best seller.

Conduct a brainstorm

Brainstorming is a technique for creating plans, finding solutions, and discovering new ideas. When you are stuck on a problem, brainstorming can break the logjam. For example, if you run out of money two days before payday every week, you can brainstorm ways to make your money last longer. You can brainstorm ways to pay for your education. You can brainstorm ways to find a job.

The overall purpose of brainstorming is to generate as many solutions as possible. Sometimes the craziest, most outlandish ideas, while unworkable in themselves, can lead to new ways to solve problems. Use the following steps to try out the brainstorming process:

- *Focus on a single problem or issue.* State your focus as a question. Open-ended questions that start with the words *what, how, who, where*, and *when* often make effective focusing questions.

- *Relax.* Creativity is enhanced by a state of relaxed alertness. If you are tense or anxious, use relaxation techniques such as those described in "Let Go of Test Anxiety" in Chapter 7: "Tests."

- *Set a quota or goal for the number of solutions you want to generate.* Goals give your subconscious mind something to aim for.

(woman) Floresco Productions/OJO Images/Getty, (words) Shutterstock

- *Set a time limit.* Use a clock to time your brainstorming session to the minute. Digital sports watches with built-in stopwatches work well. Experiment with various lengths of time. Both short and long brainstorms can be powerful.

- *Allow all answers.* Brainstorming is based on attitudes of permissiveness and patience. Accept every idea. If it pops into your head, put it down on paper. Quantity, not quality, is the goal. Avoid making judgments and evaluations during the brainstorming session. If you get stuck, think of an outlandish idea, and write it down. One crazy idea can unleash a flood of other, more workable solutions.

- *Brainstorm with others.* Group brainstorming is a powerful technique. Group brainstorms take on lives of their own. Assign one member of the group to write down solutions. Feed off the ideas of others, and remember to avoid evaluating or judging anyone's ideas during the brainstorm.

Focus and let go

Focusing and letting go are alternating parts of the same process. Intense focus taps the resources of your conscious mind. Letting go gives your subconscious mind time to work. When you focus for intense periods and then let go for a while, the conscious and subconscious parts of your brain work in harmony.

Focusing attention means being in the here and now. To focus your attention on a project, notice when you pay attention and when your mind starts to wander. Be sure to involve all of your senses. For example, if you are having difficulty writing a paper at a computer, practice focusing by listening to the sounds as you type. Notice the feel of the keys as you strike them. When you know the sights, sounds, and sensations you associate with being truly in focus, you'll be able to repeat the experience and return to your paper more easily.

Be willing to recognize conflict, tension, and discomfort in yourself. Notice them and fully accept them rather than fight against them. Look for the specific thoughts and body sensations that make up the discomfort. Allow them to come fully into your awareness, and then let them pass.

You might not be focused all of the time. Periods of inspiration might last only seconds. Be gentle with yourself when you notice that your concentration has lapsed. In fact, that might be a time to let go. *Letting go* means not forcing yourself to be creative. Practice focusing for short periods at first, and then give yourself a break. Take a nap when you are tired. Thomas Edison took frequent naps. Then the light bulb clicked on.

Cultivate creative serendipity

The word *serendipity* was coined by the English author Horace Walpole from the title of an ancient Persian fairy tale, "The Three Princes of Serendip." The princes had a knack for making lucky discoveries. Serendipity is that knack, and it involves more than luck. It is the ability to see something valuable that you weren't looking for.

History is full of people who make serendipitous discoveries. Country doctor Edward Jenner noticed "by accident" that milkmaids seldom got smallpox. As a result, he discovered that mild cases of cowpox immunized them. Penicillin was also discovered "by accident." Scottish scientist Alexander Fleming was growing bacteria in a laboratory petri dish. A spore of *Penicillium notatum,* a kind of mold, blew in the window and landed in the dish, killing the bacteria. Fleming isolated the active ingredient. A few years later,

during World War II, penicillin saved thousands of lives. Had Fleming not been alert to the possibility, the discovery might never have been made.

You can train yourself in the art of serendipity. Keep your eyes open. You might find a solution to an accounting problem in a Saturday morning cartoon. You might discover a topic for your term paper at the corner convenience store. Multiply your contacts with the world. Resolve to meet new people. Join a study or discussion group. Read. Go to plays, concerts, art shows, lectures, and movies. Watch television programs you normally wouldn't watch.

Also expect discoveries. One secret for success is being prepared to recognize "luck" when you see it.

Keep idea files

We all have ideas. People who treat their ideas with care are often labeled "creative." They recognize ideas, record them, *and* follow up on them.

Safeguard your ideas when they occur to you, even if you're pressed for time. One method is to write them down on 3×5 cards. Jotting down four or five words is often enough to capture the essence of an idea. If you carry 3×5 cards in a pocket or purse, you can record ideas while standing in line or sitting in a waiting room.

You can also use digital tools to capture ideas. Google Notebook, Zoho Notebook, and similar applications allow you to "clip" images and text from various Web pages, categorize all this content, and add your own notes. Personal information managers such as Evernote and Yojimbo serve a similar purpose. Some of them allow you to add "offline" content, such as digital photos of business cards and receipts. You can search through all this content by using tags and keywords.

No matter what method you use, collect powerful quotations, random insights, notes on your reading, and useful ideas that you encounter in class. Collect jokes, too.

27 **critical thinking exercise**
Fix-the-world brainstorm

This exercise works well with four to six people. Pick a major world problem such as hunger, nuclear proliferation, poverty, terrorism, overpopulation, or pollution. Then conduct a 10-minute brainstorm about the steps an individual could take to contribute to solving the problem.

Use the brainstorming techniques explained earlier in this chapter. Remember not to evaluate or judge the solutions

during the process. The purpose of a brainstorm is to generate a flow of ideas and record them all.

After the brainstorming session, discuss the process and the solutions that it generated. Did you feel any energy from the group? Was a long list of ideas generated? Are several of them worth pursuing?

Keep a journal. It doesn't have to be exclusively about your own thoughts and feelings. You can record observations about the world around you, conversations with friends, important or offbeat ideas—anything.

To fuel your creativity, read voraciously, including newspapers and magazines. Keep a clip file of interesting articles. Explore beyond mainstream journalism. There are hundreds of low-circulation specialty magazines and online news journals that cover almost any subject you can imagine.

Review your files regularly. Some amusing thought that came to you in November might be the perfect solution to a problem in March.

Collect and play with data

Look from all sides at the data you collect. Switch your attention from one aspect to another. Examine each fact, and avoid getting stuck on one particular part of a problem. Turn a problem upside down by picking a solution first and then working backward. Ask other people to look at the data. Solicit opinions.

Living with the problem invites a solution. Write down data, possible solutions, or a formulation of the problem on 3×5 cards and carry them with you. Look at them before you go to bed at night. Review them when you are waiting for the bus. Make them part of your life, and think about them frequently.

Look for the obvious solutions or the obvious "truths" about the problem—then toss them out. Ask yourself, "Well, I know X is true, but if X were *not* true, what would happen?" Or ask the reverse: "If that *were* true, what would follow next?"

Put unrelated facts next to each other and invent a relationship between them, even if it seems absurd at first. In *The Act of Creation,* novelist Arthur Koestler says that finding a context in which to combine opposites is the essence of creativity.[4]

Make imaginary pictures with the data. Condense it. Categorize it. Put it in chronological order. Put it in alphabetical order. Put it in random order. Order it from most to least complex. Reverse all of those orders. Look for opposites.

It has been said that there are no new ideas—only new ways to combine old ideas. Creativity is the ability to discover those new combinations.

Create while you sleep

A part of our mind works as we sleep. You've experienced this fact directly if you've ever fallen asleep with a problem on your mind and awakened the next morning with a solution. For some of us, the solution appears in a dream or just before we fall asleep or wake up.

You can experiment with this process. Ask yourself a question as you fall asleep. Keep pencil and paper or a recorder near your bed. The moment you wake up, begin writing or speaking, and see if an answer to your question emerges.

Refine ideas and follow through

Many of us ignore the part of the creative process that involves refining ideas and following through. How many great moneymaking schemes have we had that we never pursued? How many good ideas have we had for short stories that we never wrote? How many times have we said to ourselves, "You know, what they ought to do is attach two handles to one of those things, paint it orange, and sell it to police departments. They'd make a fortune." The thing is, we never realize that we are "they."

One powerful tool you can use to follow through is the Discovery and Intention Journal Entry system. First write down your idea in a Discovery Statement, and then write what you intend to do about it in an Intention Statement. Genius resides in the follow through—the application of perspiration to inspiration. ✳

Discovering assumptions

Our thinking and behavior are guided by assumptions. These are often invisible, powerful, and unconscious. People can remain unaware of their most basic and far-reaching assumptions—the very ideas that shape their lives.

ASSUMPTIONS CAN EVEN BE embedded in physical spaces. For example, go into any large lecture hall and take a look around. You'll probably see row after row of seats that face a lectern or platform in front of the room. This layout is based on some assumptions, such as:

Learning takes place in large groups.

Learning happens when one person does most of the talking and everyone else listens.

People learn best when they are sitting down.

Learning takes place in a quiet, private space rather than a busy, public space such as a workplace.

Spotting assumptions can be tricky. They are usually unstated and offered without evidence. In addition, we can hold many assumptions at the same time.

Assumptions might even contradict each other, resulting in muddled thinking and confused behavior. This makes uncovering assumptions a feat worthy of the greatest detective.

Assumptions can undermine us

Letting assumptions remain in our subconscious can erect barriers to our success. Take the person who says, "I don't worry about saving money for the future. I think life is meant to be enjoyed today—not later." This statement rests on at least two assumptions: *saving money is not enjoyable* and *we can enjoy ourselves only when we're spending money.*

It would be no surprise to find out that this person runs out of money near the end of each month and depends on cash advances from high-interest credit cards. He is shielding himself from some ideas that could actually help to erase his debt: Saving money can be a source of satisfaction, and many enjoyable activities cost nothing.

The stakes in uncovering assumptions are high. Prejudice thrives on the beliefs that certain people are inferior or dangerous due to their skin color, ethnic background, or sexual orientation. Those beliefs have led to flawed assumptions such as *mixing the blood of the races will lead to genetically inferior offspring* and *opening the armed forces to gay and lesbian people will destroy morale.*

When we remain ignorant of our assumptions, we also make it easier for people with hidden agendas to do our thinking for us. Demagogues and unethical advertisers know that unchallenged assumptions are potent tools for influencing our attitudes and behavior.

Assumptions can create conflict

Heated conflict and hard feelings often result when people argue on the level of opinions—forgetting that the real conflict lies at the level of their assumptions.

An example is the question about whether the government should fund public works programs that create jobs during a recession. People who advocate such programs might assume that creating such jobs is an appropriate task for the federal government. In contrast, people who argue against such programs might assume that the government has no business interfering with the free workings of the economy. There's little hope of resolving this conflict of opinion unless we deal with something more basic: our assumptions about the proper role of government.

Look for assumptions

In summary, you can follow a three-step method for testing the validity of any viewpoint:

1. Look for the assumptions—the assertions implied by that viewpoint.

2. Write down these assumptions.

3. See if you can find exceptions to any of the assumptions.

This technique helps detect many errors in logic. Use these three steps to liberate yourself from half-truths, think more powerfully, and create new possibilities for your life. ✳

Ways to fool yourself: Common mistakes in logic

Rich Reed/National Geographic/Getty

EFFECTIVE REASONING IS NOT JUST an idle pastime for unemployed philosophers. When you think logically, you take your reading, writing, speaking, and listening skills to a higher level.

Over the last 2,500 years, specialists have listed some classic land mines in the field of logic—common mistakes in thinking that are called *fallacies*. The following examples will help you in understanding fallacies.

Jumping to conclusions. Jumping to conclusions is the only exercise that some lazy thinkers get. This fallacy involves drawing conclusions without sufficient evidence. Take the bank officer who hears that a student failed to pay back an education loan. After that, the officer turns down all loan applications from students. This person has formed a rigid opinion on the basis of hearsay. Jumping to conclusions—also called *hasty generalization*—is at work here.

Following are more examples of this fallacy:

- *When I went to Mexico for spring break, I felt sick the whole time. Mexican food makes people sick.*
- *Google's mission is to "organize the world's information." Their employees must be on a real power trip.*
- *During a recession, more people go to the movies. People just want to sit in the dark and forget about their money problems.*

Each item in this list includes two statements, and the second statement does not necessarily follow from the first. More evidence is needed to make any possible connection.

Attacking the person. People who indulge in personal attacks are attempting an intellectual sleight of hand to divert our attention away from the truly relevant issues. The mistake of attacking the person is common at election time. An example is the candidate who claims that her opponent has failed to attend church regularly during the campaign.

Appealing to authority. A professional athlete endorses a brand of breakfast cereal. A famous musician features a soft drink company's product in a music video. The promotional brochure for an advertising agency lists all of the large companies that have used its services.

In each case, the people involved are trying to win your confidence—and your dollars—by citing authorities. The underlying assumption is usually this: *Famous people and organizations use our product. Therefore, you should use it, too.* Or: *You should accept this idea merely because someone who's well known says it's true.*

Appealing to authority is usually a substitute for producing real evidence. It invites sloppy thinking. When our only evidence for a viewpoint is an appeal to authority, it's time to think more thoroughly.

Pointing to a false cause. The fact that one event follows another does not necessarily mean that the two events have a cause-and-effect relationship. All we can accurately say is that the events might be correlated. For example, as children's vocabularies improve, they tend to get more cavities. This does not mean that cavities are the result of an improved vocabulary. Instead, the increase in cavities is due to other factors, such as physical maturation and changes in diet or personal care.

Thinking in all-or-nothing terms. Consider these statements: *Doctors are greedy. . . . You can't trust politicians. . . . Students these days are in school just to get high-paying jobs; they lack ideals. . . . Homeless people* *don't want to work.* These opinions imply the word *all.* They gloss over individual differences, claiming that all members of a group are exactly alike. They also ignore key facts—for instance, that some doctors volunteer their time at free medical clinics and that many homeless people are children who are too young to work. All-or-nothing thinking is one of the most common errors in logic.

Basing arguments on emotion. The politician who ends every campaign speech with flag waving and slides of his mother eating apple pie is staking his future on appeals to emotion. So is the candidate who paints a grim scenario of the disaster and ruination that will transpire unless she is elected. Get past the fluff and histrionics to see if you can uncover any worthwhile ideas.

Creating a straw man. The name of this fallacy comes from the scarecrows traditionally placed in gardens to ward off birds. A scarecrow works because it looks like a man. Likewise, a person can attack ideas that sound *like* his opponent's ideas but are actually absurd. For example, some legislators attacked the Equal Rights Amendment by describing it as a measure to abolish separate bathrooms for men and women. In fact, supporters of this amendment proposed no such thing.

Begging the question. Speakers and writers beg the question when their colorful language glosses over an idea that is unclear or unproven. Consider this statement: *Support the American tradition of individual liberty and oppose mandatory seat belt laws!* Anyone who makes such a statement "begs" (fails to answer) a key question: Are laws that require drivers to use seat belts actually a violation of individual liberty?

Creating a red herring. When hunters want to throw a dog off a trail, they can drag a smoked red herring (or some other food with a strong odor) over the ground in the opposite direction. This distracts the dog, who is fooled into following a false trail. Likewise, people can send our thinking on false trails by raising irrelevant issues. Case in point: Some people who opposed a presidential campaign by U.S. Senator Barack Obama emphasized his middle name: Hussein. This was an irrelevant attempt to link the senator to Saddam Hussein, the dictator and former ruler of Iraq.

Appealing to tradition. Arguments based on an appeal to tradition take a classic form: *Our current beliefs and behaviors have a long history; therefore, they are correct.* This argument has been used to justify the divine right of kings, feudalism, witch burnings, slavery, child labor, and a host of other traditions that are now rejected in most parts of the world. Appeals to tradition ignore the fact that unsound ideas can survive for centuries before human beings realize that they are being fooled.

Sliding a slippery slope. The fallacy of sliding a slippery slope implies that if one undesired event occurs, then other, far more serious events will follow: *If we restrict our right to own guns, then all of our rights will soon be taken away. . . . If people keep downloading music for free, pretty soon they'll demand to get everything online for free. . . . I notice that more independent bookstores are closing; it's just a matter of time before people stop reading.* When people slide a slippery slope, they assume that different types of events have a single cause. They also assume that a particular cause will operate indefinitely. In reality, the world is far more complex. Grand predictions about the future often turn out to be wrong. ✳

 Practice hunting for fallacies online.

28 critical thinking exercise
Explore emotional reactions

Each of us has certain "hot spots"—issues that trigger strong emotional reactions. These topics may include abortion, gay and lesbian rights, capital punishment, and funding for welfare programs. There are many other examples, varying from person to person.

Examine your own hot spots on a separate sheet of paper by writing a word or short phrase summarizing each issue about which you feel very strongly. Then describe what you typically say or do when each issue comes up in conversation.

After you have completed your list, think about what you can do to become a more effective thinker when you encounter one of these issues. For example, you could breathe deeply and count to five before you offer your own point of view. Or you might preface your opinion by saying, "There are many valid points of view on this issue. Here's the way I see it, and I'm open to your ideas."

Think critically about information on the Internet

SOURCES OF INFORMATION on the Internet range from the reputable (such as the Library of Congress) to the flamboyant (such as the *National Enquirer*). This fact underscores the need for thinking critically about everything you see online. Taking a few simple precautions when you surf the Net can keep you from crashing onto the rocky shore of misinformation.

Look for overall quality. Examine the features of the Web site in general. Notice the effectiveness of the text and visuals as a whole. Also note how well the site is organized and whether you can navigate the site's features with ease.

Look for the date that crucial information was posted, and determine how often the site is updated. Check individual pages for revision dates and notice how recent they are. If you're looking for facts, then avoid undated sources of information.

Next, take a more detailed look at the site's content. Examine several of the site's pages, and look for consistency of facts, quality of information, and competency with grammar and spelling. See whether links within the site are easy to navigate.

In addition, evaluate the site's links to related Web pages. Look for links to pages of reputable organizations. Click on a few of those links. If they lead you to dead ends, it might indicate that the site you're evaluating is not updated often—a clue that it's not a reliable source for current information.

Look at the source. Think about the credibility of the person or organization that posts the Web site. Look for a list of author credentials and publications. Go to **Amazon.com** and the Library of Congress (**catalog.loc .gov**) to see if the author has published other works.

Notice if the site shows any evidence of bias or special interest. Perhaps the site's sponsoring organization wants you to buy a service, a product, or a point of view. This fact might suggest that the information on the site is not objective, and therefore is questionable.

The domain in the uniform resource locator (URL) for a Web site can give you clues about sources of information and possible bias. For example, distinguish among information from a for-profit commercial enterprise (URL ending in .com); a nonprofit organization (.org); a government agency (.gov); and a school, college, or university (.edu).

Note: Wikis (peer-edited sites) such as Wikipedia do not employ editors to screen out errors or scrutinize questionable material before publication. Do not use these sites when researching a paper or presentation.

Also, be cautious about citing blogs. Blog authors might not review their posts for accuracy or base articles on careful research.

Look for documentation. When you encounter an assertion on a Web page or some other Internet resource, note the types and quality of the evidence offered. Look for credible examples, quotations from authorities in the field, documented statistics, or summaries of scientific studies. ✳

29 critical thinking exercise
Evaluate search sites

Access several popular search sites on the Web, such as:

Alta Vista	**www.altavista.com**
Ask.com	**www.ask.com**
Bing	**www.bing.com**
Dogpile	**www.dogpile.com**
Excite	**www.excite.com**
Google	**www.google.com**
HotBot	**www.hotbot.com**
Yahoo!	**www.yahoo.com**

Find more options by entering the keywords *search engines* into any of the sites mentioned in the list.

Next, choose a specific topic that you'd like to research—preferably one related to a paper or other assignment that you will complete this term. Identify keywords for this topic and enter them in several search sites. (Open up a different window or tab in your browser for each site.) Be sure to use the same keywords each time that you search.

Finally, evaluate the search sites by comparing the results that you get. Based on this evaluation, keep a list of your favorite search sites.

Overcome stereotypes with critical thinking

CONSIDER ASSERTIONS SUCH AS THESE: "College students like to drink heavily," and "Americans who criticize the president are unpatriotic."

These assertions are examples of stereotyping—generalizing about a group of people based on the behavior of isolated group members. When we stereotype, we gloss over individual differences and assume that every member of a group is the same. Generalizations that divide the people of the world into "us" versus "them" are often based on prejudice. You can take several steps to free yourself from such stereotypes.

Look for errors in thinking. Some of the most common errors in thinking are the following:

- *Selective perception.* Stereotypes can literally change the way we see the world. If we assume that homeless people are lazy, for instance, we tend to notice only the examples that support our opinion. Stories about homeless people who are too young or too ill to work will probably escape our attention.

- *Self-fulfilling prophecy.* When we interact with people based on stereotypes, we set them up in ways that confirm our thinking. For example, when people of color were denied access to higher education based on stereotypes about their intelligence, they were deprived of opportunities to demonstrate their intellectual gifts.

Create categories in a more flexible way. Stereotyping has been described as a case of "hardening of the categories." Avoid this problem by making your categories broader. Instead of seeing people based on their skin color, you could look at them on the basis of their heredity. (People of all races share most of the same genes.) Or you could make your categories narrower. Instead of talking about "religious extremists," look for subgroups among the people who adopt a certain religion. Distinguish between groups that advocate violence and those that shun it.

Test your generalizations about people through action. You can test your generalizations by actually meeting people of other cultures. It's easy to believe almost anything about certain groups of people as long as we never deal directly with individuals. Inaccurate pictures tend to die when people from different cultures study together, work together, and live together.

Be willing to see your own stereotypes. The Power Process: "Notice Your Pictures and Let Them Go" can help you see your own stereotypes. One belief about yourself that you can shed is *I have no pictures about people from other cultures.* Even people with the best of intentions can harbor subtle biases. Admitting this possibility allows you to look inward even more deeply for stereotypes. Every time we notice an inaccurate picture buried in our mind and let it go, we take a personal step toward embracing diversity. ✳

critical thinking exercise
Examine assumptions about diversity

On a separate sheet of paper, write down the first words that come to mind when you hear the terms in the following list. Do this now.

Musician

Homeless people

Football players

Computer programmers

Disabled person

Retired person

Adult learner

Next, exchange your responses to this exercise with a friend. Did you discover stereotypes or other examples of bias? What counts as evidence of this bias? Summarize your answers on a separate sheet of paper.

Gaining skill at *decision making*

WE MAKE DECISIONS ALL THE TIME, whether we realize it or not. Even avoiding decisions is a form of decision making. The student who puts off studying for a test until the last minute might really be saying, "I've decided this course is not important" or "I've decided not to give this course much time." In order to better understand the decision-making process, decide right now to experiment with the following suggestions.

Recognize decisions. Decisions are more than wishes or desires. There's a world of difference between "I wish I could be a better student" and "I will take more powerful notes, read with greater retention, and review my class notes daily." Decisions are specific and lead to focused action. When we decide, we narrow down. We give up actions that are inconsistent with our decision. Deciding to eat fruit for dessert instead of ice cream rules out the next trip to the ice cream store.

Establish priorities. Some decisions are trivial. No matter what the outcome, your life is not affected much. Other decisions can shape your circumstances for years. Devote more time and energy to the decisions with big outcomes.

Base your decisions on a life plan. The benefit of having long-term goals for our lives is that they provide a basis for many of our daily decisions. Being certain about what we want to accomplish this year and this month makes today's choices clearer.

Balance learning styles in decision making. To make decisions more effectively, use all four modes of learning explained in Chapter 1: "First Steps." The key is to balance reflection with action, and balance thinking with experience. First, take the time to think creatively and generate many options. Then think critically about the possible consequences of each option before choosing one. Remember, however, that thinking is no substitute for experience. Act on your chosen option, and notice what happens. If you're not getting the results that you want, then quickly return to creative thinking to invent new options.

Choose an overall strategy. Every time you make a decision, you choose a strategy, even when you're not aware of it. Effective decision makers can articulate and choose from among several strategies. For example:

- *Find all of the available options, and choose one deliberately.* Save this strategy for times when you have a relatively small number of options, each of which leads to noticeably different results.

- *Find all of the available options, and choose one randomly.* This strategy can be risky. Save it for times when your options are basically similar and fairness is the main issue.

- *Limit the options, and then choose.* This strategy works best when the number of options is overwhelming. For example, when deciding which search engine to use on the World Wide Web, visit many sites and then narrow the list down to two or three that you choose.

Use time as an ally. Sometimes we face dilemmas—situations in which any course of action leads to undesirable consequences. In such cases, consider putting a decision on hold. Wait it out. Do nothing until the circumstances change, making one alternative clearly preferable to another.

Use intuition. Some decisions seem to make themselves. A solution pops into our mind, and we gain newfound clarity. Using intuition is not the same as forgetting about the decision or refusing to make it. Intuitive decisions usually arrive after we've gathered the relevant facts and faced a problem for some time.

Evaluate your decision. Hindsight is a source of insight. After you act on a decision, observe the consequences over time. Reflect on how well your decision worked and what you might have done differently.

Think *choices*. This final suggestion involves some creative thinking. Consider that the word *decide* derives from the same roots as *suicide* and *homicide*. In the spirit of those words, a decision forever "kills" all other options. That's kind of heavy. Instead, use the word *choice,* and see if it frees up your thinking. When you *choose,* you express a preference for one option over others. However, those options remain live possibilities for the future. Choose for today, knowing that as you gain more wisdom and experience, you can choose again. ✳

Four ways to solve problems

THINK OF PROBLEM SOLVING as a process with four Ps: Define the *problem,* generate *possibilities,* create a *plan,* and *perform* your plan.

1 **Define the problem.** To define a problem effectively, understand what a problem is—a mismatch between what you want and what you have. Problem solving is all about reducing the gap between these two factors.

Start with what you have. Tell the truth about what's present in your life right now, without shame or blame. For example: "I often get sleepy while reading my physics assignments, and after closing the book I cannot remember what I just read."

Next, describe in detail what you want. Go for specifics: "I want to remain alert as I read about physics. I also want to accurately summarize each chapter I read."

Remember that when we define a problem in limiting ways, our solutions merely generate new problems. As Albert Einstein said, "The world we have made is a result of the level of thinking we have done thus far. We cannot solve problems at the same level at which we created them."[5]

This idea has many applications for success in school. An example is the student who struggles with note taking. The problem, she thinks, is that her notes are too sketchy. The logical solution, she decides, is to take more notes, and her new goal is to write down almost everything her instructors say. However, no matter how fast and furiously she writes, she cannot capture all of the instructors' comments.

Consider what happens when this student defines the problem in a new way. After more thought, she decides that her dilemma is not the *quantity* of her notes but their *quality.* She adopts a new format for taking notes, dividing her notepaper into two columns. In the right-hand column, she writes down only the main points of each lecture. In the left-hand column, she notes two or three supporting details for each point.

Over time, this student makes the joyous discovery that there are usually just three or four core ideas to remember from each lecture. She originally thought the solution was to take more notes. What really worked was taking notes in a new way.

2 **Generate possibilities.** Now put on your creative thinking hat. Open up. Brainstorm as many possible solutions to the problem as you can. At this stage, quantity counts. As you generate possibilities, gather relevant facts. For example, when you're faced with a dilemma about what courses to take next term, get information on class times, locations, and instructors. If you haven't decided which summer job offer to accept, gather information on each job's salary, benefits, and working conditions.

3 **Create a plan.** After rereading your problem definition and list of possible solutions, choose the solution that seems most workable. Think about specific actions that will reduce the gap between what you have and what you want. Visualize the steps you will take to make this solution a reality, and arrange them in chronological order. To make your plan even more powerful, put it in writing.

4 **Perform your plan.** This step gets you off your chair and out into the world. Now you actually *do* what you have planned. Ultimately, your skill in solving problems lies in how well you perform your plan. Through the quality of your actions, you become the architect of your own success.

Note that the four Ps of this problem-solving process closely parallel the four key questions listed in the article "Becoming a Critical Thinker."

Define the **problem**	**What** is the problem?
Generate **possibilities**	**What if** there are several possible solutions?
Create a **plan**	**How** would this possible solution work?
Perform your plan	**Why** is one solution more workable than another?

When facing problems, experiment with these four Ps, and remember that the order of steps is not absolute. Also remember that any solution has the potential to create new problems. If that happens, cycle through the four Ps of problem solving again. ✳

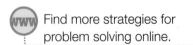 Find more strategies for problem solving online.

Define your values, align your actions

Values are the things in life that you want for their own sake. They influence and guide your choices, including your moment-by-moment decisions about what to do and what to buy. You can tell a lot about your values by looking at the ways you spend time and money.

VALUES DIFFER FROM GOALS. A goal is an outcome that you can achieve. For example, you can set a goal to lose 10 pounds, replace your car, or get a new job. Once you've achieved a goal, you can cross it off your list and replace it with a new goal.

Values, on the other hand, are constant. Instead of describing *what* we want to do or have, they describe *how* we achieve our goals. We can achieve our goals in ways that exploit other people, or we can achieve them in ways that create loving relationships. *Loving* is one example of a value. Like other values, it is never fully achieved or crossed off a list.

Some people are guided by values that they automatically adopt from others or by values that remain largely unconscious. Other people focus on short-term gain and forget about how their behavior violates their values over the long term. (This is a perspective that helped to create the recent economic recession.) When people forget or ignore their values, they miss the opportunity to live a life that's truly of their own choosing.

From Master Student to Master Employee is based on a particular set of values:

- Focused attention
- Self-responsibility
- Integrity
- Risk taking
- Contributing

You'll find these values and related ones directly stated in the Power Processes throughout the text. For instance:

"Discover What You Want" is about the importance of living a purpose-based life.

"Ideas Are Tools" points to the benefits of being willing to experiment with new ideas.

"Risk Being a Fool" is about courage—the willingness to take risks for the sake of learning something new.

"Be Here Now" expresses the value of focused attention.

"Love Your Problems (and Experience Your Barriers)" is about seeing difficulties as opportunities to develop new skills.

"Notice Your Pictures and Let Them Go" is about adopting an attitude of open-mindedness.

"I Create It All" is about taking responsibility for our beliefs and behaviors.

"Detach" reminds us that our core identity and value as a person does not depend on our possessions, our circumstances, or even our accomplishments.

"Find a Bigger Problem" is about living in ways that contribute to the happiness of others.

"Employ Your Word" expresses the value of making and keeping agreements.

"Choose Your Conversations (and Your Community)" reminds us of the power of language, and that we can reshape our lives by taking charge of our thoughts.

"Surrender" points to the value of human community and the power of asking for help.

"Be It" is specifically about the power of attitudes—the idea that change proceeds from the inside out as we learn to see ourselves in new ways.

In addition, most of the skills you read about in these pages have their source in values. The Time Monitor/Time Plan process, for example, calls for focused attention. Even the simple act of sharing your notes with a student who missed a class is an example of contributing.

Values are abstract. They do not refer to things that we can directly see, hear, or touch. To define your values, translate them into goals and visible actions that you can put on your daily to-do list.

Say that one of your values is to be healthy. To define that value, you could set a goal to exercise daily. Then you could plan to walk for 45 minutes this afternoon.

THINKING

8

One set of values

Think of values as your ultimate commitments. One way to start defining your values is to brainstorm endings for this sentence: *I am committed to being . . .*

Following is a sample list of values. Don't read it with the idea that it is the "right" set of values for you. Instead, use this list as a point of departure in creating your own list.

Value: Be accountable   This means being:

- Honest
- Reliable
- Trustworthy
- Ethical
- Dependable
- Responsible
- Able to make and keep agreements

Value: Be loving   This means being:

- Affectionate
- Devoted
- Accepting
- Considerate
- Respectful
- Inclusive
- Ethical
- Dedicated
- Equitable
- Gentle
- Forgiving
- Friendly
- Fair

Value: Be promotive   This means being:

- Nurturing
- Contributing
- Frugal
- Helpful
- Encouraging
- Reasonable
- Judicious
- Cooperative
- Appreciative

Value: Be candid   This means being:

- Honest
- Genuine
- Frank
- Spontaneous
- Free of deceit
- Able to avoid false modesty without arrogance
- Self-disclosing
- Open about strengths and weaknesses
- Authentic
- Self-expressed
- Outspoken
- Sincere

Value: Be detached   This means being:

- Impartial
- Experimental
- Open-minded
- Adaptable
- Trusting
- Joyful
- Unbiased
- Satisfied
- Patient
- Without distress
- Tolerant
- Willing to surrender

Value: Be aware of the possible   This means being:

- Creative
- Resourceful
- Foresighted
- Visionary
- Audacious
- Imaginative
- Inventive
- Holistic
- Inquisitive
- Adventurous

One wonderful aspect of defining your values is that you can start living them today. There is nothing you have to gain or buy *before* you can start being loving or honest. It might take you weeks, months, or years to achieve just one of your goals. However, you can start acting in ways that are loving and honest right now.

Defining your values and aligning your actions has a lot to do with leading a life of fulfillment and happiness. Many people define happiness as a feeling of pleasure. The problem with that definition is that we don't always control the things that happen to us or the way we feel.

In contrast, we *can* usually control our behavior. If we define happiness as taking action in the service of our values, then we can lead a worthwhile life even when circumstances and emotions are difficult.

Defining your values is also a way to create a legacy that will outlast your life. When someone dies, what

we reflect on is not what they earned or what they owned. We think about what they stood for and how they showed up for life. We recall their kindness, their wisdom, their commitments, and their contributions. In other words, we focus on their values.

Gaining a liberal education is all about choosing values and then setting goals that bring those values out into the world. As you begin to define your values, consider the people who have gone before you. In creeds, scriptures, philosophies, myths, and sacred stories, the human race has left a vast and varied record of values. Be willing to look everywhere, including sources that are close to home. Another way to define your values is to describe the qualities of people you admire.

In any case, start defining your values and aligning your actions today. ✳

THINKING

8

Making ethical decisions

EVERY DAY THAT YOU attend classes or go to work, you make choices that either reinforce or violate your core values. Your employers, coworkers, and instructors want to know that they can trust you in making these choices. Earn their trust by thinking through some potential issues now.

Making ethical choices at work

Some workplace behaviors are widely acknowledged to be unethical. Examples are submitting false expense reports, operating machinery while intoxicated, stealing from a cash drawer, diverting corporate funds for personal uses, or using work time to download explicit sexual images from the Internet.

You might find it easier to stop unethical behavior in its early stages—before it becomes habitual or widespread. According to *Setting the Standard*, published by the Office of Ethics and Business Conduct at Lockheed Martin Corporation, people might be walking on thin ethical ice when they make the following statements to justify an action:

- "It doesn't matter how the job gets done as long as it gets done."
- "Everyone does it."
- "Shred that document."
- "We can hide it."
- "No one will get hurt."
- "This will destroy the competition."
- "We didn't have this conversation."[6]

Making ethical decisions at school

Students in higher education face many situations that call for ethical decision making. While living away from home for the first time, some students choose to have casual sex, use illegal drugs, or drink alcohol before they reach the legal drinking age.

To get practice in ethical decision making, think through an issue that directly affects your grades and prospects for graduation: cheating.

Cheating on tests can be a tempting strategy. It offers the chance to get a good grade without having to study. Instead of studying, we could spend more time watching TV, partying, sleeping, or doing anything that seems like more fun. Another benefit is that we could avoid the risk of doing poorly on a test, which could happen even if we *do* study.

Cheating carries costs. Here are some intentions, actions, and consequences to consider.

We risk failing the course or getting expelled from school. The consequences for cheating are serious. Cheating can result in failing the assignment, failing the entire course, getting suspended, or getting expelled from college entirely. Documentation of cheating may also prevent you from being accepted to other colleges.

We learn less. While we might think that some courses offer little or no value, we can create value from any course. If we look deeply enough, we can discover some idea or acquire some skill to prepare us for future courses or a career after graduation.

We lose time and money. Getting an education costs a lot of money. It also calls for years of sustained effort. Cheating sabotages our purchase. We pay full tuition and invest our energy without getting full value for it.

Fear of getting caught promotes stress. When we're fully aware of our emotions about cheating, we might discover intense stress. Even if we're not fully aware of our emotions, we're likely to feel some level of discomfort about getting caught.

Violating our values promotes stress. Even if we don't get caught cheating, we can feel stress about violating our own ethical standards. Stress can compromise our physical health and overall quality of life.

Cheating on tests can make it easier to violate our integrity again. Human beings become comfortable with behaviors that they repeat. Cheating is no exception. Think about the first time you drove a car. You might have felt excited—even a little frightened. Now driving is probably second nature, and you don't give it much thought. Repeated experience with driving creates familiarity, which lessens the intense feelings you had during your first time at the wheel.

We can experience the same process with almost any behavior. Cheating once will make it easier to cheat again. Furthermore, if we become comfortable with compromising our integrity in one area of life, we might find it easier to compromise in other areas.

Cheating lowers our self-concept. Whether or not we are fully aware of it, cheating sends us the message that we are not smart enough or responsible enough to make it on our own. We deny ourselves the celebration and satisfaction of authentic success.

An alternative to cheating is to become a master student. Ways to do this are described on every page of this book.

8

THINKING

Create an ethics checklist

You don't have to be a philosopher in order to make sound ethical decisions at work and school. Start with the working definition of ethics as using moral standards to guide your behavior. Next, turn your own moral standards into a checklist of pointed questions. Then use your checklist to make choices in daily life.

Although there is no formula for making ethical decisions, you can gain clarity with questions that can be answered either yes or no. Following is a sample checklist:

Is this action legal?   [   ]Yes [   ]No

Is this action consistent with my organization's mission, goals, and policies?   [   ]Yes [   ]No

Is this action consistent with my personal values?   [   ]Yes [   ]No

If I continue to make choices such as this, will I be happy with the kind of person I become?   [   ]Yes [   ]No

Will this action stand the test of time? Will I be able to defend this action tomorrow, next month, and next year? [   ]Yes [   ]No

In taking this action, am I setting an example that I wish others to follow?   [   ]Yes [   ]No

Am I willing to make this decision public—to share it wholeheartedly with my boss, my family, and my friends? Would I feel confident if an article about my decision was published in tomorrow's newspaper? [   ]Yes [   ]No

Has everyone who will be affected by this decision had the chance to voice his or her concerns?   [   ]Yes [   ]No

Avoiding plagiarism

Using another person's words, images, or other original creations without giving proper credit is called *plagiarism*. Plagiarism amounts to taking someone else's work and presenting it as your own. This is the equivalent of cheating on a test. Consequences of plagiarism can range from a failing grade to expulsion from school.

The basic guideline for preventing plagiarism is to cite a source for each phrase, sequence of ideas, or visual image created by another person. While ideas cannot be copyrighted, the way that any idea is *expressed* can be. The goal is to clearly distinguish your own work from the expressions of others.

Identify direct quotes   If you're taking notes and use a direct quote from another writer or speaker, then put that person's words in quotation marks. Do the same when copying sentences or paragraphs from a Web page and pasting them directly into your notes.

Paraphrase carefully   Instead of using a direct quote, you might choose to paraphrase or summarize an author's words. Paraphrasing means restating the original passage in your own words, usually making it shorter and simpler. Remember that copying a passage and then just rearranging or deleting a few words creates a serious risk of plagiarism. Cite a source for paraphrases and summaries, just as you do for direct quotes.

Note details about each of your sources
Include the author, title, publisher, publication date, and page number (for printed materials). Ask your instructor for what details to record about online sources. Also ask about how to cite your sources—as endnotes or footnotes—and get examples of the format to use.

Submit only your own work   Turning in materials that have been written or revised by someone else puts your education at risk.

 Find more ways to prevent plagiarism online.

Find a Bigger Problem

It is impossible to live a life that's free of problems. Besides, problems serve a purpose. They provide opportunities to participate in life. Problems stimulate us and pull us forward.

When problems are seen from this perspective, our goal becomes not to eliminate them, but to find problems that are worthy of us. Worthy problems are those that draw on our talents, move us toward our purpose, and increase our skills. Solving these problems offers the greatest benefits for others and ourselves. Viewed in this way, bigger problems give more meaning to our lives.

Problems expand to fill whatever space is available. Suppose that your only problem for today is to write a follow-up letter to a job interview. You could spend the entire day thinking about what you're going to say, writing the letter, finding a stamp, going to the post office—and then thinking about all of the things you forgot to say.

Now suppose that you get a phone call with an urgent message: A close friend has been admitted to the hospital and wants you to come right away. It's amazing how quickly and easily that letter can get finished when there's a bigger problem on your plate. True, the smaller problems still need to be solved. The goal is simply to solve them in less time and with less energy.

Bigger problems are easy to find—world hunger, child abuse, environmental pollution, terrorism, human rights violations, drug abuse, street crime, energy shortages, poverty, and wars. These problems await your attention and involvement.

Tackling a bigger problem does not have to be depressing. In fact, it can be energizing—a reason for getting up in the morning. A huge project can channel your passion and purpose.

When we take on a bigger problem, we play full out. We do justice to our potentials. We then love what we do and do what we love. We're awake, alert, and engaged. Playing full out means living our lives as if our lives depended on it.

Perhaps a little voice in your mind is saying, "That's crazy. I can't do anything about global problems." In the spirit of critical thinking, put that idea to the test. Get involved in solving a bigger problem. Then notice how you can, indeed, make a difference. And just as important, notice how your other problems dwindle—or even vanish.

 Learn more about finding bigger problems online.

Career Application

Maria Sanchez graduated with an associate's degree in legal assistance and has been working for two years as a paralegal at a large law firm.

Maria's work is supervised by an attorney who is ultimately responsible for the documents she produces. As a paralegal, she cannot set legal fees, give legal advice, or present cases in court. Except for these restrictions, however, she does many of the same things that lawyers do. Maria's current job centers on legal research—identifying laws, judicial decisions, legal articles, and other materials that are relevant to her assigned cases.

Maria is one of three paralegals who work with her supervising attorney. Recently she applied for a new paralegal job that opened up in the firm. In addition to legal research, this job involves drafting legal arguments and motions to be filed in court. Getting this job would mean a promotion and a raise for Maria.

Maria has formally applied for the job and expressed strong interest in it. She believes that her chances are excellent. One of the paralegals she works with is not interested in the job, and she knows that the other one plans to announce next month that she's quitting the firm to attend law school.

One day, Maria finds the first draft of an e-mail that her supervisor has printed out and accidentally placed in a stack of legal documents for Maria to file. The e-mail is a note of congratulations that offers the new paralegal job to the person who plans to quit.

Reflecting on this scenario

Does Maria face an ethical dilemma in this situation? Explain your answer.

_____

_____

_____

_____

_____

© Andresr/Shutterstock

Review the guidelines for decision making given in this chapter—particularly the suggestions for ethical decision making. Choose one and explain how Maria could apply it.

_____

_____

_____

_____

_____

_____

_____

_____

_____

_____

Quiz

Name _____ Date ____/____/____

1. List the four questions from this chapter that can guide you to becoming a critical thinker.

2. Briefly describe one strategy for answering each question you just listed.

3. Define the word *plagiarism* and explain one method for preventing it.

4. The goal of the Power Process in this chapter is to help you eliminate problems. True or false? Explain your answer.

5. Briefly describe three strategies for creative thinking.

6. Explain the difference between values and goals.

7. List two types of logical fallacies, and give an example of each type.

8. List an assumption behind the following statement: "Why save money? I want to enjoy life today."

9. Name a logical fallacy involved in this statement: "Everyone who's ever visited this school agrees that it's the best in the state."

10. According to the text, the words *choose* and *decide* have the same meaning. True or false? Explain your answer.

Focus on Transferable Skills

Now that you've experimented with some new strategies for thinking, take a few minutes to revisit your responses to the "Thinking" section of the Discovery Wheel in Chapter 1: "First Steps." Also reflect on ways to extend your thinking skills.

You might want to prepare for this exercise by reviewing the articles "Jumpstart Your Education with Transferable Skills" on page 58 and "101 Transferable Skills" on page 60.

CREATIVE AND CRITICAL THINKING

When I'm asked to come up with a topic for a paper or speech, the first thing I do is . . .

When choosing how to vote in an election, the first thing I take into account about a candidate is . . .

PROBLEM SOLVING AND DECISION MAKING

When faced with a major decision, such as choosing a career or declaring my major, my first step is usually to . . .

One of the biggest problems I face right now is . . .

To come up with a solution for this problem, I will . . .

NEXT ACTION

The most important thing I could do to become a more skilled thinker is . . .

To develop this skill, I intend to . . .

Master Student PROFILE

Irshad Manji

. . . is courageous

© Colin McPherson/CORBIS

It's to be expected that an author with a book on the verge of publication will lose her cool over a last-minute detail or two. Some might get nervous that their facts won't hold up and run a paranoid, final check. Others might worry about what to wear to their book party. When Irshad Manji's book was about to hit the stands, her concern was a bit different. She feared for her life.

Certain her incendiary book *The Trouble with Islam* would set off outrage in the Muslim community, she called the police, told them she was working on a book that was highly critical of Islam, and asked if they could advise her on safety precautions.

They came to visit her Toronto apartment building several times and suggested she install a state-of-the-art security system, bulletproof windows, and hire a counterterrorism expert to act as her personal bodyguard.

In her short, plucky book she comes down hard on modern-day Islam, charging that the religion's mainstream has come to be synonymous with literalism. Since the 13th century, she said, the faith hasn't encouraged—or tolerated—independent thinking (or as it's known in the faith, *ijtihad*).

The book, which is written like a letter, is both thoughtful and confrontational. In person, Ms. Manji embodied the same conflicting spirit. She was affable and wore a broad smile. Her upbeat, nervous energy rose to the task of filling in every potentially awkward pause. (One of her favorite factoids: "Prophet Mohammed was quite a feminist.")

Her journey scrutinizing Islam started when she was an 8-year-old and taking weekly religious classes at a *madrasa* (religious school) in suburban Vancouver. Her anti-Semitic teacher Mr. Khaki never took her questions seriously; he merely told her to accept everything because it was in the Koran. She wanted to know why she had to study it in Arabic, which she didn't understand, and was told the answers were "in the Koran."

Her questioning ended up getting her kicked out of school at 14, and she embarked on a 20-year-long private study of the religion. While she finds the treatment poured on women and foreigners in Islamic nations indefensible, she said that she continues to be a believer because the religion provides her with her values. "And I'm so glad I did because it was then I came to realize that there was this really progressive side of my religion and it was this tradition of critical thinking called *ijtihad*. This is what allows me to stay within the faith."

She calls herself a "Muslim refusenik" because she remains committed to the religion and yet she doesn't accept what's expected of Muslim women. As terrorist acts and suicide bombings refuse to subside, she said it's high time for serious reform within the Islamic faith.

She said many young Muslim supporters are still afraid to come out about their support of her. "Even before 9/11 it was the young Muslims who were emerging out of these audiences and gathering at the side of the stage. They'd walk over and say, 'Irshad, we need voices such as yours to help us open up this religion of ours because if it doesn't open up, we're leaving the mosques.'"

She wants Muslims to start thinking critically about their religion and to start asking more questions. "Most Muslims have never been introduced to the possibility, let alone the virtue, of asking questions about our holy book," she said. "We have never been taught the virtue of interpreting the Koran in different ways."

Lauren Mechling, "The Trouble with Writing About Islam," as appeared in *New York Sun*, November 26, 2004. Copyright © 2004. Reprinted with permission of the author.

(1969–)
Controversial journalist, broadcaster, and author of *The Trouble with Islam*, who uses her "Muslim voice of reform, to concerned citizens worldwide" in an effort to explore faith and community, and the diversity of ideas.

Learn more about Irshad Manji and other master students at the Master Student Hall of Fame.